No. 1738
$15.95

FLEA MARKET TREASURE

BY DAN D'IMPERIO

TAB BOOKS Inc.

BLUE RIDGE SUMMIT, PA. 17214

To Jeff, Beth, and Janice.

FIRST EDITION

FIRST PRINTING

Library of Congress Cataloging in Publication data

D'Imperio, Dan.
    Flea market treasure.

    1. Collectibles—United States—Catalogs.
2. Flea markets—United States. I. Title.
AM303.5.D56   1984   790.1′32   84-12374
ISBN 0-8306-0738-2
ISBN 0-8306-1738-8 (pbk.)

Some Illustrations by C. R. Mansfield

Front cover: Tiffany lamp and jack-in-the-pulpit vases appear courtesy of the William Doyle Galleries, 175 East 87th Street, New York, NY.

Contents

Acknowledgments

A special thank you to Dolores Kephart and Helen Kippax for their gracious cooperation on this project.

Introduction

Are you a collector of Shirley Temple mementos, depression glass, Elvis Presley items, or Golden Oak furniture? Then perhaps you are among the thousands of Americans suffering from "flea market fever." Attending a market can be an exhilarating experience. Seasoned shoppers have been trained to expect the unexpected; both beginning and advanced collectors are usually intent on bagging a bargain.

Due to the intense interest in collectibles, prices in most categories have been on the upswing. This is because the collectibles business is primarily governed by the supply and demand syndrome. This book, which covers collectibles in an A to Z format, includes a value guide for each entry. The price quotations are based on a nationwide survey of sales transactions at flea markets. Please remember that prices vary slightly based on condition and geographical location.

Whether you have a piece of sheet music, a Dick Tracey Big Little Book, a calendar plate, or any other collectible stored away in the attic, this book has been designed to offer background information and current prices for your enjoyment and enlightenment.

If the book prompts continued or beginning participation in flea marketeering, then it has accomplished its mission. Why not put a little fun in your life and try collecting? It really is a rewarding hobby.

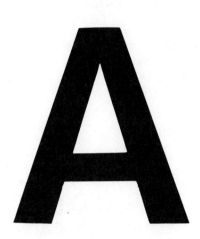

ABG DOLLS

A display of ABG bisque-headed dolls at the Chicago World's Fair of 1893 drew appreciative glances from visitors. They originated at the Alt, Beck, & Gottschalck pottery of Germany, which had been

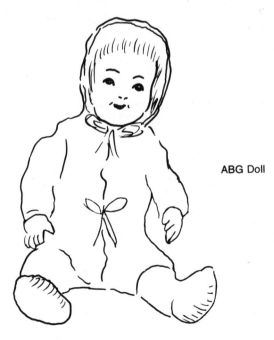

ABG Doll

1

established in 1854. Child dolls, customarily having the mold number 1362, were found under many American Christmas trees in the 1890s. By the early 1900s, character dolls brought the ABG pottery fame in the field of playthings. Produced in a variety of sizes, many of these bisque-headed beauties had sleep eyes, open mouths, and composition bodies. George Borgfeldt, the respected American doll importer, commissioned ABG to make bisque heads for his dolls. Locating a fine quality ABG doll is no longer as simple as "ABC." *Value guide: character doll, bent-limb body, 22" tall, circa 1913, $450.*

ACME SLEEVE BOARDS

Work-weary homemakers of the late 1800s relied on a variety of homemade sleeve boards. These wooden ironing devices were usually covered with flannel or muslin, and many stood on bases. As a rule, they were slightly narrower than the average sleeve to facilitate ironing chores. One handy helper was the Acme Sleeve Board patented in 1899, by C. H. Smith of Boston. Mr. Smith had something up his own sleeve, for his model came complete with an iron clamp. Thus, sleeves could be slipped on and off the board with relative ease. *Value guide: Acme Sleeve Board, $30.*

ACTORS' FAIR SPOONS

Theatrical history was made at New York's Madison Square Garden, between May 2-7, 1892, when the Actors' Fair was held. The Gorham Silver Company issued a set of star-studded actress spoons honoring the occasion. Each spoon bore a cut-out bust of a theatrical great with a scroll beneath bearing a replica of the subject's autograph. Etched laurel leaves enlivened the stems, while the bowls were gold washed. Honored on these silver souvenirs were such legendary ladies as Lillian Russell, Sarah Bernhardt, and May Robson. *Value guide: May Robson, $30.*

ADAM PATTERN

When bread lines were forming in many metropolitan areas in 1932, the Jeannette Glass Company of Pennsylvania introduced the Adam pattern. Depression customers purchased luncheon and dinner sets in pink, green, and crystal. This mold-etched glass design had cut-off corners that blended beautifully with art deco interiors. Dinner plates boasted centers comprised of alternating feathers and plumes; at the point where the center met the rim, wide radial ridges appeared. Border areas were enhanced with garlands of flowers. By 1934, Adam tablewares and apples were part and parcel of the depression. *Value guide: bowl, pink, 5¾" diameter, $25; sugar and creamer, green, $45.*

Adam Pattern Bowl

ADVERTISING PAPER DOLLS
No one can deny it! The advertising paper doll can stand on its own as a cherished collectible. Despite its humble beginning as a pre-

Advertising Paper Doll

3

mium item around the turn of the century, these advertising pieces have enormous appeal. Hundreds of American companies relied upon them to promote products and services. Young snippers were treated to paper dolls from such prestigious firms as Clarks O.N.T., Diamond Dyes, Columbia Bicycles, Duplex Corsets, and Worcester Salt. Each company had its own mascot or symbolic figure. While McLaughlin Coffee perked up sales with a paper doll in every package, the rival Lion Coffee concern bolstered business with the Brownies. *Value guide: Lion Coffee-Jack & Jill, $14; McLaughlin's Coffee-Czarina of Russia, $12.*

AGNEW ELEPHANT BOTTLE

The Agnew elephant bottle from the James Beam Distilling Company rates as an unforgettable collectible and one of the rarest Beam bottles. This Republican elephant bottle was designed specifically to honor former Vice President Spiro Agnew's appearance at a $100-a-plate fund-raising dinner on November 12, 1970. The elephant formed the bottle's stopper, while embossed stars encircled the base. Only 96 bottles were made for this political happening. Beam collectors, sensing their scarcity, were waiting outside when the guests departed. Their offers for a single bottle often exceeded $100. Whether empty or full, Agnew elephant bottles can stand on their own as colossal collectibles. *Value guide: Agnew elephant bottle, $2,750.*

AKRO AGATE GLASS COMPANY

George Rankin, Gilbert Marsh, and Horace Hill were the founders of the Akro Agate Glass Company. This Akron, Ohio, concern was established in 1911. Just three years later the company relocated to Clarksburg, West Virginia. Through the early 1930s, Akro Agate became the largest marble producing company in America. When competition entered the picture, officials decided to diversify. Ashtrays, garden pots, bowls, and other novelties were added to production schedules. Those highly coveted children's dishes were introduced about 1942. During the war years, the curtailment of Japanese imports permitted Akro Agate to become a major maker of children's tea sets. When the factory failed in 1952, pieces bearing the trademark of a crow flying through the letter "A" landed on flea market tabletops. *Value guide: figurine, Scotty, pink, $70; tea set, jade luster, 24 pieces, $150.*

ALADDIN LAMPS

Kerosene lamps were the rage of the late 19th century. A typical lamp of the 1890s used round wicks; the air was supplied to the flame through a central tube. A German improvement of 1905 featured a mantle that fit over the burner to afford the user a better source of light. Victor Johnson, of Missouri, was so impressed that he established a Chicago factory to manufacture lamps. His Mantle Lamp Company introduced the Aladdin lamp. The public responded enthusiastically, for his lamps burned less fuel and furnished more light. Between 1909 and 1968, approximately 16 models of Aladdin lamps were produced. This included hanging, table, bracket, and floor lamps. The art deco examples, dating from the 1920s and 1930s, light up collectors' lives. *Value guide: desk lamp, reverse painted tree scene, 13½" tall, $250; table, Model#8, #401, paneled globular satin shade, $175.*

ALICE B. TOKLAS COOKBOOK

Celebrity cookbooks represent a specialized field for cookbook collectors. This Harper & Row publication, illustrated by Sir Francis Rose, therefore, is assured of tempting collectors' tastebuds. In addition to Alice B. Toklas' culinary philosophy, the text also provides tasty tidbits pertaining to her life in Paris with Gertrude Stein during the 1920s and '30s. The recipes and the reminiscences make this book a collectible on two counts. For those intent upon knowing what was cooking with the literary set during this era, a copy of the *Alice B. Toklas Cookbook* is a necessity. *Value guide: book, $18.*

ALICE IN WONDERLAND

Walt Disney's classic "Alice in Wonderland" premiered on July 28, 1951. Although it triggered a considerable amount of character merchandise, box office receipts were sluggish. Alice in Wonderland cards (1-48) were issued by Carreras Ltd. The rare animated watch, which was marketed by Ingersoll, features Alice in color, along with the Mad Hatter who rocks back and forth on the second hand. Decca Distributing Corporation issued the Alice in Wonderland album. One must assume that while the movie received only lukewarm reception, novelties marketed from the film drew just the opposite response. *Value guide: cookie jar, $35; Alice in Wonderland doll, jointed, vinyl, 12" tall, $30.*

ALTWASSER PORCELAINS

Victorian homemakers stocked their china closets with the finest continental porcelains; those with taste often chose tablewares from the Tielsch & Company pottery of Altwasser, Silesia (Germany). They impressed ceramic critics with their porcelain presentations at the Great London Exhibition of 1851. These so-called

C. T. Germany wares were extensively exported to America in the late 19th century. Lobster dishes, bowls, plates, serving pieces, and other articles surrendered to the finest quality ornamentation. Attribution is possible, for most bore their trademark of an eagle with outstretched wings enclosing the letters "CT." The Hutschenreuther family assumed control of the works about 1918. *Value guide: bowl, cherubs, 10" diameter, $75; lobster dish, red and gold, large, $80.*

ALUMINUM

Aluminum, that most modern of metals, has been commercially produced since the 1850s. According to reports, the first aluminum article was a rattle crafted for the infant son of Napoleon III. In fact, Napoleon also ordered some aluminum knives and forks. (At that time aluminum was far more expensive than gold or silver.) When a less costly electrical production method was developed in the 1880s, aluminum prices tumbled into the affordable range. Collectors have now begun to seek the hammered aluminum articles dating from the 1930s and 1940s. Flea marketeers have been warming up to accessories from such aluminum greats as the Kensington, Inc. and Wendell August Forge. *Value guide: ice bucket, Chrysanthemum, $20; percolator, lucite handles, Continental, $45.*

AMBROTYPES

The ambrotype was developed in England by Frederick Scott Archer (1813-1857), in 1852. Two years later it was patented in America by James Cutting. The ambrotype was a collodion negative on glass that was bleached and set against a dark background, thus giving the appearance of a positive. They were customarily housed in daguerrean cases. Portraits of historical, stage, military, or other identifiable subjects always receive a positive reception. In addition, collectors pay premium prices for outdoor scenes, as few were attempted during this era. *Value guide: soldier holding pistol and saber, $165; lady wearing ruffled bonnet, $20.*

AMERICAN ENCAUSTIC TILING COMPANY

What company was regarded as the foremost maker of wall and floor tiles around the turn of the century? Undoubtedly, the American Encaustic Tiling Company of Zanesville, Ohio. Between 1875 and 1936, they floored the public with hundreds of relief tiles. Art director Hermann Mueller worked with chemist Karl Lanegnbeck during the 1890s to fashion some fantastically beautiful tiles. The gold medals awarded to them at the Paris Exhibition of 1900 and the Pan American Exhibition of 1901 brought added stature to this tile maker. Novelties were also executed, including a wine bottle with a removable head. Tiles and other treasures typically bore the initials "A.E.T. Co.". *Value guide: tile, hunting dogs, 6" × 18", $275; tile, Roman figures, 6" × 6", $200.*

AMERICAN FLYER

In 1907, a factory was established in Chicago, Illinois, where cast-iron carriages imitative of Ives were produced. This successful toy venture was operating under a new partnership by 1910, known as the American Flyer Company. In the period before World War I, electric trains were added to production schedules. Until 1936, their trains were made in 2⅛" gauge. Executives acquired the Ives stock in the late 1920s. When A. C. Gilbert purchased American Flyer in 1938, he became one of America's foremost manufacturers of model trains. In 1967, the company was absorbed by Lionel. *Value guide: car, 982, State of Maine box car, S gauge, $35; locomotive, 477, Silver Flash, S gauge, $65.*

AMERICAN SWEETHEART PATTERN

Depression glass collectors have been staging a love affair with the

American Sweetheart Pattern Plate

7

American Sweetheart pattern from the MacBeth-Evans Glass Company. The mold-etched design was produced between 1930 and 1936. Table settings were available in pink, red, blue, crystal, Monax (opaque white), and Cremax (opaque with ivory tint). The festoons, ribbons, and scrolls forming the central motif were repeated on the border. Those short radial lines separating the border area formed a ruffled effect. Engaging, but elusive, American Sweetheart finds include the two- and three-tier trays, footed salt and pepper shakers, and 80-ounce pitchers. *Value guide: console bowl, Monax, $300; plate blue, 15½" diameter, $325.*

AMERICAN TWIN ICE CREAM FREEZER

The first American patent for an ice cream freezer was issued in 1848. For the duration of the century, patent offices were inundated with requests for new and improved freezers, because, despite the availability of commercially made ice cream, many homemakers

American Twin Ice Cream Freezer

preferred making it at home. Each new freezer promised to make "the lightest and purest ice cream ever." The Arctic Blizzard, Freezo, White Mountain, and Lightning lured customers with various advertising gimmicks. Around the turn of the century, the North Brothers Manufacturing Company scored a triumph with the finger-licking set with its American Twin, for it was capable of producing two different flavors of ice cream at the same time. *Value guide: American Twin Freezer, $45.*

AMERICAN WALTHAM WATCH COMPANY

On February 4, 1859, the American Watch Company of Massachusetts was incorporated, an outgrowth of several different partnerships dating from 1850. After a shaky start due to the Civil War, the company rallied in the 1870s. In 1885, it was reorganized as the American Waltham Watch Company. Until World War I, the business was quite successful; however, by the early 1920s, the company faced insolvency. In 1925, after merging its interests with the local Waltham Clock Company, the firm operated as the Waltham Watch Company. Electric clocks and speedometers were manufactured until about 1940. Between 1860 and 1957, when the company ceased producing watches in favor of imported models, over 34 million watches were in circulation. *Value guide: Crescent Street, 17 jewels, M#1870, key wind, $375; George Washington, M#1875, key wind, $325.*

AMERICAN WRINGER COMPANY

During early times, water was wrung from clothes by hand. Subsequently, crank-handled wringers with wooden rollers, and later with rubber rollers, eased washing chores. One of the foremost turn-of-the-century makers was the American Wringer Company of New York City. Their various horseshoe-brand wringers bore individual trade names, such as Novelty or Empire. Identification problems seldom existed, for their horseshoe trademark enclosed the letters "AWC." The company customarily crafted them of hard maple, with plain or ball bearings. They could be used, of course, on round or square tubs. Few consumers experienced any hand wringing anxiety over the prices, which generally fell between $10 and 20. *Value guide: Novelty wringer, $50.*

AMOS AND ANDY

It has been estimated that the Amos and Andy radio program had an audience of 40 million listeners between 1929 and 1935. Historically speaking, it was the most popular program in the annals of American broadcasting. Charles Correll and Freeman Gosden played the famous pair, who happened to be personal favorites of

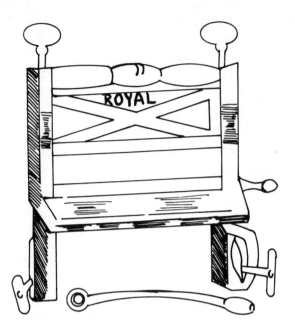

Royal Clothes Wringer

President Hoover. By 1932, restaurants and stores added radios so that customers could listen to the program, which aired nightly Monday through Friday between 7:00 and 7:15. Pepsodent toothpaste was the sponsor of this National Broadcasting Company hit. Amos and Andy remembrances rate as dandy acquisitions, especially Marx's "Fresh Air Taxicab of America." *Value guide: toy, Amos and Andy Fresh Air Taxi, complete, $575; sheet music, Pepsodent theme song, $14.*

Amos & Andy Walking Toys

AMPHORA

The potteries located in the Turn-Teplitz area of Central Europe won lavish praise from ceramic critics in the late 1800s, because their porcelain presentations, which adorned many American mantels, exhibited great originality. They were especially proficient at figurines. One active works, the Amphora Porzellanfabrik (Amphora Porcelain Works), was owned by Reissner, Stellmacher, and Kessel. Varying trademarks identifying the ware included the initials "RSK" or "Amphora," often accompanied by a crown. Closely related wares were manufactured at the nearby Alexandra Works. That individualistic expression, inherent in art nouveau themes, found fullest exposure in these exotic procelains. *Value guide: camel rider figurine, 24" tall, $750; vase, woman's head, beaded effects, 10" tall, $300.*

Amphora Camel Rider Figurine

ANDY GUMP

Destined to become one of America's most widely read comic strips of the 1920s, Sidney Smith's "The Gumps" first appeared as a daily Strip on February 12, 1917, in the *Chicago Tribune*. The Gumps were supposed to portray everyday life in Chicago during the flapper age. Andy, Min, the dedicated housewife with purse and umbrella, and son, Chester, with hoop and stick, were the principal members of the strip. As might be expected, the Gumps began appearing on penny banks, playing cards, mechanical toys, lampshades, and other novelties. Following Sidney Smith's untimely death in 1935, the strip was assigned to Gus Edson. The Gumps galloped into obscurity when the strip faltered in 1959. *Value guide: figurine, bisque, Andy Gump, 13" tall, $85; toothbrush holder, Andy & Min, bisque, $65.*

ANIMAL HORN FURNITURE

Exotic animal horn furniture experienced a revival in America that coincided with the Western movement. This organic furniture had been deemed proper for hunting lodges and masculine interiors at an earlier date. Those who hunt animal horn pieces usually uncover steer or buffalo horn chairs, settees, footstools, and tables. Zoological decorating fads were not strictly limited to masculine tastes, however, for some were upholstered in pink or lavendar floral damask and finished with braid and fringe. These pieces, often the result of a successful hunt, were presented as gifts to Abraham Lincoln and Theodore Roosevelt. *Value guide: armchair, steer horns, $650; footstool, buffalo horns, $250.*

Animal Horn Chair

ANSONIA CLOCKS

The Ansonia Clock Company of Ansonia, Connecticut, was founded in 1851. The entire works moved to New York City in 1879. Their timepieces, both wall and shelf clocks, were executed in the Connecticut style. They kept abreast of the public's taste, making OG clocks, versions of the French four-glass regulator clocks, drop-dial clocks with visible pendulums, and ticket clocks. China case clocks in rococo styles were imported from the Royal Bonn works in

Ansonia Mantel Clock

Germany. Upon arriving in America, they were fitted with Ansonia movements. The factory remained active until 1930. Clock collectors scour the market attempting to locate timepieces having their A within a diamond within a circle trademark. *Value guide: Mantel, black marble, exposed escapement, $350; wall clock, Queen Elizabeth, time and strike, walnut, $750.*

APPLE PARERS

The earliest American apple parers were made completely of wood,

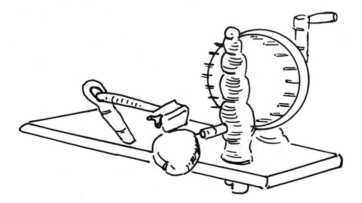

Apple Parer

13

except for the blades and prongs. By the mid-1800s, cast-iron apple parers supplanted the earlier wooden varieties in popularity. A Winslow Homer illustration, dated 1859, featured a young boy working with a new-fangled apple parer. The apple bee, like the quilting bee, was an American way of life. Each new patent promised to pare and cut the apple in record-breaking time. Collectors have unearthed a bushel and a peck of parers having a maker's name or patent date. The complicated Hudson and Vermont innovations proved capable of paring, coring, and slicing apples. But those left-handed parers from the 1890s really reached the core of the matter! *Value guide: Hudson, Little Star, $40; Reading Hardware, 1890s, $50.*

ARCADE MANUFACTURING COMPANY

Between the 1860s and 1920s, the Arcade Manufacturing Company of Freeport, Illinois, produced a variety of household essentials. Within collecting circles their toy cars, traffic signs, gasoline pumps, and other novelties rate as admirable acquisitions. Their die-cast iron cars rode into American homes in sizable quantities, and they are regarded as the most heavily cast of any toy cars. In addition, these vehicles were realistically painted, because designers gave considerable attention to every detail. These cars are so popular that the Arcade decal has been forged. Many traffic signals and gasoline pumps bore the Arcade Mfg. Co., Freeport, Ill.," mark on the case. *Value guide: City Ambulance, 6" long, 1920s, $135; Yellow Cab, 5" long, 1920s, $325.*

Arcade Toy Sedan

ARNOLD PRINT WORKS

Between 1876 and 1919, the Arnold Print Works of North Adams, Massachusetts, was a major American maker of prints and dress fabrics. In 1892, printed figures on cotton were sold by the yard to be sewn and stuffed into rag dolls. A pasteboard base was suggested

14

to make them stand erect. The sew and stuff crowd had a choice of subjects including Tatters and Little Tatters, Little Red Riding Hood, Rooster and Owl, Hen and Chickens, Floss, Jocko, Bunny, and Topsy. Even the Palmer Cox Brownies were sold by the yard for home assemblage. The fabric cost between 12 and 20 cents per yard. The number of dolls each yard would yield varied, depending on their size; most, however, had two to eight subjects per yard. Dolls having the "Arnold Print Works, North Adams, Mass., Incorporated 1876" trademark rate as fun finds. *Value guide: Red Riding Hood, circa 1900, $75.*

ASHTRAYS

The humble ashtray has become a formidable collectible. Activity in this field accelerated with the expansion of the tobacco industry about 1865. Practically overnight, glass, metal, and ceramic ashtrays were pressed into service. They surrendered to a full range of decorative techniques. By the 1880s advertising types proliferated, mainly from liquor and cigarette companies. Matching sets, comprised of an ashtray, cigarette box, and match holder, were in demand with those sending up smoke rings in drawing rooms. Serious ashtray aficionados have little difficulty discovering marked examples from Louis Comfort Tiffany, Dirk van Erp, and the Roycroft Shops among others. *Value guide: ashtray, Mr. Peanut's 50th Anniversary, $50; bronze, Tiffany, gold dore, scalloped, nest of four, $450.*

AUBURN RUBBER CORPORATION

Automobile tires were the major product of the Double Fabric Tire Corporation of Auburn, Illinois, when it was founded in 1913. In the mid-1930s, however, in order to improve profits, the company entered the molded rubber toy field. This resulted in a line of toy soldiers which marched right into American toy shops. Subsequently, wheeled vehicles, baseball players, and armies of soldiers brought them fame as toymakers. The title Auburn Rubber Corporation was adapted. The toy division, later sold to the town of Deming, New Mexico, remained active until 1968. *Value guide: Cadillac, 1936, $25; Oldsmobile sedan, 6" long, 1940, $45.*

AURENE

Unquestionably, Aurene glass was inspired by the iridescent glass objects attributed to Louis Comfort Tiffany. A rage for this art glass spread through America in the early 1900s. The Aurene trademark was registered by Frederick Carder for the Steuben Glass Works in 1904, the name apparently derived from the Latin *aureus,* a Roman gold coin. Until 1934, Aurene objects with a smooth, uniform,

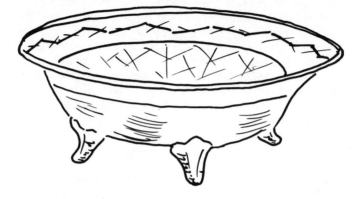

Aurene Footed Bowl

iridescent surface appeared in gold, blue, or silvery blue. Ornamental and utilitarian items often bore the mark "Aurene," "Steuben," or both. Occasionally, a piece bore the name "Carder." As for those original paper labels, they have all but vanished with time. *Value guide: bowl, loop decor, 8" diameter, $400; vase, gold, ruffled top, 5" tall, $275.*

AURORA WATCHES

The Aurora Watch Company, founded in 1883, wanted one jeweler in every town selling its pocket watches. This Aurora, Illinois, based concern had the good fortune of having the ground for its plant donated by the city fathers. Within one year, Aurora watch movements were being sold in sizable numbers. They made 11 grades of hunter cases and open faces with stem wind. Seven grades of key wind watches were kept in stock. Strong competition from fellow watchmakers, however, forced them to wind down production by 1892. *Value guide: pocket watch, 18 size, 7 jewels, open face, key wind, circa 1885, $250; Guild watch, 18 size, $450.*

AUTRY, GENE

Gene Autry, affectionately known as "America's Favorite Singing Cowboy," was born in Texas on September 29, 1907. Following his graduation from high school, he became a telegrapher. Will Rogers walked into the station to send a telegram one day and heard Gene singing. Rogers persuaded Autry to pursue a career, preferably in radio. Gene accepted his advice, becoming known as "Oklahoma's Yodeling Cowboy." Record contracts, radio programs, and a film career followed. Between 1937 and 1942, Autry's name ranked with the top ten money-makers in the United States. Trivia buffs will be quick to mention that his stint in films spanned 19 years and 56 features. With nostalgia buffs, the sun never sets on his artifacts. *Value guide: cap pistol, boxed, $40; ranch outfit, boxed, unused, $50.*

AUTUMN LEAF

American homemakers have been falling for the Autumn Leaf dinnerware service since 1933. Originally, this Hall China Company pattern of floral decals was sold exclusively through Jewel Tea outlets. Prior to 1940, it circulated under several names. Other potteries eventually produced the design for various retailers. Mixing or matching a set could conceivably uncover backstamps from such potters as The Harker Potteries, Crooksville China Company, and Paden City Pottery. The Autumn Leaf motifs apparently proved somewhat contagious, because fabrics, flatware, glassware, and cooking utensils in this perennial pattern have appeared over the years. *Value guide: bean pot, handled, $140; coffee server, 8½" tall, $32.*

AVON PRODUCTS

The "Avon Calling" selling concept had its origins in 1886, when Dr. H. McConnell founded the California Perfume Company. Early products bearing this original Avon name are eagerly sought. McConnell seemed blessed with an adventuresome spirit, for he hired women to sell his products—a radical approach for the period. Products were sold door-to-door, starting with a set of five perfumes called "Little Dot." The company prospered, becoming the Avon Corporation in 1929. Collectors compete for perfume bottles, figural containers, food coloring kits, vanity sets, silver cream polish containers, soaps, and an array of other Avon attractions. *Value guide: beauty basket, 1947, $95; Black Sheep set, 1955, $70.*

BABY SANDY DOLLS

Dedicated movie-goers remember Baby Sandy, widely publicized as "The Wonder Baby" by Universal Pictures. Ralph Freundlich, an American doll maker, conceived the all-composition Baby Sandy

Baby Sandy Doll

doll. It appeared in sizes ranging from 7 to 26 inches. This chubby toddler doll with a smiling face was a big ticket item at toy shops between 1939 and 1941. She had a swivel head, jointed shoulders and hips, and molded hair. Cinema buffs compete with doll collectors over Baby Sandy dolls, which explains why she remains a star attraction at markets. *Value guide: Baby Sandy doll, composition, swivel head, molded hair, sleep eyes, dressed, 14" tall, $250.*

BAD ACCIDENT BANK

Prolific toy bank designer Charles A. Bailey worked exclusively with the J. & E. Stevens and Company in the late 1800s. It has been estimated that he was partially responsible for over 30 different banks. His Bad Accident bank features a man wearing a blue jacket and red pants and driving a yellow mule cart with orange wheels. After placing a penny between the feet of the driver, a lever is pressed next to his coattails. Suddenly a small boy darts in front of the donkey, which rears up. As the cart and driver tip backward, the coin is deposited in the bottom of the cart. As for the boy, he is unharmed and ready to face the possibility of another accident at the sight of another penny. The words "Bad Accident" appear on the base of the bank. *Value guide: Bad Accident, cast iron, 6" tall, $650.*

BALTIMORE & OHIO CHINA

D. William Scammel, of the Lamberton Works, Trenton, New Jersey, executed a stunning blue and white dinner service to commemorate the 100th anniversary of the Baltimore & Ohio railroad. Accessories in the Baltimore & Ohio 1827-1927 service were clearly marked "Scammel's Lamberton/China/Patent Applied for." Dining car patrons had every reason to be impressed, for the design had well known locomotives around the border and boasted center subjects of famous landmarks along the railroad's routes. This pattern was later produced by other American potters. More than one piece of this railroad china has traveled the dining car to dining room route. *Value guide: platter, Diesel 51 center decor, 10½" diameter, $70.*

BAMBI

Walt Disney's dearly loved deer, Bambi, lit up the screen when the feature premiered on August 13, 1942. Bambi buffs hunt for cels and stills from the film. The Evan K. Shaw factory issued ceramic figurines of the film's characters. Feeding dishes picturing Bambi were also made by this firm. The American Pottery Company of Los Angeles, California heralded a line of Bambi childrens' dinnerware in the later 1940s. Even the New York Graphic Society had fun with this fawn in a series of colored lithographs, available with or without frames. Perhaps one of the most engaging Bambi items was the Ingersoll wristwatch, which retailed for $6.95 in 1948. *Value guide: comic book, Horlick's Malted Milk premium, 1941, $60; figure, Steiff, 4½" tall, 1940s, $55.*

BAMBOO FURNITURE

The bamboo craze, which began in America at the time of the Centennial, reached a fever pitch by the 1880s; real and imitation bamboo was declared acceptable for furnishing a country house. Furniture crafted of imported bamboo was made by many companies, notably Nimura and Sato of Brooklyn, and J. E. Wall of Boston. Imitation bamboo made of maple or bird's eye maple also proved popular with such makers as George Hunzinger, C. A. Aimone, and the Kilian Brothers. The latter offered an imitation bamboo chair for $8.67. In America, bamboo and pseudo-bamboo furniture was especially suited for bedroom areas. In fact, the *Decorator and Furnisher* magazine, the last word in home furnishings, declared in 1886 that bamboo made a room "light and bright, summery and inviting." *Value guide: chair, side, circa 1890, $225; easel, circa 1900, $200.*

Bamboo Side Chair

BANGLE BRACELETS

Fashion-minded ladies of the late 19th century always armed them-

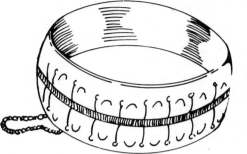

Bangle Bracelet

selves with an assortment of gold, gold-filled, or silver inflexible bracelets. By the 1860s, the hinged bangle was a jewelry-box staple. Conservative ladies selected the plainer engraved types, while more adventuresome ones purchased those displaying semi-precious stones. In the early 1900s, a vogue developed for narrow bangles, worn in sets of six or more. The bangle moved up in popularity in the late 1930s when slave bangles ornamented upper arms. *Value guide: gold 14K, florentine bangles, $250; sterling silver, repousse work, $90.*

BARBER BOTTLES
Beautiful barber bottles sold at a fast clip in the late 1800s and early

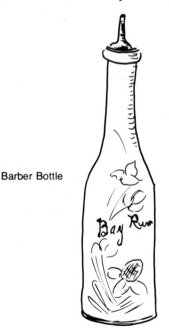

Barber Bottle

1900s. European and American glasshouses fashioned them in an endless variety of styles. These handsome containers, essential to a gentleman's grooming, held tonic, shampoo, cologne, witch hazel, and other preparations. Some had long, narrow necks suitable for holding a sprinkling device. Practically every type of decoration was employed, principally engraved, etched, and enameled effects. Pressed and milk glass bottles were also within easy reach of many barbers. The Mary Gregory, art glass, and gilded varieties fetch razor-sharp returns. *Value guide: Clambroth bottle, 9" tall, $50; enameled florals, amethyst, original top, 9½" tall, $120.*

BARBIE DOLLS

When Barbie, the world's best-selling doll, was introduced in 1958, she retailed for $3.00. Some of Barbie's costumes, which were sold separately, were more expensive than the doll. Most ranged from $1.00 to $5.00, with an entire wardrobe of 19 costumes retailing for $51.10. This ensemble included a Barbie-Q outfit, Easter Parade, Peachy Fleecy Coat, and Wedding Day attire. Originally, there were blonde and brunette Barbie's, but in recent years only blondes have been manufactured. A Barbie "family" originated, starting with the boy friend Ken in 1960. He was followed by Barbie's little sister, Skipper, a cousin, Francie, and friends Midge, Christie, Stacey, P. J., Steffie, and Kelley. Additional relatives and friends were gradually added as Barbie's popularity persisted. *Value guide: Barbie #1 mint, in box, 1959, $900; Barbie #2 mint, in box, 1959, $450.*

BARCLAY MANUFACTURING COMPANY

Prior to World War II, the Barclay Manufacturing Company of New Jersey ranked as America's foremost maker of toy soldiers. The firm was founded in the 1920s. Several types of soldiers were made through 1941: small mounted figures with moving arms; 3½" versions with separate tin helmets (known as short strides), and die-cast figures with "cast helmets." In 1938, following complaints from retailers, a clip held on the helmets. Frank Krupp, a Barclay employee, was the principal designer and sculptor during the 1930s. Their toy cars customarily bore the trademark "Barclay, Made in U.S.A." This prolific toymaker marched into oblivion in 1971, when the firm shuttered. *Value guide: soldier, standing, rifle, $10.*

BARNEY GOOGLE

Billy De Beck originally introduced Barney Google as Aleck, one of the harrassed spouses in a feature entitled "Married Life," for the *Chicago Tribune* in 1916. The first daily sequence of "Take Barney

Google, For Instance" appeared on the sports pages of the *Herald-Examiner* on June 17, 1919. By the following week it was renamed "Barney Google, F'Instance." A sports-oriented guy, he was more interested in prize fighters, horses, and baseball diamonds than in family life. Barney became devoted to a race horse named "Sparkplug." The horse was always covered with a blanket. Why? To keep his knock-knees from showing! The exploits of this feisty, tophatted character were typically featured on the sports pages. During the Roaring Twenties he was the subject of that snappy toe-tapper, "Barney Google with the Goo-Goo-Googly Eyes." *Value guide: cereal bowl, ceramic, Germany, $40; candy container, Sparkplug, $85.*

Barney Google & Sparkplug Toy

BASSETT-LOWKE

A meeting between W. J. Bassett-Lowke of England and Stefan Bing of Germany at the Paris Exhibition of 1900 had a profound effect upon the model railway industry when Bing entered into an agreement to manufacture realistic models for Bassett-Lowke. These models were not to be sold in Germany. Henry Greenly, consulting engineer, designed many early models. A perfected version of the Black Prince, the initial Bing-Bassett-Lowke model, was introduced in 1910. Through skillful promotion this Northampton, England, company became synonymous with superior model railways until the founder's death in 1953. In fact, Bassett-Lowke's London showroom was called the "Mecca of the Model Railway." *Value guide: "Streamlinia," live-steam launch, 39" length, 1930s, $3,500.*

Bassett-Lowke Model Locomotive

BATMAN

That man Batman was created by writer Bill Finger and artist Bob Kane for the May, 1939, issue of *Detective Comics, No. 27.* Unlike Superman, Batman did not possess super powers. Actually, the Batman character who roamed about the alleys of Gotham City by night relentlessly stalking criminals was millionaire Bruce Wayne in his civilian identity. His unique batlike cape and cowl made him instantly recognizable. He took a ward, Robin, known as The Boy Wonder. Readers multiplied as villains, such as The Joker, The Penquin, The Riddler, Two-Face, and The Cat Woman, (who lost her heart to Batman), appeared. Two Batman serials surfaced in the 1940s, along with a radio program. The 1966 television series starring Adam West brought about the issuance of a bundle of Batman novelties. *Value guide: buckle, utility belt radio, 1941, $85; game, Bradley, complete, 1960s, $40.*

BATTERY-OPERATED TOYS

Certain members of the toy-collecting fraternity get a charge from acquiring Japanese battery-operated toys. Many date from between the late 1940s until about 1960. It was not unusual for these toys to be made on a cottage industry basis. Models in working condition are preferred, since repair work can be a tedious job. Also, many batteries leaked over the years, causing damage to the toys. Perhaps the most familiar toy in this category is the drinking and smoking Charlie Weaver. Hundreds of other varieties exist, many depicting human figures, comic characters, and animals. Others, displaying a degree of originality, included a trotting Teddy Bear, an Indian beating drums, and a smoking Popeye. *Value guide: peanut vendor, original box, $165; Teddy the Artist, original box, $150.*

BAUMGARTEN'S TAPESTRIES

America's first tapestry works was established by William Baumgarten in 1893 on Fifth Avenue, New York City. Mr. Foussadier, a former weaver at the Royal Windsor Tapestry Manufactory, became an associate in the enterprise. Initially only furniture panels were made on low-warp looms. One of the original pieces was a Louis XV chair seat. After relocating to Williamsbridge, New York, Mr. Foussadier recruited a number of French weavers from Aubusson. At this point, decorative tapestries and reproductions of Francis Gobelin designs were crafted. Although they received numerous commissions, the factory shuttered in 1912. *Value guide: Aubusson panel, vase, flower medallion, 8½' × 3½', circa 1900, $350.*

BAWO AND DOTTER

Frances Bawo and Charles Dotter became New York importers during the mid-1860s. They represented W. H. Goss, W. T. Copeland, and Simon & Halbig, among others. During the 1880s, they acquired two European decorating studios. Objects marked "Elite Works" originated at their Limoges location, while "Carlsbad China," accompanied by a shield, denotes production at Fishern bei Carlsbad. Further expansion was undertaken in 1888, when the partners purchased a glass factory at Steinshoenau, Bohemia. A decade later Bawo and Dotter became internationally known with retail outlets in Paris, London, Berlin, Hamburg, and Brussels. *Value guide: cake plate, roses, Elite, 12" diameter, $50; powder box, Napoleon's portrait, "Carlsbad China," 3½" tall, $45.*

BEADED BAGS

Flappers of the 1920s never ventured far without a colorful beaded bag. These bags, usually with linings of cloth or chamois, had fancy beads arranged in eye-catching patterns. Society matrons generally carried bags with sterling silver frames, while others satisfied their

Beaded Bag

buying urges with nickel silver frames. Many of the better bags were embellished with semiprecious stones. The fanciest bags, of course, fetch the fanciest figures. Some bear a maker's mark on the frame. Those small narrow netted purses slit at the center known as "miser's purses" are also sought. In the post-World War I era, beaded bags moved faster than feet to the beat of the Charleston. *Value guide: beaded, butterfly decor, Czechoslovakian, 1920s, $50; beads, multi-colored florals, sterling frame, Gorham, 1920s, $100.*

BEATLES

Americans fell in love with the Beatles when the "lads from Liverpool" made an appearance on "The Ed Sullivan Show" on February 9, 1964. Already a sensation, they had recorded the two top songs in the country. Three months later they had the top five songs and the top two albums. Between this time and 1970, when they disbanded, John Lennon, Paul McCartney, George Harrison, and Ringo Starr reigned supreme as a musical force. Beatle wigs sold rapidly, because many fans emulated them in this fashion. Bubble gum cards, lunch boxes, dolls, buttons, paperback books, banjos, rings, coloring books, bedsheets, and tote bags are just a few of the countless items traded annually at Beatlefest, the official Beatles Fan Celebration held in major cities across the country. *Value guide: bandana, $25; lunch box, $30.*

BEER CANS

Prior to prohibition, beer was typically stored and shipped in kegs and dispensed in returnable bottles. Following the repeal of the Prohibition Act in 1933, it became necessary to store beer for longer periods of time. The American Can Company began experiments, culminating in a patent for a lined can for its "Keglined" process issued on September 25, 1934. The Gottfried Kruger Brewery Company, Newark, New Jersey, became the first firm to use the can. Pabst followed suit, becoming the first major company to join the beer can revolution. The cone-top beer can was introduced by the Continental Can Company in 1935; Schlitz was the first brewery to use this type of can. Highly collectible cone-top cans were everyone's favorite through 1950; then the aluminum can reached the marketplace, followed by the lift-top aluminum can in the late 1950s, and the tab-top in 1962. Collectors prefer cans that have been opened from the bottom, with no signs of rust or dents. *Value guide; Acme Boch, Los Angeles, flat-top, 12-ounce, $100; Ballentine's Ale, Newark, cone-top, 33-ounce, $65.*

BENTWOOD ROCKING CHAIR

Bentwood rockers have been in continuous production since they were developed by the Thonet Brothers of Austria in 1860. Throughout the years, they have earned respect in the comfort and stability departments. Their long, gently curved seats, along with convoluted underframing, enabled them to furnish maximum support for tired bodies. By the 1880s, they were on sale in most English furniture shops. Subsequently, their fame spread to the United States. Most had caned seats and backs; quite often, the framework was painted black or brown. Some had button upholstery. Variations were inevitable, including an early 20th century Spanish version. *Value guide: bentwood rocker, cane seat, and back, Thonet, circa 1885, $750.*

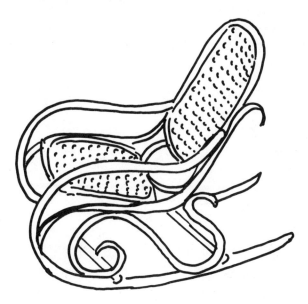

Bentwood Rocker

BERGEN, JAMES D.

James D. Bergen and Thomas Niland founded a glass-cutting concern in Meriden, Connecticut, in 1880. Shortly thereafter, Bergen assumed full ownership. He had sharpened his glass-cutting skills while toiling for the Mt. Washington Glass Company and the New England Glass Company. By the early 1900s, Bedford, Glenwood, Dallas, Elain, Claremont, Wabash, and Logan ranked as fast-selling cut-glass patterns. The firm flourished until 1916. Objects marked "Bergen" lightly etched in script or "Bergen" running across two world globes with the wording "Cut Glass" are considered a notch above the rest. *Value guide: cheese dish, Elaine pattern, $425; olive dish, Caprice pattern, 7" diameter, $175.*

BERRY BOWLS

Richly ornamented cut, engraved, clear, and colored glass fruit dishes, fruit stands, berry bowls, and centerpieces began appearing on dining room tables in the mid-1870s. At first, the silverplated stands housing the bowls were unpretentious, but later they became quite grand. As glass craftsman introduced art glass specialties in the 1880s, silversmiths matched their accomplishments with a full array of attractive stands. Mary Gregory, Agata, Amberina, Burmese, Peachblow, Pomona, and Satin glass bowls were supported by a bevy of beautiful mounts. Many glass inserts had fluted or ruffled edges. Favored as wedding gifts, many people referred to them as "Bride's Baskets." *Value guide: basket, enameled flowers, ruffled edges, Meriden silverplated frame, 10" diameter, circa 1885, $375; bowl, satin glass, butterscotch, flowers, silverplated frame, circa 1895, $285.*

Berry Basket with Frame

BETTY BOOP

That scandalous Betty Boop, the sexy star of animated cartoons, was introduced in Max Fleischer's "Betty Co-Ed" in 1931. Bouncy Betty scored such a hit that a series of cartoons emerged from Paramount Pictures. A comic strip was syndicated in 1935 by King Features, but the feature was dropped three years later because

Betty Boop Statuette

conservative elements found Betty a trifle too suggestive. Her last film was defiantly called, "Yip, Yip, Yippy." Fleischer profited from such character items as dolls, games, toys, and pocket watches. Articles pertaining to this Paramount prettie fetch a pretty penny. *Value guide: playing cards, complete, $65; soap, boxed, $85.*

BIG LITTLE BOOKS

At the time Americans were humming "Brother, Can You Spare a Dime," the Whitman Publishing Company of Racine, Wisconsin, introduced the ten-cent Big Little Books. These cube-shaped books had cartoons on the right page and text on the left pages and resembled hardcover "comic books." They measured 3½ × 4½ × 1½ inches. Sam Lowe's original six titles, based on comic characters, met with such success that approximately six new titles were issued monthly between 1934 and 1941. The subject matter broadened to include radio and movie titles. Sales topped the 12 million mark annually by 1938. During the early 1940s, "flip art" was introduced to create the illusion of movement when the pages were flipped. A serious paper shortage of World War II curtailed production on these pulp-paper pleasers. *Value guide: Jack Armstrong and the Ivory Treasure, 1937, $15; Tailspin Tommy and the Hooded Flyer, $30.*

BING AND GERBRUDER

The Gerbruder-Bing toy works was founded in Germany in the mid-1860s by Ignaz and Adolf Bing. They had the largest stand at the Bavarian Trades Exhibition of 1882. Trains were manufactured from this date; they were early sheet metal types with cast brass wheels that ran on zinc rails. By the 1890s, a factory for manufacturing enameled toys was founded at Grunhaim, Saxony. Warehouses and administrative buildings were centrally located in Nuremburg. By the early 1900s, they employed 4,000 workers. Especially sought are the soft toys in fur fabrics, velvet, and felt. For the American market they conceived lithographed metal, clockwork-powered cars, such as Checker and Yellow cabs, and five clockwork Ford Model Ts. Their toys were marked "GBN" until 1919, when the mark changed to "BW." *Value guide: Magic Lantern, tin, painted, circa 1902, $150; Orient Express, five piece, gauge "one" electric train set, circa 1910, $2,500.*

Bing Touring Car

BISMARCK BANK

Americans became enraged when, in 1883, Germany's Chancellor

Otto von Bismarck passed legislation placing import restrictions on pork products. Newspaper headlines voiced nationwide disapproval over his actions. A retaliatory toy bank was conceived by Charles A. Bailey, a noted designer of the era. This pig-shaped mechanical bank had a coin slot above the pig's tail. It was activated by placing a coin in the slot and pressing the tail, whereupon Chancellor Bismarck's head popped from the pig's body—much to the delight of pork lovers. *Value guide: Bismarck bank, $2,000.*

Bismarck Bank

BISSEL'S 39 CARPET SWEEPER

Were you among the 45 million visitors who browsed through the 1,500 exhibits at the 1939 New York World's Fair? Then perhaps you arrived home with one or more souvenirs depicting the fair's two symbols: the 200-foot ball known as the Perisphere, and the Trylon Tower. They were prominently featured on Bissel's '39 carpet sweeper. This sweeper, made expressly for this event, was decorated in the fair's blue and orange color scheme. They seldom gather any dust at markets, for existing examples are in short supply. *Value guide: Bissel's 39 carpet sweeper. $150.*

BLACK FOREST CLOCKS

Modestly priced German wall clocks from the Black Forest region have been regarded as trusty timekeepers since the 1600s. Three centuries later, weight-driven varieties, notably the cuckoo, trumpeter, and picture frame models, were being exported to America in increasing numbers. A change from wooden to brass movements occurred during this period. Heavy production schedules necessitated a shift from cottages to factories. As im-

31

ports threatened their livelihood, some makers crafted timepieces imitative of American models. The German-made OG clocks fall into this category. Reproductions of German medieval clocks, dated 1492, were crafted in honor of the 1892 Columbian Exposition. Statistics show that over 4,000 clocks were crafted every 24 hours by clever Black Forest clockmakers during the 1890s. *Value guide: OG Clock, German, circa 1875, $265.*

BLACKINTON & COMPANY

Sterling silver and 14 karat gold novelties, flatware, holloware, and dresserware from the R. Blackinton & Co. of North Attleboro, Massachusetts, have been favored since the early 1860s. It is still owned and operated by members of the same two founding families. Around the turn of the century, the company began to create costume jewelry articles displaying art nouveau forms. A belt pin or buckle of the times might sport a woman's head surrounded by swirls, plants, and leaf forms. Ever alert to changing public tastes, Blackinton announced in the early 1900s that over "200 new patterns were now in production." *Value guide: belt pin, lady's head, sterling silver, circa 1905, $75.*

Blackinton Silver Buckle

BLISS MANUFACTURING COMPANY

Dollhouses from the Bliss Manufacturing Company of Pawtucket, Rhode Island, keep collectors in a state of bliss. Founded in 1832, the company manufactured wooden toys, games, and architectural toys. By the 1890s, their lithographed dollhouses boasted an abundance of decoration. As a general rule, they were quite complex. Gingerbread facades, skyscrapers, stables, and mansions were fabricated of brightly colored papers glued to wood. Paper printed windows adorned smaller models, while larger versions boasted mica windows. Some dollhouse furnishings were also produced. Many of these beloved bygones bear the Bliss title for easy identification. *Value guide: townhouse, gingerbread facade, marked Bliss, circa 1900, $650.*

Bliss Dolls' House

BLOCK OPTIC PATTERN

In 1929, when Marlene Dietrich captivated cinema-goers in "The Blue Angel," executives at the Hocking Glass Company were surveying sales on Block Optic table settings. This machine-pressed and blown pattern captured the spirit of the '30s with its wide concentric circles set apart and divided into blocks. Until 1933, depression-weary buyers purchased tablewares in green, pink, yellow, and crystal. Despite a bulky appearance, Block Optic proved fragile. The geometric pattern echoes the spirit and splendor of art deco. *Value guide: compote, green, 4" diameter, $12; salt and pepper shakers, yellow, $65.*

Block Optic Pattern Creamer

BLONDIE

Remember those Saturday matinee "Blondie" films starring Penny Singleton? Did you realize that Blondie Boopadoop was created by Chic Young? She made her debut on comic pages as a bird-brained flapper being pursued by Dagwood Bumstead, playboy son of a railroad tycoon on September 15, 1930. On February 13, 1933, they were married, and readers have lived happily ever after. became a devoted wife, rescuing Dagwood from untold difficulties. A son, Alexander, appeared in 1934, followed, in 1941, by a sister, Cookie. Eventually, when the strip was internationally read, Blondie's readers totaled into the hundred millions. In addition, the strip inspired 28 movies, a television series, a novel, and bounty of Blondie mementos. *Value guide: Blondie Comics #12, David McKay Publications, fine condition, $95; wind-up toy, Dagwood in the Airplane, Marx, $575.*

BONE DISHES

Bone dishes, sold singly or as part of a dinner service, became tabletop staples in the late 1800s. They were crafted in an endless variety of motifs by American and European potters. One was placed on the table in front of each diner to accommodate fish bones. Those crescent shapes were developed so that they could curve around dinner plates. Haviland specimens generally bore florals, while scalloped edges were widely preferred by German potters. Brides of the period were often presented with one or more sets of these oddities. Bone-dish buffs will be fast to concur: those fish shaped versions represent quite a catch. *Value guide: Flow Blue, Lorne, Grindley, $25; Haviland, roses, $15.*

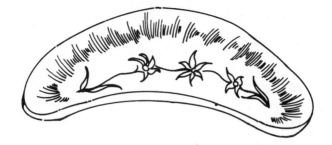

Bone Dish

BONNET DOLLS

By the 1860s and 1870s, Bonnet dolls began appearing in company catalogs. Apparently they were ahead of their time, for these bisque dolls failed to attract an audience until the turn of the century. Bonnet dolls were sold in various sizes, sporting a veritable "Easter Parade" of bonnets. Due to their headgear, they were originally called "hooded," "fancy hatted," or "princess" dolls. Most were crafted of coarse bisque by German makers. According to reports they failed to find favor with children. Why? Because the hair and hats on these dolls were not removable, but rather molded into the overall design. *Value guide: doll, large bonnet, molded hair, German, 13" tall, circa 1905, $265.*

Bisque Bonnet Doll

BOOKMARKS

Looking for an affordable collectible? Then investigate the opportunities vintage bookmarks can provide. There are many one-of-a-kind varieties, including crocheted, embroidered, hand-painted, and woven types. Bookmark buffs also seek the manufactured silver, silverplate, silk, or lithographed versions. Knowledgeable collectors expect the unexpected, for some silver versions had their own knives. Woven silk bookmarks represent another choice category, particularly those ascribed to Thomas Stevens of Coventry, England. Be assured, when an advertising, commemorative, or souvenir bookmark pops from the pages of a family Bible, there is a bookmark enthusiast ready to purchase it. *Value guide: sterling silver, florals, circa 1910, $50; Thomas Stevens, "Home Sweet Home," woven silk, $140.*

BOSS WASHING MACHINE

No homemaker could dispute it: the electrically powered washing machine was an improvement over the primitive washboard and tub. The Boss, patented by the Heunfield Company of Cincinnati,

Boss Washing Machine

Ohio, on July 5, 1888, was a giant step forward in combating the Monday morning blahs. This early, hand-operated model was shaped to resemble a cradle. An iron wheel with a wooden handle was at one side of the machine; when set in motion it caused the two grooved wooden cradles to rock back and forth. Rival manufacturers did them dirty by immediately marketing similarly constructed washing machines. *Value guide: The Boss, circa 1892, $350.*

BOSTON CARD

The Boston Card was a fifth place winner in Louis Prang's competition of 1884. This annual event was held in that year at the Richards Gallery of New York City. The design was executed by Miss L. B. Humphrey, the noted late-Victorian greeting card artist and illustrator. On the front of the card was a charming chromolithographed Christmas scene, while the back, which was printed in monochrome, has the message along with a view of Boston. This view provided this Christmas card with its Boston Card title. *Value guide: the Boston Card, $20.*

BOWLING ALLEY BANK

Kyser and Rex of Philadelphia were leading hardware specialists of the 1870s. About 1880, they were the recipients of numerous patents including one for the coveted Bowling Alley penny saver. This orange bank, featuring touches of gold, has a male bowler outfitted in a white shirt and black trousers. The somewhat predictable action consists of placing the ball in the bowler's hand and inserting the coin in the box behind him. The bowler poises himself; the ball leaves his hand, rolls down the alley, and —you guessed it —he gets a strike. Just as the ball hits the pins, a ringing bell sounds to signal his bowling accomplishment. *Value guide: Bowling Alley bank, iron and wood, 5¾" tall, $18,500.*

BOX CAMERAS

Family photography took a giant step forward with the introduction of the first Kodak box camera in 1888. At first, the development charge was absorbed in the cost of the camera. Through the 1930s, cameras of wood, cardboard, leather, or leatherlike materials clicked with shutterbugs. Subsequently, plastic types supplanted all others. Some early cameras were loaded with glass plates or special film packs rather than the familiar roll films. Over the years variations such as detective cameras, plate-loading cameras, and extra-wide versions for panoramic views appealed to the "watch the birdie" set. *Value guide: Blair Weno Hawkeye, No. 6, $75; Kodak Quick Focus, 1906, $90.*

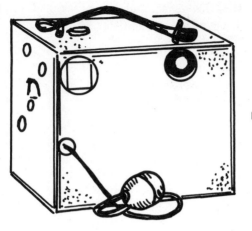

Box Camera

BOY ON TRAPEZE BANK

Children of the late 19th century became captivated with this brightly colored, cast-iron mechanical bank from the J. Barton Smith Company of Philadelphia. When originally issued, it was known as French's Automatic Toy Bank. The action of the bank was described as follows on an advertising card: "The more money the boy gets, the more he will do to earn it. For one penny dropped in the head the boy revolves once, for a nickel twice, for a quarter dollar three times, for a half dollar six times." The action is triggered by the weight of the coin. Dimes were precluded, because they did not possess sufficient weight to activate the boy, who was clad in a red shirt and blue pants. The base was of blown lacquer. Company promotions mentioned that this bank was the "children's choice." *Value guide: Boy on trapeze bank, cast iron, 9" tall, $875.*

BOY ROBBING BIRD'S NEST BANK

Charles Bailey, that ingenious late 19th century bank designer, was responsible for the Boy Robbing Bird's Nest mechanical bank. It bore such familiar Bailey characteristics as a realistic tree, lush foliage, and vines. The bank features a tree with two birds and a boy far out on one limb about to rob a bird's nest. To set this J. & E. Stevens & Company creation in motion, a penny is placed in the slot on the tree trunk located just below the branch. The lever appears beneath the left bird. As the branch falls down, taking the boy and nest, the penny is knocked into the bank. In the early 1900s, this cast-iron novelty was called "The Tree Bank." *Value guide: Boy Robbing Bird's Nest Bank, 8" tall, circa 1895, $1,250.*

BRASS BAND HARMONICA

What harmonica billed itself as "The King of All Harmonicas" in the early 1900s? None other than the Brass Band Harmonica. Musically inclined individuals discovered that it furnished hours of musical melodies. Advertisements mentioned that "this instrument has no equal." Furthermore, "it was perfectly tuned." The Brass Band has 10 double holes, 40 bell metal reeds, brass plates, reeds, and extension ends. To tempt buyers, this harmonica rested securely in a handsome wood-lined case. With all of this hoopla, who can believe it retailed for $1.00! *Value guide: Brass Band Harmonica, $18.*

BRASS BEDS

The brass bed began appearing in rural English communities in the second quarter of the 19th century. Following a successful showing at the Great London Exhibition of 1851, middle-class English and American families began ordering them. Early examples boasted Renaissance Revival details, such as cherubs at the corners and canopies. Eventually, designs became more open and symmetrical. Birmingham, England, became the world's brass bed center. The all-brass seamless versions usually had straight lines, while the iron-tubing types wrapped with brass sheet metal showed a seam on the rod where the end of the brass was crimped. A magnet will stick to this type of bed. The least desirable ones were made from brass-plated metal. Although some art deco styles had rectilinear designs, brass beds were holding fewer slumberers by the 1930s. *Value guide: double, standard tubular style, circa 1885, $800; single, standard tubular style, circa 1895, $450.*

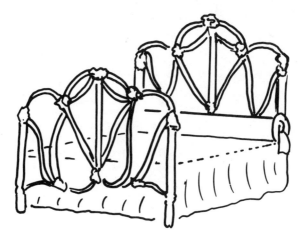

Brass Bed

BRINGING UP FATHER

When "Bringing Up Father" first hit newspapers in 1913, it appeared irregularly, although its creator, George McManus, had already established himself as a first-rate cartoonist. The strip became a daily feature in 1916, with a Sunday version launched by 1918. The theatricality of the feature, with its witty dialogue, zany characters, and unusual situations brought it world-wide acclaim. The basic plot, set against Art Nouveau furnishings, centers around Jiggs running out of the house while ducking Maggie's rolling pin. It has been adapted to the screen, animated cartoons, and reprinted in book form. During the war, Jiggs became the official emblem of the Eleventh Bombardment Squadron. *Value guide: ashtray, Jiggs, German, $60; wood figure, 39" tall, "Dec. 25, 1927," $400.*

BRITAIN'S

Since 1893, Britain's of London has made a vast number of model soldiers and military processions. Individual figures are somewhat more plentiful than complete boxed sets. William Britain introduced hollow cast figures that were light to handle and inexpensive to produce. From the outset, the company placed emphasis upon accurate renderings of colors and uniforms; many were sold in shiny

Britains Model Soldier

red boxes. The Lifeguards appeared first, followed by the Grenadiers and kilted Highlanders. Early "plug-handled Highlanders" had a separate sword or rifle plugged into the cuff of the right hand. As a dating guide, The City Imperial Volunteers were the first to bear the label "Copyright Wm. Britain Jun. 1 1900," and from the 1900s the company's mark was embossed on horses. By 1902, 104 different regiments were in production. *Value guide: Red Army Cavalry, set #2028, $550; U.S. Army Infantry, set #2033, original box, $90.*

BROOKLYN BRIDGE SHEET MUSIC

In the late 19th and early 20th centuries, developments, inventions, topical events, passing fads, and political happenings all served as a source of inspiration for Tin Pan Alley dwellers. In 1883, the completion of the Brooklyn Bridge afforded travelers a gracefully arched exit from the crowded isle of Manhattan. Overnight the very same travelers found themselves humming the "Brooklyn Bridge Grand March." This E. Mack ditty was published by the Oliver Ditson Company. It bore a panoramic cover view of the famed bridge. Do not be dismayed if a flea entrepreneur tries selling you the Brooklyn Bridge. *Value guide: "Brooklyn Bridge Grand March," $25.*

BROWNIES

The Brownies cavorted into the hearts of Americans upon their introduction in *St. Nicholas* magazine in 1883. Through the early

Brownie Cloth Dolls

1900s, they populated the pages of countless childrens' periodicals. The first Palmer Cox book, *The Brownie's Their Book* was published in 1887. Twelve other books followed, chalking up sales in excess of $1 million. Palmer Cox copyrighted and patented 12 Brownie figures on January 15, 1982. These figures adorned many novelties including paper dolls from the Frederick F. Stokes Company, as well as cloth dolls from the Arnold Print Works. Brownie rubber stamps, silverware, scarf pins, spoons, childrens' dishes, figurines, and games followed in swift succession. *Value guide: bowling pins, Palmer Cox, complete set, $425; tray, advertising ice cream, $65.*

BUBBLE PATTERN

The Bubble depression-glass pattern burst on the scene in 1934. Originally, this Hocking Glass Company staple was called "Bull's Eye." The lengthy history of the design, with its overall bull's eye dots, attests to its prolonged public acceptance. Pink table settings became available between 1934 and 1937, followed by green and crystal renditions. Light blue opaque accessories abounded during

Bubble Pattern Creamer & Sugar

the 1940s. A decade later, a milk glass version was being marketed, followed by a dark red and crystal reissue. Avowed depression-glass buffs naturally prefer the earlier specimens. *Value guide: creamer, pink, $20; platter, oval, blue, $14.*

BUCKLES

When Americans fell under the influence of Art Nouveau, buckle makers were besieged with orders. Suddenly they adorned belts, shoes, capes, cloaks, and even girdles. Brass, silverplated, and sterling silver types won top awards in fashion circles. Especially popular were those possessing florals, butterflies, peacocks, leaves, and nudes set against naturalistic backgrounds. Marked examples abound from leading domestic and European factories. The Gorham Silver Company and the Unger Brothers were two American concerns who found themselves waist deep in the buckle business. *Value guide: belt, brass, Art Nouveau florals, circa 1900, $75; shoe, French cut steel, pair, circa 1915, $35.*

Sterling Silver Art Nouveau Buckle

BUCK ROGERS

America's first science-fiction comic strip landed from outer space onto comic pages on January 7, 1929. Initially it was called "Buck Rogers in the year 2429 A.D." Later it became known as "Buck Rogers in the 25th Century," and finally "Buck Rogers." It was adapted by Phil Nowlan from his novel *Armageddon 2419 A.D.* The artist was Dick Calkins; the distributor, John F. Dille Company. Readers were stunned by such futuristic objects as rocket pistols, disintegrator guns, rocket ships, and space satellites. Soon copies of these imaginative items were being sold on the planet Earth. The strip was the basis for a radio series, a movie, and a comic book. Participants in the Buck Rogers "cult" seek early buttons, books, Big Little Books, chemistry sets, pop-up books, games, helmets, paint boxes, rings, rocket pistols, telescopes, and timepieces. *Value guide: pop-up book, complete, $190; disintegrator gun, Daisy Mfg., $135.*

Buck Rogers Rocket Pistol

BUDDY "L"

Fred Lundahl, owner of the Moline Pressed Steel Company of
Moline, Illinois, introduced Buddy "L" toys in 1921. They were

Buddy L Model T

affectionately named for his son. The so-called "indestructible" heavy steel toys capable of supporting a child's weight were distributed through 1932. The majority measured between 21 and 24 inches in length. Collectors enjoy wheeling and dealing for early trucks, pile drivers, concrete mixers, fire engines, and road rollers. Subsequently, modified, lighter weight vehicles were marketed. Various name changes have been instituted over the years, including "Buddy 'L' Corp." "Buddy 'L' Toy Co.," and in recent years those quotation marks have disappeared. *Value guide: Curtis Candy truck, $265; trencher, 1928-31, $300.*

BUFFALO POTTERY

The Buffalo Pottery of Buffalo, New York, was founded by John Larkin, of the Larkin Soap Company, in 1901. It was established to provide pottery and ceramics for premium use, as well as for general sale. Dinner sets, toilet sets, a poppy-decorated chocolate pot and cracker jar, and a three-piece oatmeal set were among the first semivitreous pieces made at the pottery. In 1905, they introduced an underglaze Blue Willow, which was considered superior to the imported ware. Each piece of Blue Willow dated 1905 bore the wording, "First Old Willow Ware Manufactured in America." A series of advertising and commemorative plates appeared about this time, along with various pitchers or jugs. The latter were made through 1909. Deldare Ware was marketed in 1908. The pottery changed from semivitreous to vitrified china in 1915, stamping wares "Buffalo China" rather than "Buffalo Potter." *Value guide: cup and saucer, Blue Willow, demi-tasse, $25; pitcher, Robin Hood, $300.*

Deldare Ware Pitcher

45

BULLDOG SAVINGS BANK

In the 1880s, the brown-lacquered Bulldog savings bank was taking a bite of youngsters' budgets, for it was prohibitively priced at $3.50. This Ives, Blakeslee, & Company penny saver was patented by Enoch R. Morrison in 1878. Activated by a clockwork mechanism, the bank depicted a man at one end and a crouching bulldog above the main section. After placing a coin in the man's outstretched hand, the key to the spring is wound. Next, a lever is pressed below the figure. Children anticipated the action, which involved the dog springing forward, taking the coin from the man's hand, and swallowing it. *Value guide: Bulldog savings bank, iron, 7" tall, $950.*

Bulldog Savings Bank

BUSTER BROWN

Buster Brown, that impeccably dressed little boy with long blonde hair and a knowing smile, was created by Richard Felton Outcault. Buster Brown participated with his trusty sidekick, bulldog Tige, in a never-ending series of pranks. They were never malicious, though, and Buster Brown was always forgiven for his harmless mischief. The strip made its appearance in 1902, in the *New York Herald.* Shortly thereafter, it went into national syndication. Buster Brown and Tige became overnight celebrities, spawning a stream of advertising and souvenir articles. These two cohorts promoted shoes, buttons, liquor, hats, and even cigars. Their faces had

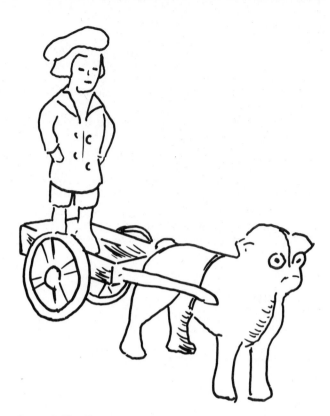

Buster Brown & Tige Toy

obtained immortality when the strip was discontinued in 1926. By
that time, however, sufficient mementos had been circulated to fill a
museum—or maybe even two. *Value guide: Buster Brown box
camera, $30; wristwatch, $135.*

BUTTER PATS

In the pre-bread-and-butter-plate period, small, individual butter
pats were placed on tabletops in front of diners. Although the shapes
varied, most were round or square. While enjoying worldwide
production, the sizes generally held at about 2½" diameter. A
representative assortment would reveal backstamps reading like a
"Who's Who" in potting circles, since Wedgwood, Copeland, Haviland, Coalport, and other prestigious European and American potters offered them as part of a complete dinnerware service. Delft,
Rose Medallion, Ironstone, and majolica examples also abound,
often at affordable prices. *Value guide: Etruscan majolica, lily pad,
$18; Rose Medallion, eight-sided, $40.*

BUTTON HOOKS

Why were button hooks deemed absolute essentials in the late 1800s? Because they facilitated fastening buttons on clothing, gloves, and high-button shoes. The hooked shafts were typically made of steel, but the decorative handles of silver, mother-of-pearl, wood, or ivory gave button hooks their distinctive look. Affluent buyers became hooked on the fanciful sterling silver models. Most measured up to 13 inches in length. The advertising types appeared in an infinite variety. Members of the button-hook brigade rarely allow an Art Nouveau style to slip through their fingers. *Value guide: silverplate, figural woman's leg, 6" long, $65; sterling silver, Art Nouveau florals, 9" long, $75.*

Silver Button Hook

BYE-LO BABY DOLLS

Grace Storey Putnam's Bye-Lo Baby doll is said to have been modeled after a three-day-old baby. The designer secured four copyrights: the first in 1922, two others in 1923, and yet another in 1924. She apparently endeavored to incorporate minor design changes over the years. The dolls, with celluloid, bisque, rubber, or composition heads were distributed by George Borgfeldt. Various factories produced the heads and bodies. As for size, most ranged between 13 and 20 inches. Dolls bearing the mark "Bye-Lo" or "Grace Putnam" can easily be converted into dollars. *Value guide: Bye-Lo Baby doll, bisque head, celluloid hands, cloth body, dressed, 18" tall, $1,100; doll, socket head, original body, dressed, 13", $750.*

Bye-Lo Baby Doll

48

C

CADOT et CIE

When the conversation shifts to French pewter ice-cream mold makers, the Cadot et Cie name springs to attention. Founded in

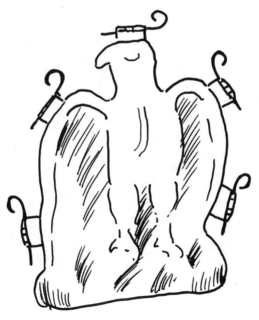

Eagle Ice Cream Mold

1826, it was one of the earliest European makers. This Paris-based maker executed molds in shapes ranging from beguiling to bewildering, a tribute to a combination of skills. Some of their ice cream treats, in fact, were too beautiful to eat. While the sculptor fashioned the original image, the craftsman did the chasing on the master mold in order to hold the detail of the design. Any mold bearing the letters "CC" accompanied by a handcranked ice cream freezer symbol can be safely attributed to Cadot et Cie. *Value guide: calla lily, $65; doves cooing, $70.*

CAKE BASKETS

American silversmiths made a variety of cake baskets around the turn of the century. They were deemed as ideal gifts for brides. Basically, the shape remained unchanged, although some subtle changes occurred as designers displayed a trace of originality. Round or oval types consistently won popularity awards. Some were set on low pedestals; others were footed. Cake baskets boasting engraved, chased, embossed, or pierced work were considered just a cut above the rest. Sterling and silverplated varieties were made and marked by a host of superior silversmiths. *Value guide: silverplated, William Rogers, vintage motif, ornate, 11" diameter, $85; sterling silver, Kirk, repousse work, florals, 12" diameter, $450.*

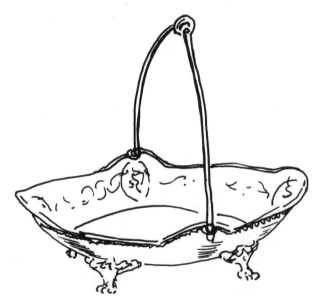

Silverplated Cake Basket

CALENDAR CLOCKS

Who was America's foremost maker of calendar clocks between 1865 and 1915? None other than the Ithaca Clock Company of Ithaca, New York. These timepieces were also made by such giants in the field as Seth Thomas, E. N. Welch Manufacturing Company, E. Ingraham, and the Waterbury Clock Company. Wall and shelf clocks in this category kept track of the date, as well as the time. While some required adjustments, others ostensibly remained accurate for up to 400 years. The cases, which varied depending upon the maker, were often of rosewood or walnut. For some inexplicable reason, this style of timepiece failed to attract a European audience. Calendar clocks bearing the name of a highly respected clockmaker are never outdated. *Value guide: Ingraham, rooster head, eight-day oak, $325; Seth Thomas, calendar, double dial, walnut, 36" tall, $1,400.*

CALENDAR PLATES

Those with a preference for dated collectibles scour the marketplace for calendar plates. While examples have been located dating from 1889, collector interest centers around plates from 1906 to 1921. They were circulated as "compliments of the season" by merchants and business establishments who thus benefitted from some subtle advertising. Most of these semi-vitreous creations bore calendar leaves along with selected center subjects. Gibson Girls, presidential portraits, airplanes, and even Betsy Ross proved popular as central themes. The potters of East Liverpool, Ohio, including D. E. McNicol; Dresden; Sterling; A. Harker; and Knowles, Taylor, and Knowles appear to have kept calendar plates in production 365 days of the year! *Value guide: Santa with holly, 9 ¼" diameter, $65; 1914, Betsy Ross, 8" diameter, $45.*

CALLING CARD CASES

Throughout the late 19th century people made a ritual of visiting friends and neighbors and leaving them with a calling card. The cards were customarily housed in small gold, silver, leather, mother-of-pearl, or tortoise-shell cases. Handsomely engraved or monogrammed types were preferred by affluent users. Many bore typical late Victorian or Art Nouveau modes of ornamentation. When this gracious custom fell from favor in the early 1900s, the cases became "beloved bygones." *Value guide: tortoise shell, mother-of-pearl effects, $50; sterling silver, engraved fish, circa 1890, $70.*

CALUMET BAKING POWDER BANKS

Do you remember the Calumet Kid? Edward Barnes of Chicago,

Illinois, patented a bank based on this lovable character on September 16, 1924. All tin versions, as well as cardboard and tin variations, now rank as rarities. Simply by depositing a coin in the bank, the Calumet Kid rocked back and forth on this mechanical marvel. The red can bore blue lettering pertaining to the product along with the wording, "You Save Time and Money by Using Calumet Baking Powder." Since few have survived in fine condition, collector interest has been compounding daily. *Value guide: cardboard and tin, $150; all tin, $200.*

CAMBRIDGE ART TILE WORKS

Those who treasure tiles hold marked specimens from the Cambridge Tile Works in high esteem. This Coventry, Kentucky, maker was established in 1887. Two years later they merged with the Mount Casino Tile Works. Following a decorating fad that started at the Centennial, tiles were used everywhere—in parlor, bedroom, and bath—and in woodwork and on furniture. One New York townhouse of the era was termed "a paradise of tiles." At present, some exquisitely embossed and enameled Cambridge tiles repose in museum collections. In the 1920s, a move was made to relocate the factory to Cincinnati, Ohio, but the production of art tiles was abandoned. *Value guide: warrior head, green glaze, 6" square, $65.*

CAMBRIDGE GLASS COMPANY

The National Glass Company of Cambridge, Ohio, began operating

Cambridge Seagull Candleholder

in 1902. Following a bankruptcy, Arthur Benett assumed control of the works, renaming it the Cambridge Glass Company in 1910. Under his guidance the company prospered with pressed, carnival, art glass, plus scores of novelties and stemware. Special recognition is due the firm for its Crown Tuscan production of the '20s. Through the years, designers maintained a contemporary look to the lines. Cambridge's animal figurines would fill a zoo. The factory, which ceased functioning in 1954, used a variety of trademarks, notably "Near-Cut," 1904-1940s; the letter "C" within a triangle, 1915-1930; and a paper label during the 1930s. *Value guide: compote, Crown Tuscan, emerald, 7" tall, $90; figurine, swan, crystal, 9" tall, $85.*

CAMEO PATTERN

The Cameo depression design has the honor of being the only pattern featuring a human figure. Small dancing girls wearing long draped scarves accompanied by festoons and ribbon bows encircled the borders. These figures have been responsible for some collectors nicknaming it Ballerina or Dancing Girl. Between 1930 and 1937, Cameo accessories waltzed into American emporiums in green, yellow, pink, and crystal. Some crystal specimens boasted platinum rims. Rumors abound that the draped figure, which appeared on over 40 different tableware items, was inspired by Isadora Duncan. *Value guide: pitcher, green, 5 ¾ " tall, $120; syrup, green, 5 ¾" tall, $135.*

Cameo Pattern Cookie jar.

CAMPBELL KIDS

The Campbell Kids have been cavorting about since the turn of the century. They first appeared on street car ads. Grace Gebbie Drayton, known professionally as Grace Gebbie Wiederseim, created these lovable characters, and as their fame spread, Campbell Kids were depicted on dozens of mementos. Various dolls have been marketed over the years, including, between 1911 and 1914, the E. I. Horsman versions with "Can't Break 'Em" heads. Other items, such as silverplated flatware, Buffalo Pottery childrens' dishes, pens, pencils, and potholders, also stir up interest as Campbell Kid keepsakes. *Value guide: doll, Horsman, composition head and hands, 11" tall, circa 1910, $125; soup spoon, girl, $10.*

Campbell Kids Doll

CAN OPENERS

Can openers, particularly any having a patent date, can open the path to unexpected collecting profits. Patent models proliferated in the late 1800s and early 1900s. By the 1890s, the iron "Delmonico" and "Peerless" styles became kitchen helpers. They were followed in close pursuit by the redoubtable "Never Slip" in 1892. To facilitate jar opening chores, the J. C. Foster Company of Pittsburgh, Pennsylvania, had a quadruple threat in its "Four-in-One" opener of 1910. All early types intrigue those smitten by kitchen keepsakes. The Roaring Twenties ushered in the "King" and "None-Such" just in time to please flabbergasted flappers. *Value guide: "Never Slip," circa 1894, $15; "Peerless," circa 1895, $18.*

Perfection Can Opener

CANDY CONTAINERS

Although the candy container fad had its birth during the Centennial Exposition of 1876, these glass toys won widespread acceptance about 1900. While earlier versions were intended for adults, the emphasis gradually shifted to the younger generation. The containers, which held tiny pellets of sugar candy, could still amuse a child after the candy had been consumed. Some earlier ones had corks or stoppers; later a small metal cap was preferred. The development of the automatic bottling machine enabled manufacturers to produce these glass containers in a wide variety of shapes. Candy containers depicting boats, animals, Santa Claus, pistols, trains, automobiles, carpet sweepers, and countless comic and celebrity figures rate as dandy acquisitions. *Value guide: Greyhound bus, $40; Happifats on Drum, $200.*

Windmill Candy Container

CANED-SEAT ROCKERS

That American institution, the rocking chair, rocked out of most American furniture factories in the late 19th century. Smaller makers, along with country craftsmen, showed a fondness for rectangular or oval backs, typically framed in maple or other hardwoods, with backs and seats of cane. These caned seats were subjected to heavy usage; thus many require recaning. Made with or without arms, some rockers had intricate carving on the crest rails. These rockers, which currently rate as super sitters, were loved by one and all, because they furnished maximum comfort. *Value guide: rocker, caned seat and back, maple, carved details, circa 1890, $275.*

CANES

As dress accessories, canes became fashion essentials for affluent gentlemen around the turn of the century. From a collecting standpoint, the major interest centers around the handles. Wealthy individuals preferred gold walking aids, often devoid of ornamentation except for a crest or monogram. For the masses, silver handles proved popular. They bore various decorative themes including armorial and spontaneous Art Nouveau subjects. Fragile glass canes, along with others of wood, brass, ivory, or horn, bore sufficient motifs to please the most discriminating buyer. *Value guide: sterling silver, dog's head handle, $150; wood, carved horse's head handle, $190.*

CAN'T BREAK 'EM DOLLS

In 1892, Solomon Hoffman of Brooklyn, New York, patented the composition "Can't Break 'Em" dolls. Undoubtedly, they were greeted with a hint of cautious optimism by parents. Although these

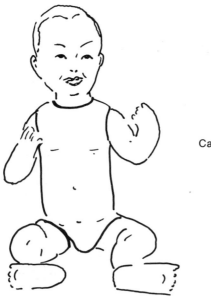

Can't Break-em Doll

composition heads had a reputation for durability, most show signs of cracking and peeling. Originally, they were imported from Germany, but by the early 1900s they were being manufactured domestically by the American Doll & Toy Manufacturing Company and the Aetna Doll & Toy Company. About 1910, Horsman became the sole distributor. By 1911 there were over 50 dolls in the line including Baby Bumps, Peterkin, Chinkee, Little Billy, Fluffy Ruffles, and the Campbell Kids. Were they popular? Apparently so, for by 1912, over 1 million "Can't Break 'Em" heads were being produced annually. *Value guide: Baby Bumps, composition head, molded hair, painted features, 12" tall, circa 1910, $125; Billiken, composition head, watermelon mouth, slanted slits for eyes, 12" tall, $250.*

CAPTAIN AMERICA

Captain America, created by Jack Kirby and Joe Simon, made his debut in Timely's *Captain America No. 1* in 1941. The first issue is a valuable collectors' item. Dressed in a star-spangled red, white, and blue flag-inspired outfit, he became the symbol of American patriotism during World War II. This larger-than-life super hero, Steve (Captain America) Rogers, conquered hordes of German enemies. When the war ended, Captain America floundered. The Captain's escapades terminated after May 1949 upon the publication of the 74th issue. Several revivals occurred over the next few decades, including a new Captain America magazine in 1968. In addition, the fearless Captain America was depicted in paperback, animated cartoons, and a 1943 movie serial. *Value guide: Captain America Comics #5, Marvel Comics Group, fine condition, $350.*

CAPTAIN MARVEL

The Captain Marvel feature appeared in 155 issues of Whiz Comics and 150 issues of Captain Marvel's Adventures. His adventures ended in January, 1954, in *Marvel Family #89*. The feature had been successful since 1940. Captain Marvel was actually Billy Batson. When he went to see the wizard Shazam, Billy spoke his name and was transformed into "The Big Red Cheese." This orange and gold long-underwear-clad super hero was the subject of a Republic serial in 1940. Various artists were employed under the direction of C. C. Beck, including Jack Kirby. One must acknowledge Captain Marvel as being the classic example of America's underlying optimism. His success spawned an entourage of Marvels. *Value guide: racing cars, Lightning, $350; tattoos, complete, original envelope, 1940s, $35.*

CAPTAIN MIDNIGHT

Wilifred Moore and Robert Muri premiered the Captain Midnight radio program on September 30, 1940. His first comic book ap-

pearance was in July, 1941, in Dell's *The Funnies, Number 57.*
Fawcett purchased the character, and it appeared in *Captain Midnight, Number 1,* in September, 1942. Captain Midnight was really Captain Albright, a crack flyer assigned to defeat Nazi official Ivan Shark prior to midnight. At the stroke of midnight, the mission was accomplished; hence the name. Between 1940 and 1949, when Ovaltine sponsored Captain Midnight's Secret Squadron radio program, various premiums were distributed. Big Little Books were also available at the same time that the Captain Midnight movie serial reached Saturday matinee crowds. *Value guide: decoder, 1940, $75; Ovaltine shaker, $35.*

CARD RECEIVERS

Silverplated card receivers became essentials during the era of the calling card. The earliest models were simply made, composed of a small tray mounted on a pedestal. Were they well received? Evidently, for in 1861, the Meriden Britannia Company offered four designs; that figure increased to 31 by 1879. They became ever fancier with ornate pedestal-supporting trays featuring elephant, owl, frog, peacock, cat, dog, and floral ornaments. Some depicted animals dressed as humans. Many had gold-washed highlights. Others boasted colorful art glass flower vases rising majestically

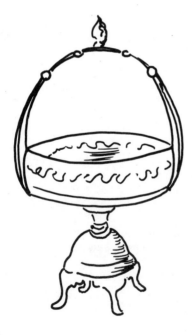

Silverplated Card Receiver

from the center tray. By the early 1900s, when the calling-card custom was considered old fashioned, card receivers were relegated to oblivion. *Value guide: Meriden Britannia receiver, dogs, Moorish, circa 1885, $165; Reed & Barton, cherub holding tray, gold lined, 1887, $175.*

CARLTON WARE

From the 1890s, Carlton Ware was produced at the Carlton Works, Stoke-on-Trent, by Wiltshaw and Robinson. Those who covet English ceramics prize their output, which often bore enameled or gilded effects. Fans and flowers were among the foremost decorative devices. Their Oriental luster wares have attracted many antiquarians. Although various trademarks were utilized, many objects have the circular "W & R/Stoke-on-Trent" mark enclosing a swallow topped by a crown. Quite frequently, the handpainted Carlton Ware symbol was incorporated into the backstamp. This prestigious pottery was renamed Carlton Ware Ltd. in 1958. *Value guide: cracker jar, white figures, blue ground, silverplated cover, $140; candleholder, Rough Royale, $50.*

CARNIVAL GLASS

Art nouveau glass designers, including Louis Tiffany, started a vogue for iridescent glass. Pressed glasshouses responded by marketing inexpensive wares in a multitude of exciting patterns. Some pieces bore one design on the interior and another on the exterior of an object. This iridescent glass, made by such factories as the Northwood Glass Company, Fenton Art Glass Company, Millersburg Glass Company, and the Imperial Glass Company, was destined for mass consumption. Full sets of tableware were pro-

Carnival Glass Bowl

duced; so specialization is possible. Countless patterns, some quite exotic, were marketed in various colors, notably shades of marigold, amber, cobalt blue, amethyst, purple, white, clambroth, red, green, smoky, peach, aqua, Vaseline, ice blue, or ice green. Carnival glass, once a giveaway at fairs and carnivals, qualifies as a choice collectible. *Value guide: Butterfly and Berry water set, blue, $325; Good Luck plate, marigold, 9" diameter, $150.*

CARPET BEATERS

Flea marketeers beat a path to any early carpet beater. Some of the earliest were home crafted of wood or wire. By the late 19th century, however, most general stores offered them in a variety of pleasing patterns. The all-wire or wire-with-wooden-handle versions, were twisted into wickedly wonderful shapes. Other, all-wooden, varieties sometimes bore a patent date or maker's trademark. There were also rattan and flexible hickory switch beaters capable of keeping the dust flying in every direction. At present, carpet-beater buffs fan out in all directions at the sight of an unusual specimen. *Value guide: all-wire, The Niagara, heavy steel, circa 1910, $25; all-wood, The Batwing Beater, 1920s, $35.*

The Niagara Carpet Beater

CARRETTES, GEORGES

Between 1886 and 1917, Georges Carrette & Cie was a major Nurenburg tin toy maker. Although a rivalry existed between Bing and Carrette, Bing became a backer in the venture. Carrette was the son of a Parisian photographer. Early toys of brass and tin often bore a hand-enameled finish. By the early 1900s, Carrettes' catalogues showed modified toys, less intricate than those being manufactured by his contemporaries. Tin cars, boats, planes, buses, and railways were being promoted at this point. Georges Carrettes, who had maintained his French citizenship, returned to his native country in 1914. About three years later the factory bearing his name shuttered. *Value guide: boat, clockwork, original paint, 8½" length, circa 1915, $300.*

60

Carette Toy Gunboat

CARTE DE VISITES

Cartomania was an international rage that persisted in the second half of the 19th century. The *carte-de-visite* photograph, usually full length, was taken with a multi-lens camera. Thus, anywhere from 8 to 12 exposures were made from a single collodion plate. The negative was cut up to achieve an equal number of prints. due to lower production costs, the *carte-de-visite* photograph, mounted on cardboard, became America's first mass-produced photograph. In fact, Queen Victoria triggered a vogue for these somber-faced portraits in England by collecting them. Celebrities, politicians, and heroes were afforded widespread circulation, because newspapers could only reproduce line drawings or etchings. According to statistics, over 1,000 prints were made each day at the É. and T. H. Anthony studios. *Value guide: Andrew Johnson, $22; Tom Thumb and his wife in wedding dress, Brady, $265.*

CAST-IRON FURNITURE

American foundries benefitted financially when a fad for cast-iron furniture swept through the United States in the second half of the 19th century. Neighbors cast an appreciative eye at gardens exhibiting cast-iron chairs, tables, settees, and urns. These cast-iron confections typically bore naturalistic patterns plucked from Mother Nature's bounty. Rustic and grape designs were offered, along with rococo and Renaissance Revival styles. Other forms such as umbrella stands, hall stands, and footstools were deemed proper as indoor accents. Fortunately, some foundries marked their products. *Value guide: armchair, grape decor, circa 1890, $325; settee, rustic, 4' long, circa 1895, $450.*

Cast-Iron Umbrella Stand

CHAD VALLEY

Anthony Binn founded the Chad Valley firm in Birmingham, England, about 1820, initially specializing in printed material and stationery. An 1897 catalog featured toys. Expansion was undertaken when a move to Chad Stream at Harbourne, outside Birmingham, became a reality. The Chad Valley trademark came into general use at this time, when they operated as Johnson Brothers, Harbourne, Ltd. In 1913, "The Card House and Fort Builder" construction set was marketed. One year later, their "Brick Building Sets" were available to would-be architects. Craft sets were a factory specialty through the 1930s. Yet another milestone was scored by this still active doll and toy maker in 1947, with its "Uhilda Motor Car" assembly set. *Value guide: Brick Building Set, complete, $70; doll, Happy, 7" tall, 1939, $75.*

Chad Valley Steam Roller Toy

CHAFING DISHES

Around the turn of the century, homemakers were bombarded with booklets on chafing dish cookery. Chafing dishes of silverplate and sterling silver, however, had been occupying space in silver company catalogs for several decades. Earlier versions came complete with alcohol burners. Most bear a maker's trademark for positive identification. Chafing dishes were suggested as suitable gifts for young homemakers and college girls. Collectors have acquired an appetite for early specimens, especially complete units. *Value guide: chafing dish, silverplate, Smith, Patterson, & Co., complete, $90.*

Chafing Dish

CHAPLIN, CHARLIE

Movie mogul Mack Sennett discovered Charlie Chaplin, An English born actor-dancer, in New York in 1913. Chaplin's comic talents carved a niche in the nation's funny bone with such films as *Tillie's Punctured Romance* and *Between Showers*. Between 1914 and 1917, a daily and Sunday strip, "Charlie Chaplin's Comic Capers" hit newspapers. Chaplin-inspired toys were inevitable, some of the finest originating in Germany. The Charlie Chaplin wind-up tin and cast-iron toy and the Whistling Charlie clockwork toy qualify as amusing acquisitions. Pencils, dolls, playing cards, figurines, movie posters, and other Chaplin creations never fail to bring a smile to the face of flea-market shoppers. *Value guide: doll, walking, composition head, cloth body, wind-up, $1,250; poster, Gold Rush, 60" × 40", $600.*

Charlie Chaplin Doll

CHARLIE McCARTHY

On May 9, 1937, the "Charlie McCarthy Show," featuring ventriloquist Edgar Bergen, premiered on NBC radio; W. C. Fields appeared on the program through December. The show continued on NBC through 1948, becoming a CBS program between 1949 and 1954. At the height of Charlie's radio and movie fame in 1938, Marx introduced the Charlie-McCarthy-in-His-Benzine-Buggy wind-up toy. The toy depicted Charlie in his inimitable top hat, tuxedo, and monocle in a black luxury car ready to "mow you down." The McCarthy Strut was another immensely successful toy. Both were packaged in colorful boxes with pictures of Charlie and Edgar in their show biz attire. The animated Charlie McCarthy Alarm Clock from Gilbert is another reminder of this lap-sitting wise-cracker. Other items also appeared, some distributed as premiums by the show's sponsor, Chase & Sanborn. *Value guide: game, "Charlie McCarthy's Radio Party," complete, $50; wind-up car, $350.*

CHASE CHROME

The chase is on for Chase chrome articles of art deco vintage. Between 1930 and 1942, the Chase Brass and Copper Company of Waterbury, Connecticut, cashed in on the chrome craze. Chrome household items, like glass furniture, became the "last word" in the '30s. To satisfy the craving for chrome, serving trays, pancake sets, corn sets, salt and pepper shakers, electric buffet servers, lamps, bowls, smoking stands, and countless other items were issued. Of course, quite a number of pieces were designed to quench the thirst for that art deco addition: the cocktail. *Value guide: coffee pot, black handle, $65; warming pan, electric, $150.*

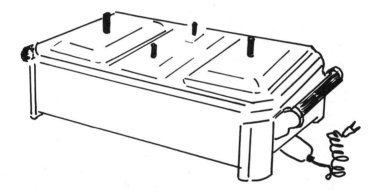

Chase Chrome Warming Pan

CHASE STOCKINETTE DOLLS

Martha Chase began crafting here dolls for friends and family in the late 1800s. As the demand increased, commercial production methods were instituted. Chase Stockinette Dolls were aptly named; they had a piece of stretched stockinette pulled taut over the facial features, which prepared the doll for the details that were realistically applied in oils. The earliest Chase dolls had pink sateen bodies; subsequently, white cotton cloth bodies were stuffed with cotton batting. In 1909, R. H. Macy advertised Chase dolls in sizes 16, 17, 21, and 24 inches tall at prices ranging between $2.49 and $4.96. Knowledgeable collectors examine the arm or thigh for the

65

Chase Stockinette Doll

following trademark: "The Chase Stockinette Doll. Made of Stockinette and cloth. Stuffed with cotton. Made by hand. Made especially by trained workers." *Value guide: child, stockinette head and limbs, cloth body, jointed at shoulder, bobbed hair, 15" tall, $400.*

CHATELAINES

The chatelaine, worn at the waist and suspended by a long chain, was an 18th century style revived with vigor by 19th century jewelry designers. It can best be described as a hooked ornament composed of a varying number of drops suitable for carrying a multitude of personal possessions. Watches, seals, scissors, and keys were among the items usually found dangling from a chatelaine. They became fashion musts in Europe and America, concurrent with the rage for Renaissance Revival styles from the 1870s through the 1890s. The gold varieties often bore diamonds or semi-precious stones. *Value guide: sterling silver, three drops, circa 1890, $150; sterling silver, mother-of-pearl inlay, five drops, circa*

Sterling Silver Chatelaine

1900, $185.

CHAUTAUQUA FURNITURE

The premium-minded Larkin Soap Company of Buffalo, New York, offered Chautaugua furniture premiums to customers around the turn of the century. Golden Oak pieces were suitable for almost any

Chautauqua Desk

room in the home. The famous Chautauqua desk was offered absolutely free with a $10 case of Larkin soap. Was it popular? Apparently, for a mid-1890s catalog noted this desk "has gladdened more than half a million hearts." Another premium freely distributed with a $10 case of Larkin soap was the ever popular Morris chair. It was available in oak or birch with a mahogany finish and fitted with corduroy cushions. The current fad for Golden Oak furniture has transformed these one-time premiums into treasured possessions. *Value guide: Chautauqua desk, oak, carved details, mirror panel above, circa 1895, $500.*

CHEIN INDUSTRIES

Lithographed toys and banks attributed to Chein Industries of Burlington, New Jersey, delight toy devotees. Imaginative tin containers were also produced, some based on antique designs such as the Roly Poly tins. The factory began operating in 1903. Their wind-up toys, including ferris wheels, drum majors, alligators, and clowns, were handsomely lithographed in vivid colors. Many were derived from celebrated comic characters such as Happy Hooligan and Donald Duck. In fact, they are responsible for the highly desirable 2nd National Donald Duck Bank, featuring Donald, Mickey Mouse, and Minnie Mouse. Chein banks form another specialized collecting category for the serious seekers of prized playthings. *Value guide: ferris wheel, 1930s, $175; Popeye, tin wind-up, 6½" tall, $130.*

Chein Toy Penguin

CHERRY BLOSSOM PATTERN

Early Jeannette Glass Company ads for the Cherry Blossom pattern pictured cherry trees blooming by the Washington Monument; presumably, the design was inspired by the Cherry Blossom festival. Needless to say, the major decorative element featured cherry blossoms and foliage. Between 1930 and 1938, this mold-etched ware appeared in green, pink, crystal, and opaque blue. The latter, known as Delphite, made its debut in 1936. A limited amount of Jadite, an opaque green, was also issued. At the height of the depression, the Cherry Blossom pattern proved a perennial favorite. *Value guide: bowl, green, 8" diameter, $22; sugar and creamer, pink, $20.*

Cherry Blossom Pattern
Footed Tumbler

CHERRY STONERS

According to advertising claims, most late 19th century cherry stoners seeded from 20 to 30 quarts an hour. Some were activated by a spring-driven knife, which removed seeds without cutting or disfiguring. Many spring-driven stoners were designed to clamp onto table tops. These gadgets were able to work on any size cherry. Cherry pitters often showed a preference for the cast-iron, crank-handled table models with legs or clamp-on devices. Occasionally, a maker exhibited a whimsical attitude by enameling one in red. Rust-resistant, heavily tinned, or japanned stoners surfaced as fruit picker's favorites. In 1910, Enterprise stoners were "recommended for those desiring rapid and effective work." *Value guide: Enterprise No. 1, $45; The Family Cherry Stoner, Goodell, $50.*

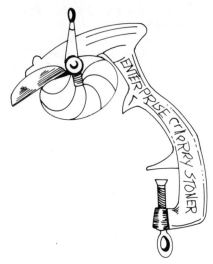

Enterprise Cherry Stoner

CHINA CASE CLOCKS

The china case clock became a favored timekeeper in the late 19th century. While larger models rested on mantels, smaller versions

Royal Bonn China Case Clock

were deemed ideal for use in the boudoir. Around the world, potters capitalized on the craze, many specializing in elaborate rococo cases delicately ornamented with florals. Delft and Dresden models fetch premium returns, as do those ascribed to the Haviland works of France. The Royal Bonn works of Germany made some of the most desirable models, many fitted with Ansonia movements. Belleek clock cases from the Willets Manufacturing Company of Trenton beguile buyers. A hanging version from the New Haven Clock Company was priced at $19 in the early 1900s. Without exception, marked china case clocks sell at alarming figures. *Value guide: Belleek, Willits, 10" tall, circa 1895, $275; Royal Bonn, florals, 17" tall, $400.*

CHRISTOPHER COLUMBUS STATUETTE

When the World's Columbian Exposition of 1893 opened in Chicago, it prompted a stream of souvenir items. Christopher Columbus was afforded tremendous honors, for the fair celebrated the 400th anniversary of the discovery of America. Chicago-based liquor stores were not to be denied their fair share of Columbus mementos: a plaster-of-Paris statue of the noted discoverer advertising Christopher Columbus Rum could be spotted in many store windows. One must acknowledge it as being one of the more spirited reminders of the 40-acre fair. *Value guide: statuette, $225.*

CHRONOGRAPHIC WATCHES

E. D. Johnson earned respect in watchmaking quarters by perfecting the chronographic watch in 1855. This unique timepiece, utilized primarily for measuring intervals in sporting events, was a precision-timed instrument. Although related to the stopwatch in a sense, the chronograph was more complex and costlier. By the 1890s, the Waltham Watch Company had a model on the market featuring a gold case. It was a bargain priced at $2.50. Present day prices reveal that the chronograph can be termed a timely investment. *Value guide: Waltham Chronograph, circa 1895, $600.*

CIGAR BOXES

Statistically speaking, there were over 20,000 different brands of cigars being made in America by the third quarter of the 19th century. As might be expected, each had its own colorful label, crafted by the stone lithography process, and involving over 20 different colors per label. Victorians adored cigar boxes with attractive paper labels on the sides and inner lids. Many were converted into stash boxes by sentimentalists. Did you know that the finest boxes were made of cedar? Labels boasting embossed highlights accompanied by gold trim are branded best by collectors. *Value guide: cigar box with 40 cigar labels, $75.*

CITRÖEN, ANDRE

Andre Citröen made model cars as promotional aids from 1923. Every effort was taken by this French motor car company to manufacture toy cars that emulated real-life prototypes. These detailed models bore lights, doors that opened, and realistic windows. Sheet metal wheels found on earlier cars were supplanted by rubber wheels on later versions. Those bearing Citroen's stenciled trademark are speeding into private collections today. After 1936, the production of toy cars was undertaken by CIJ (Compagnie Industrielle du Jouet) and later by JRD. Many different models were produced. The last cars to carry the Jouets Citroen mark were "Petite Rosalie" and "Rosalie V," dating from 1935. *Value guide: Petite Rosalie, fine condition, circa 1937, $1,050.*

CLIFTON WARE

One late 19th century critic noted that majolica objects from the Chesapeake Pottery "were pronounced equal to the famous Wedgwood of that grade." High praise for the owners of the Chesapeake Pottery of Baltimore, Maryland! A majolica interpretation, introduced in 1882, bore the backstamp "Clifton" and had an

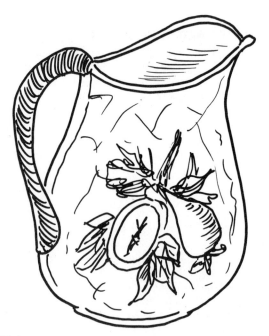

Clifton Ware Pitcher

ivory tint and soft rich glaze. The finely detailed ware had painted, raised motifs of strawberries, grapes, blackberries, and geraniums. A similar ware, known as "Avalon," bore floral sprays. With marked American majolica in short supply, these Chesapeake pottery articles have won a loyal following. *Value guide: cake plate, Clifton, geranium, 12" diameter, $85; platter, Avalon, florals, 13" diameter, $60.*

CLOVERLEAF PATTERN

The Waldorf Astoria, the Chrysler Building, and the Empire State Building were all opened in 1931, the same year that Hazel-Atlas introduced Cloverleaf. Table settings were produced at this Clarksburg, West Virginia, glasshouse through 1936. Various accessories were issued in pink, green, yellow, crystal, and black. The latter earns a place in the scarce category. Those cloverleafs obviously provided depression-era consumers with a tinge of optimism. Some rarities in this design possess the Hazel-Atlas trademark. *Value guide: ashtray, black $60; salt and pepper shakers, pink, $25.*

Cloverleaf Tumbler

CLOVERLEAF SCALES

Lucky indeed is the flea marketeer who uncovers a Cloverleaf tea and counter scale. Although grocers had a choice of scales in the early 1900s, many selected this Jones of Binghampton, New York, model. Each scale in the Cloverleaf line had a polished brass beam

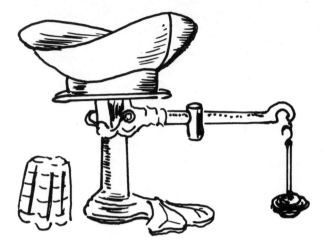

Cloverleaf Scale

and poise. To blend with their cloverleaf trademark, each scale was beautifully finished in green enamel. Many pounds of tea and coffee could be weighed, for the tin scoops were heavy and durable. The Cloverleaf boasted absolutely accurate scale and weights. The 25-pound capacity version weighed in at just $4.50. *Value guide: Cloverleaf, complete, circa 1910, $140.*

CLOWN, HARLEQUIN, AND COLUMBINE BANK

Collectors mesmerized by mechanical banks regard the Clown, Harlequin, and Columbine model as one of the most inventive banks ever conceived. From 1906, it was extensively promoted by the J. & E. Stevens Company. The colorful figures were borrowed from Italian pantomine shows. The masked harlequin; his sweetheart, the light-footed columbine; and the clown are featured in realistic fashion. Turning the platform resets the bank, placing columbine between the two figures. When a coin is deposited between the clown and harlequin, a lever is pushed on the right of the base. As the platform revolves, columbine twirls to a position on the outside next to the clown whose hand she is grasping over her head. The clown, harlequin, and Columbine staged many a matinee performance for the playroom set. *Value guide: Clown, Harlequin, and Columbine bank, cast-iron, $12,000.*

COCA-COLA

Coca-Cola was first offered for sale in Atlanta, Georgia, in 1886. John S. Pemberton, a local pharmacist, formulated the syrup, selling it to local druggists. Frank S. Robinson, his bookkeeper.

utilized the wording "Coca-Cola" in script. Asa G. Chandler acquired ownership of Coca-Cola in 1891, making it a popular 5-cent soft drink. The trademark "Coca-Cola" in script was patented in 1893. By 1895, Chandler advised the world that "Coca-Cola is now sold in every state of the union." The drink was bottled for the first time in 1899. The distinctive bottle that was to identify it for the next 58 years was introduced in 1916. It was a slimmer version of the waist-bulging bottle of 1913. From the outset, Coca-Cola was heavily promoted; any object bearing the company's name rates as a refreshing acquisition. *Value guide: bookmark, Lillian Russell, 1904, $80; tray, "Girl in Afternoon," 10½" × 13", 1938, $65.*

COFFEE GRINDERS

With the advent of coal stoves, specially designed coffee bean roasters were devised to fit into the round openings of the stove top. After roasting, beans were ground in coffee grinders or mills. By

Universal Coffee Mill

the late 19th century, cast-iron wall and lap grinders were made by the Sun Manufacturing Company, Enterprise Manufacturing Company, and Landers, Frary, & Clark, among others. The familiar boxlike versions were produced by countless firms, many having Britannia hoppers and brass covers. Some had sheet steel hoppers designed to be clamped on a table. Larger table and floor models were destined for store use. Coffee mills and grinders have blossomed into full-bodied collectibles. *Value guide: Ever-Ready mill, wall type, $45; Universal No. 110, steel case, $55.*

75

Enterprise Coffee mill

COLOGNE BOTTLES

Cologne bottles of every description permitted American and European glasshouses to partake of the sweet smell of success in the late 19th century. They appeared in square, rectangular, globular, and barrel shapes. Typically sold in pairs, they were slightly larger than standard perfume bottles. Prior to the 1870s, engraved bottles

Enameled Cologne Bottle

adorned many dresser tops. Thereafter, glassmakers became more daring, experimenting with cut, pressed, handpainted, and enameled variations. Milk glass containers having embossed and gilded highlights beautified bureau tops of the era. *Value guide: Bristol glass, green opaque, gold medallions, 8½" tall, $50; ruby glass, enameled florals, 7" tall, circa 1900, $90.*

COLONIAL PATTERN

Despite its 19th century appearance, Colonial was a Hocking Glass Company design dating between 1934 and 1938. It was an adaptation of the traditional Knife and Fork motif. This pressed pattern had a bulky, heavy look and appeared in crystal, pink, and green. Plates had wide panels of glass separated by narrower radiating ridges. Occasionally, gold or platinum rims were utilized. Original listings mentioned a celery holder and spoon holder, seldom found on tabletops of the 1930s. *Value guide: celery holder, green, $110; salt and pepper shakers, pink, $95.*

Colonial Pattern Water Pitcher

COLONIAL REVIVAL STYLE

Clarence Cook wrote in 1881, "All this resuscitation of 'old furniture' has been for 20 years working its way down from a circle of rich, cultivated people, to a wider circle of people . . . who bore natural good taste." It was the Centennial Exposition of 1876 that fostered a revival of faithful reproductions of "the Colonial days." This growing enthusiasm for antiques made "colonial" a catch phrase for past styles that did not always fall into the Colonial span. Furniture from the late 1500s, through William and Mary, Queen Anne, Chippendale, Hepplewhite, and Sheraton styles was authentically copied. Reproductions of Windsor chairs and Empire forms abounded. After all, "nice old fashioned chairs make a parlor look very cozy and old-timey." *Value guide: Chippendale style armchair, mahogany, pierced slat, circa 1885, $325; chest of drawers, William and Mary style, two small, 3 long drawers, 1 pine, inlaid, circa 1890, $575.*

COLUMBIA FAMILY SCALES

The ever-dependable Columbia Family Scale from Landers, Frary & Clark of New Britain, Connecticut, was available with straight or slanting dials. Various models were offered, typically of sheet steel with a black enamel finish ornamented with gilt. They had white enameled dials and square or round steel tops. A tin scoop could be purchased for an additional 20 cents. They scooped competitors price-wise with most selling for $1.20 to $3.25. The highest-priced scale weighed up to 60 pounds. No weighty decision is involved in purchasing a Columbia Family Scale, for all are sought by shoppers. *Value guide: 24-pound size, $75.*

Columbia Family Scale

COLUMBIA PATTERN

The Columbia design rates as one gem of a depression glass pattern. This Federal Glass Company creation was in production between 1938 and 1940. Budget-minded buyers could acquire crystal and pink table settings for practically pennies. Presently, the pink pieces are far from plentiful. Plates had bull's eye centers, flanked by a sunburst with large beading within the rim. Wide outer rims possessed radial rows of graduated circles that became smaller toward the edge. Those butter dishes having flashed blue, red, or iridescent lids melt collectors' hearts. *Value guide: butter, covered, crystal, $30; plate, pink, 9 ½ " diameter, $8.*

COLUMBIA PHONOGRAPH COMPANY

In the early 1900s, the Columbia Phonograph Company, with offices in most major American cities, was touting its Graphophone talking machine. Advertisements accented the fact that "The Graphophone reproduced perfectly and delightfully the music of bands, orchestras, and vocal and instrumental soloists. It is all musical instruments in one." To further entice would-be buyers, the company proclaimed that, "Only on talking machines manufactured under Graphophone patents can sound be recorded, the performances of other so-called talking machines being limited to reproduction of records of cut and dried subjects made in laboratories." This obvious reference to rival concerns was quite commonplace during this era, for there was a price war in effect among "talking-machine" companies. *Value guide: Princess model, refinished, $400; phonograph, Columbia Graphonola, Regent, desk type, $550.*

Columbia Graphophone

COLUMBIAN MAGAZINES

Fashion-conscious Victorian ladies were never without their favorite fashion magazine. In some quarters, *The Columbian Magazine*, founded by Israel Post in 1844, was considered must reading. Their fashion plates such as Les Modes Parisiennes, La Sylphide, and Le Follet bore a notation at the bottom which read, "Engraved expressively for Columbian magazine." Despite that claim, some believe that they were second-hand or used plates from fellow publisher George Graham. Few readers cared, for these plates by noted European artists kept them well informed about the seamier side of life. *Godey's Ladies Book*, however, was a tough act to follow, for *The Columbian* folded in 1849. *Value guide: single issue, 1845, $20.*

COLUMBUS POCKET WATCHES

The highly imaginative Ingersoll brothers began selling inexpensive watches through mail order channels about 1892. Their initial effort, manufactured by the Waterbury Clock Company of Connecticut, attracted about 10,000 orders. Prompted by this response they asked Waterbury to fabricate a watch in honor of the Columbus Exposition of 1893; thus was born the Christopher Columbus watch. It depicted three ships, surrounded by a pictorial likeness of Columbus, an American Indian, Columbia, and the Exposition Building. This unmistakable storytelling watch sails out of markets in record time. *Value guide: pocket watch, working order, $250.*

COMBS

Between the 1860s and 1880s, many combs had jeweled headings,

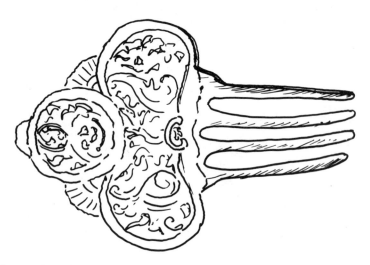

Tortoise Shell Comb

either hinged or designed to be worn just above the forehead. Others were worn in a chignon. Those who comb the markets for finds seek examples having gold, silver, or gemstone additions. Gentlemen callers were bedazzled by elaborate combs boasting "waterfall mounts" during this time, which often rivaled tiaras in both size and craftsmanship. When Bizet's "Carmen" won standing ovations from opera buffs in the late 1870s, pierced open-work tortoise shell combs received top billing from fashion followers. Even the later silver versions sporting engraved or punched motifs fetch hair-raising returns. *Value guide: silverplated, engraved floral, 9" across, circa 1900, $50; tortoise shell, handcarved, 7" across, circa 1890, $60.*

COMPETITION MANDOLIN

Competition mandolins adorned the pages of Sears, Roebuck, & Company catalogs in the early 1900s, causing budget-minded musicians to consult their catalogs with regularity. These mandolins were made "by skilled experts, the highest paid mechanics in the country." Each instrument had been constructed on the "most scientific principles." The neck was fabricated of imitation mahogany, while the patent heads were of the finest quality brass. Both adults and children found the Competition a competent instrument. What did it cost to purchase this super strummer? Just $2.65. *Value guide: Competition, working condition, $85.*

CONCERT ROLLER ORGANS

In the first decade of the 20th century, American mail order catalogs

Concert Roller Organ

were singing the praises of the Concert Roller organ. It was billed as being "of a somewhat higher grade than the Gem Roller organ." Furthermore, "it is better constructed and a finer instrument in every way." Who could ask for anything more for a mere $7.60? The Concert Roller organ produced melodious sounds, and, because the cylinders were removable, a number of different selections could be played. This instrument undoubtedly prompted more than one family sing-along. *Value guide: Concert Roller organ, circa 1910, $450.*

CONDENSED MILK CAN HOLDERS

Oddities abounded in silver company catalogs of the late 1800s. Silverplated condensed milk can holders vied for space with such beloved bygones as spoon holders and hat pin holders. These cylindrical containers with lids had bases to catch the drippings. Most makers fitted them with handles for portability. While plainer versions proliferated, the répoussé, or engraved, types are regarded as being the cream of the crop. Although marked examples exist from many makers, the Adelphia Silver Company of New York City appears to have milked the market dry. *Value guide: silverplated, engraved motif, Adelphia, $65.*

CORKSCREWS

The corkscrew, that device used to draw a cork from a bottle, has been known for centuries. During the Victorian era, however, designers uncorked countless inventive models. Occasionally, one had a frame for steadying the bottle, or arms for levering out the cork. The handles of silver, brass, gold, wood, ivory, mother-of-

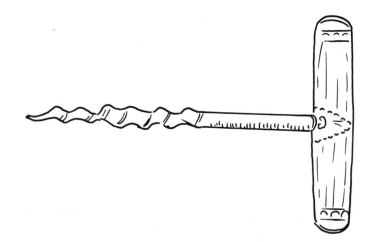

Corkscrew

pearl, or horn submitted to a variety of decorative techniques. The fanciest types are the most difficult to pry from their owners. Naturalistic art nouveau motifs abounded between 1890 and 1910. By the early 20th century, the familiar combination corkscrew/ bottle opener appeared in amazing and amusing varieties. *Value guide: brass, Cheshire cat, 6 ½ " long, $65; wood, hand turned cherry, 6" long, $40.*

CORONATION

To tap topical events for potential profit, the introduction of Hocking Glass Company's Coronation pattern coincided with the abdication of King Edward VIII in 1936. Subjected to a rather limited production run, however, only nine tabletop items have been discovered by collectors. Those devoted to depression glass have uncovered pink, crystal, and ruby red articles. The finely mitered, pressed-glass plates had a central theme, consisting of a narrow sunburst of radial lines surrounded by widely spaced lines. Borders had an inner circle of ridges and a plain outer band. Banded Fine Rib and Saxon are other acceptable names for this regal favorite. *Value guide: plate, pink, 8 ½" diameter, $12; sherbet, crystal, footed, $4.*

CORSETS

Corset is the more refined French word for "stays." The term described a tightly fitted, boned, and laced bodice reaching from the bosom to the waist. Victorian examples typically hooked in the front and laced in the back. Much to the chagrin of those who forgot to

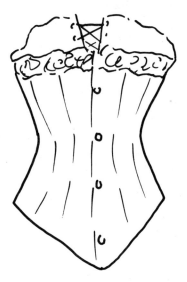

Corset, Circa 1890

count calories, corsets became longer and more rigid by the 1870s. Two decades later, they became shorter and more decorative as ladies endeavored to emulate Lillian Russell. Heavy cotton and boned corsets were preferred by those desiring the fashionable 18-inch wasp waist. *Value guide: corset, heavy cotton, circa 1895, $25.*

COSSACK CLOCKS

When dramatic black shelf clocks gained favor in America during the late 19th century, the Waterbury Clock Company had the time of its life offering various models. One collectible in this category is their Cossack clock. This 8-day, half-hour strike, cathedral gong style with a porcelain dial sold for just $12.50. A marble appearance was achieved by painting the polished wood case. The Cossack resembled costlier models, due to its gilt engraved areas and attached bronze ornaments. One critic of the period observed that a clock in the dining room was simply "a rebuke to those who came down late for breakfast." *Value guide: Cossack, working condition, $175.*

COWAN POTTERY

Following in the family tradition, R. Guy Cowan opened a pottery studio in Cleveland, Ohio, in 1913. Shortly thereafter, he moved to larger quarters in Lakewood, Ohio. After World War I, the Cowan Pottery Studio relocated to Rocky Mountain, Ohio; a few years later their pottery was being sold by over 1,200 major American retail outlets. Table settings, candlesticks, lampshades, teapots, cups and saucers, figurines, and vases were made at the pottery. Imaginative art deco designs dominated their output. Through 1931, various marks identified the pottery, including the incised "Cowan Pottery" on early redware, Cowan's monogram, "Cowan" stamped in black, "Cowan Pottery" stamped in black, or "Lakewood" (between 1927 and 1931). *Value guide: candleholders, seahorse, blue, pair, $70; figurine, nude, 6" tall, $110.*

CRACKER JACK

F. W. Rueckheim and his brother Louis introduced Cracker Jack to the American public in Chicago, about 1896. Prior to this time the brothers had operated a popcorn stand for about 20 years. Labeled "cracker jack" by an enthusiastic salesman, this candy-coated popcorn adopted it as their slogan, "The More You Eat, the More You Want." The firm received a giant sales boost when the 1908 toe tapper, "Take Me Out to the Ballgame" mentioned the product. Boxes containing coupons for redeemable prizes appeared about 1910. Just two years later, those Cracker Jack prizes made their debut in containers. Although Jack and his dog Bingo began appearing on ads in 1916, they failed to adorn boxes until 1919. *Value guide: Cracker Jack prize, delivery truck, $20; Cracker Jack prize, wheelbarrow, turning wheels, $25.*

CRAZY QUILTS

What are the necessary ingredients for a crazy quilt project? A piece of brocade, a bit of silk, a little strip of velvet, a satin remnant, or perhaps an outdated necktie. These fabric catch-alls quickened the hearts of quilt makers, especially in late 19th century. Crazy quilts were a variation of the earlier patchwork quilt, and ladies crafted them in various sizes and patterns, some quite spontaneous. As bed covers, they proved impractical, but when draped across a horse-hair sofa they drew rave reviews. Few crazy quilt makers could perceive that a century later their handiwork would find favor as wall hangings. *Value guide: crazy quilt, silks and satins, dated 1890, 60"× 66", $200; wedding bell center, dated 1895, 64"× 68", $1,250.*

CREEDMOOR

The Creedmoor, acknowledged as the first American shooting bank, scored a direct hit with depositors upon its introduction in 1877. Its realistic action gave birth to a number of other finely modeled shooting banks. The bank, designed by James H. Bowen, was manufactured by the J. & E. Stevens Company. It's name was

Creedmoor Bank

85

derived from the Long Island rifle range used by the New York National Guard during this period. The soldier holding the rifle wears a red tunic and hat, and a dark blue cape. When a penny is placed on the barrel of the rifle, the soldier's right foot is pressed and he shoots the coin into the tree. On a later version known as "The New Creedmoor," the soldier was replaced by William Tell. *Value guide: Creedmoor, cast-iron, circa 1885, $400.*

CUBE PATTERN

In the late 1920s, cubism surfaced as a dominant force with art deco artisans. By issuing the Cube design in crystal, executives of the Jeanette Glass Company were obviously alert to this abstract phase of the movement. This revival of an earlier diamond-cut crystal pattern was named Cube or Cubist. In truth, the name had a far more contemporary ring than the design. Table settings were available in green, pink, and crystal. The green articles are scarce, for they were the first to be discontinued. This pressed design, an outgrowth of the prevailing craze for cubistic geometry, was produced between 1929 and 1934. *Value guide: candy dish, footed, pink, $30.*

Cube Pattern Covered Candy Dish

CUCKOO CLOCKS

A cuckoo clock craze developed in America following a successful showing of German wall clocks at the Philadelphia Centennial Exposition of 1879. Anton Ketterer of Schonwald, Germany, perfected these timepieces about 1730. Over the centuries, the crafting of cuckoo clocks evolved into a Black Forest cottage industry. The carved wooden frames, featuring leaf decorations, usually had iron arbors. As a general rule, the hours and half-hours were struck on a gong, triggering the emergence of a wooden cuckoo through the top door. When a second bird appeared, it was usually a quail. By the early 1900s, cuckoo clocks were popping from the pages of Sears, Roebuck, and Company catalogs. *Value guide: cuckoo clock, single bird, ornate, 24" tall, circa 1900, $450.*

Cuckoo Clock, German

CUSPIDORS

The lowly cuspidor has achieved high-ranking status with collectors. Tobacco chewers of the late 19th and early 20th centuries had a choice of brass, copper, silver, pewter, glass, earthenware, or graniteware varieties. The smaller versions were deemed suitable for liberated lady tobacco chewers. A basic form evolved with a globular jug base and a wide, funnel-shaped mouth. Collectors aim to acquire the Rockingham, scroddled-ware, or flint-enamel types ascribed to the potters of Bennington, Vermont. Marked cuspidors

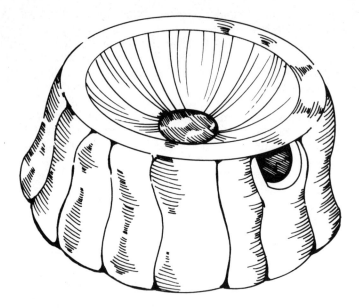

Brownware Cuspidor

from renowned potters are coveted. *Value guide: Bennington, Rockingham, swimming ducks, $130; brass, 12" diameter, circa 1900, $85.*

CUSTARD GLASS

Custard glass, a variant of milk glass, obtained its name from the color, which resembled an egg custard. It became fashionable in England during the 1880s. One of the first American glasshouses to make Custard glass tablewares was the La Belle Glass Works of

Custard Glass Maple Leaf Creamer

Bridgeport, Ohio. Numerous patterns were produced by such factories as the Northwood Glass Company, Jefferson Glass Company, Heisey Glass Company, and Fenton Art Glass Company. Premium prices have been recorded for objects bearing Northwood's capital "N" trademark in varying forms. While most patterns are in demand, special attention focuses on such fast sellers as Argonaut Shell, Chrysanthemum Sprig, Inverted Fan and Feather, Louis XV, and Winged Scroll. Did you wonder how that delicious looking custard color was achieved? Adding uranium salts to the molten glass made the difference! *Value guide: butter dish, Grape and Gothic Arches, $225; compote, jelly, Beaded Circle, enameled florals, $375.*

DAGUERREOTYPES

The daguerreotype, named for its inventor Louis Daguerre, was the first practical and commercial photograph taken with a camera. After Daguerre's *Historique et Description des Procedes du Daguerreotype et du Diorama* was published in 1839, the process became "free to the world." The world accepted enthusiastically, for a daguerreotype craze reached international proportions during the 1840s and 1850s. Morse, Draper, and Wolcott became noted American daguerreotypists, followed by the Langenheim Brothers, Fontayne, Caralho, Vance, and Babbitt. American makers excelled in portraits, landscapes, and urban views. Traveling daguerreotypists visited towns too small to have a studio of their own. *Value guide: Confederate soldier, medium size, $65; woodworker with tools, medium size, $85.*

DAGUERREOTYPE CASES

Daguerreotypes were housed in small cases of wood, covered with embossed papers in a multitude of motifs. Later, the so-called Union cases, cast in dark brown thermoplastic, housed portraits of both the famous and infamous. The first Union case was patented, in 1854, by Samuel Peck. These small, hinged presentation cases generally bore designs relating to nature, religion, history, and patriotism. According to statistics, over 800 Union case designs were utilized. An interesting side product of the daguerreotype was Daguerreville on the Hudson, which was known as the thriving center for photographic materials. *Value guide: gutta percha, double*

Daguerreotype Case

type, roses, 3" × 4½", $100; gutta percha, Rebecca at Well, 4" × 5", $140.

DAISY PATTERN

When the Daisy depression design sprouted in the Indiana Glass Company's catalog in 1933, it was listed as Number 620. This variation of a traditional Sandwich pattern originally appeared in crystal. By the 1940s, table settings became available in amber. Plates had radial sunburst center motifs, surrounded by a waffle band to the edge. Daisies alternating with foliage and scroll elements adorned the borders. At present, reproductions abound in dark olive green and milk glass, requiring cautious consumerism when picking up Daisy pieces. *Value guide: cup and saucer, amber, $7; tumbler, footed, green, 12 ounces, $6.*

DARKTOWN BATTERY BANK

The Darktown Battery mechanical bank of the 1880s, depicting three baseball players, scores a home run with bank buffs. Although the name "Darktown Battery" appeared on the base of this James H. Bowen design, some prefer the more descriptive title "Baseball Bank." The pitcher, batter, and catcher are poised to play when the lever behind the catcher is pressed. As the pitcher's arm swings forward, the batter turns to watch the ball whiz past. At the same time the catcher lowers his head and moves his right hand to catch the ball. The penny enters the catcher's body where it is deposited into the base of the bank. This J. & E. Stevens Company novelty rates as a rarity. *Value guide: Darktown Battery bank, cast-iron, 7¼" tall, $800.*

DAUM NANCY

The Daum Brothers, Auguste (1853-1909) and Antonin (1864-1930), were ardent followers of fellow French glass craftsman Emile Galle and members of the Ecole de Nancy. Upon founding their glassworks at Nancy, they proceeded to excel in cameo creations, often employing mottled or streaky backgrounds. Always experimenting, they mastered enameled techniques as well as the tedious *pate-de-verre* style. A variety of Galle-inspired glassware originated at this presently existing glasshouse. As art deco motifs held sway in the 1920s and 1930s, countless etched and geometrical pieces captured the mood of the movement. Glass objects bearing the "Daum Nancy" mark suggest superior workmanship. *Value guide: Bowl, enameled oranges and foliage, 7" diameter, $500; vase, autumn leaves, gold ground, signed, 13" tall, $750.*

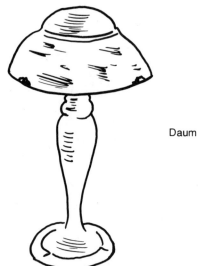

Daum Nancy Lamp

DAVENPORT SOFAS

The davenport sofa, capable of being converted from a sofa to a bed, was widely touted by furniture factories scattered in and around Grand Rapids, Michigan in the early 1900s. The Jamestown Lounge Company of Jamestown, New York, however, had an exclusive on

92

the Simplicity. It was described as being "useful and handsome," and easily changed into a "luxurious bed." To blend with prevailing themes, it was offered in "many beautiful styles, Mission, Modern Oak, and Colonial." Present day apartment dwellers realize that few sleepers exist in Davenport sofas. *Value guide: Simplicity, oak, circa 1910, $350.*

Davenport Sofa

DAVY CROCKETT

The solid ratings winner in the Disneyland television programs of the 1954 season was the trilogy of Davy Crockett shows: "Davy Crockett, Indian Fighter," "Davy Crockett Goes to Washington," and "Davy Crockett at the Alamo." Fess Parker became the idol of television viewers. A feature film starring Parker, "Davy Crockett, King of the Wild Frontier," was released to theaters on May 25, 1955. The Crockett television fad lasted until 1956. It has been estimated that within six months after the initial airing, approximately $100 million worth of character merchandise was in circulation. "The Ballad of Davy Crockett" chalked up sheet music sales in the area of ¾ million copies. Most memorable of all the Davy Crockett artifacts, however, is the coonskin hat. *Value guide: lunchbox, $15; scarf, with slide, $30.*

DEDHAM POTTERY

When the Chelsea Ceramic Works moved from Chelsea to Dedham, Massachusetts, in 1895, the firm was renamed Dedham Pottery. Under the direction of Hugh Robertson, a Chinese crackleware was potted with "a soft gray glaze and curiously crackled with a blue in-glaze decoration and fired at a heat of from 2,000 to 25,000 degrees." Uniform designs were chosen to provide artisans with guidelines. Tablewares had repetitive borders, with only the crackle lines through the center. Of the over 60 hand-executed border motifs, only the rabbit was kept in stock. Others including Duck, Polar Bear, Iris, Magnolia, Butterfly, Clover, Swan, and Crabs had to be specially ordered. Locating pieces bearing the pottery name and rabbit trademark can keep a collector hopping.

Dedham Pottery Knife Rest

Value guide: bowl, turtle, 7½" diameter, $240; cup and saucer, duck, $120.

DEGENHART GLASS

John and Elizabeth Degenhart were the guiding lights behind the Crystal Art Glass Company of Cambridge, Ohio, between 1947 and 1978. They concentrated the bulk of their efforts on paperweights and reproductions of pressed glass novelties. The Degenhart family had been actively producing paperweights since the early 1900s. John continued crafting them, including the famed "window" weight and rose weight. Numerous colors were introduced, including well over 200 crystal, opaque, and slag variations. Although some pieces were hand-stamped with the block letter "D" at an earlier date, in 1972 the logo of a "D" inside a heart outline was adapted. Many traditional pressed-glass designs, including the beloved Daisy and Button pattern, were used on their reproductions. *Value guide: heart jewel box, nile green, $28; owl, carnival, red, $120.*

DEMOREST'S MAGAZINES

The Curtis sisters, Ellen and Kate, of Saratoga Springs, New York, dreamed of fashion careers. A major step in this direction occurred at the Crystal Palace Exhibition of 1851, when their model dress charts won an award. Ellen's marriage to William Jennings Demorest brought about the opening of "Madame Demorest's" at 375 Broadway, New York City, in the late 1850s. Between 1860 and

1899, Demorest's publications flourished in America. They were sold under such titles as *Madame Demorest's Mirror,* and after 1864, as *Demorest's Illustrated Monthly Magazine,* and *Mme. Demorest's Mirror of Fashions.* These publications were well read by every well-bred Victorian lady. *Value guide: "Demorest's Illustrated Monthly Magazine," single issue, 1860s, $20.*

DETECTIVE CAMERAS

Photographic sleuths are constantly on the prowl for detective cameras. During the 1880s and 1890s, they were responsible for capturing some of America's first candid photographs. These giant, boxy street cameras were larger than a shoebox. Makers fitted them with additional storage space for glass plate film holders. As an incentive, most manufacturers included the film and processing with the purchase price. Street photographers were easily spotted carrying these wooden cameras covered in leather. When smaller box cameras came on the scene, detective cameras disappeared without a trace. *Value guide: Scovill & Adams, Knack Detective Camera, circa 1889, $675.*

DIANA PATTERN

Swirled designs were a continuing favorite with depression-glass designers. Reportedly, the Diana pressed-mold pattern was named for the daughter of a Federal Glass Company employee. Between 1937 and 1940, Diana luncheon and dinner sets swirled onto American table tops. Produced in pink, amber, and crystal, Diana can be distinguished from very similar designs because it had two spiral motifs, one in the center and another on the rim. Demi-tasse sets with their own metal stands, similar to Diana, were marketed by Federal. They are sometimes mistaken for children's dishes by novice collectors. *Value guide: candy dish, covered, amber, $40; sugar and creamer, pink, $18.*

DICK TRACY

Gangsters and G-men were grabbing headlines in 1931, when Chester Gould's Dick Tracy hit the comic strips. He became the first realistic policeman to appear in strip form. As he bested his adversaries, he was depicted in films, on a radio program, and in a television series. Early strips are often matted and framed by those who appreciate Gould's art. Super sleuths scour the markets hoping to locate a complete set of 144 cards issued for Walter H. Johnson in the early 1930s. Another set was issued by the Whitman Publishing Company to promote Dick Tracy Big Little Books. The Dick Tracy Junior Detective Kit and the Dick Tracy Police Station are among the other finds featuring this character with the bent nose and

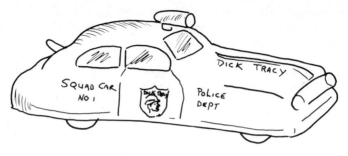

Dick Tracy Toy Squad Car

wide-brimmed fedora. *Value guide: printing set, boxed, 1935, $100; wristwatch, boxed, $200.*

DINKY TOYS

Dinky Toys were introduced by Meccano Limited Industries of England about 1933. This Liverpool toymaker had previously earned a fine reputation for innovative playthings. Despite their small scale, tremendous attention to detail and decoration was apparent on every Dinky toy. Production was curtailed at the outbreak of hostilities in the early 1940s. By 1946, however, newly modeled planes and trains rolled off assembly lines. In the post-war

Dinky Toy Airplane

era, the Dinky Toy name was utilized on many models. When the Lines Brothers acquired the works in 1964, every effort was made to continue the quality of excellence associated with the Dinky name. *Value guide: car transporter, two autos: Studebaker Commander and Rambler wagon, $90; military vehicles, set of six, including two Centurion tanks, $120.*

DIONNE QUINTUPLETS

The Dionne Quintuplets, Emilie, Yvonne, Cecile, Marie, and Annette were born on May 28, 1934. Newspaper headlines reminded readers that they were the first surviving quintuplets. Elzire Dionne became a 24-year-old mother of six; her physician was Allen DaFoe. The quints weighed in at an average of 2 pounds, 11 ounces. A collecting cult has developed around the quintuplets, as markets are scoured for scrapbooks, games, fans, handkerchiefs, paper dolls, silverplated spoons, Brown & Bigelow calendars, books, and feeding dishes. All-composition dolls were marketed by Madame Alexander in various sizes. Quintuplet memorabilia quickens the heart of many a flea marketeer. *Value guide: Paper dolls, uncut, All Aboard for Shut Eye Town, $95; silverplated spoons, set of five, $90.*

Dionne Quintuplet Doll

DOGWOOD PATTERN

Blossoming pink and white dogwood trees furnished inspiration for this aptly named MacBeth-Evans depression design. Between 1928 and 1932, this overall mold-etched pattern was issued in pink, green, crystal, yellow, Cremax, and Monax. Dogwood blossoms and leaves enlivened table settings. Three large dogwood blossoms and foliage highlighted the centers of plates; similarly sized blossoms adorned the rims. Slight variations may be noted; occasionally tumblers and pitchers devoid of mold-etched decoration were hand-ornamented in the silk-screen method by Japanese artisans. *Value guide: bowl, pink 10¼" diameter, $135; sugar and creamer, green, $65.*

Dogwood Pattern Creamer and Sugar

DOMINICK & HAFF

The Dominick & Haff silvermaking concern was an outgrowth of William Gale & Son, New York silversmiths since 1821. The succession of the business was as follows: Gale & North, 1860; North & Dominick, 1868; and Dominick & Haff, 1873. With such an outstanding beginning, it is understandable why their finely crafted hollow ware and flatware were prominently displayed in Victorian interiors. By the 1890s, they were earning swoons for their souvenir spoons. Throughout the Art Nouveau era (1890-1910), their output reflected this influence. In 1928, this New York City and Newark, New Jersey, concern was acquired by Reed & Barton. That "D & H" trademark is a desirable one with silver sleuths. *Value guide: candlestick, cigar lighter, hammered, circa 1910, $125; pitcher, foliage, hammered, circa 1895, $800.*

Dominick & Haff Silver Water Pitcher

DONALD DUCK

Although *The Adventures of Mickey Mouse* (Book 1) contained a
reference about Donald Duck, he did not appear on screen until
1934, in Disney's Silly Symphony, *The Wise Little Hen.* Daisy Duck
reached the screen in 1937, in *Don Donald,* but was not referred to
as Daisy until *Mr. Duck Steps Out,* in 1940. Donald's nephews
Huey, Louie, and Dewey came into action in 1938, in *Donald's*

Donald Duck Wind-Up Toy

99

Nephews. Everything was just ducky, especially when Butch the Bulldog joined the clan in *Bone Trouble* in 1940. Those desiring to get their feet wet with Donald Duck artifacts search for banks, brush and comb sets, dolls, figurines, comic books, paint books, jewelry, pedal cars, rail cars, statues, watches, and wind-up toys. *Value guide: celluloid, Donald Duck in Santa Claus Suit, full figure, $120; toy, Donald Duck Cart pulled by Pluto, wind-up, $850.*

DOOR KNOCKERS

Throughout the late 19th century, door knockers were fashioned in a variety of forms. These tappers were typically crafted of copper, brass, wrought iron, or cast iron. Visitors were greeted by knockers shaped to resemble birds, ropes, hands, humans, anchors, and animal's heads. In England, some were designed to represent the hands of royal children; occasionally, one bore the English registry mark, providing a clue to age and origin. The Coalbrookdale Company, Britain's major manufacturer of cast-iron furniture, knocked out customers in America and France with knockers of every description. *Value guide: bronze, Charles Dickens, circa 1900, $100; Will Rogers, brass, circa 1935, $85.*

DORIC PATTERN

Doric, based on classic Greek architectural forms, was manufactured at the Jeanette Glass Company between 1935 and 1938. Store

Doric Pattern Covered Candy Jar

owners stocked this pressed-glass depression favorite in pink, green, yellow, crystal, and opaque blue, or Delphite. Amber berry sets were submitted to a short production run. Plates had small stars in the center surrounded by 4 motifs of 4 loops each. Twelve lines radiated to the border, where 12 miniature panels housed motifs similar to the center subject. Although made from original Doric molds, the shite pieces denote a later date of production. *Value guide: creamer, crystal, $25; salt and pepper shakers, green, $30.*

DOUBLE YANKEE COOKS

The Double Yankee Cook from Orbeton & Lang's of Haverhill, Massachusetts, was a double treat to the late 19th-century homemaker. This "Yankee Baker, Yankee Cook" did the cooking for an entire family at ⅛ the cost of an ordinary stove. Its cost, therefore, could be absorbed in a matter of weeks. It was scientifically devised to enhance the highest merits of first class cooks, with a number of valuable improvements. In addition, it was capable of heating the meat, but not the whole room. This elaborate iron cooker, with its own fuel container in the base, rates as a sizzling flea market conquest. *Value guide: Double Yankee Cook, circa 1885, $135.*

Double Yankee Cook

DOUGHTY, DOROTHY

Dorothy Doughty, famed English artist, garnered international acclaim by sculpting birds in their natural habitat for the Royal Worcester Manufactury of England. The first in the series, Redstart on a Hemlock Spray, landed into private collections in 1935. Through 1960, over 30 different birds were distributed in limited editions. Each bore the artist's signature, along with the Worcester trademarks. Working in her Cornwall studio, the artist became inspired by the birds surrounding her home. American birds, studied while she traveled through America for three weeks in 1953, included the scarlet tanager, Benwick's wren, parula warbler, and the phoebe. Since Miss Doughty's death, prices have soared on her bird sculptures. *Value guide: blackbirds, yellow headed, on spiderwort sprays, pair, 10½" tall, $2,500.*

Dorothy Doughty Cardinal

DR PEPPER

Dr Pepper was introduced in 1886 as the "King of Beverages, Free of Caffeine" by Waco, Texas, chemist R. S. Lazenby. It was an outgrowth of a soft drink formula developed at the town's Old Corner Drug Store by a fountain man who had named his concoction "Dr. Pepper's Phos-Ferrates." Through skillful advertising, the drink became a national favorite. Collectors suffering from an acute case of "advertising fever" seek early promotional premiums from this firm. Over the years, the Dr. Pepper logo has changed from script to printed letters. In 1950, the period was removed from Dr. *Value guide: sign "Dr Pepper Good for Life," porcelain, 27"× 10", $100; thermometer, Dr Pepper, tin, $35.*

DUKE CLOCK

When the Warren Telechrome Company of Ashland, Massachusetts, advertised its timepieces in the mid 1930s, "New Models for the New Deal" was mentioned. A subtle reference to the depression could also be noted, for the public was advised that their timepieces "ran quietly and faithfully through good times and bad." The cleverly conceived Duke electric clock had a gold-finished case which measured 4¾" tall. It proved to be the perfect accent for a dressing table or desk. Originally, this art deco delectable sold for $4.50. *Value guide: Duke clock, 1936, $60.*

DUMBO

Walt Disney's animated feature-length film about an elephant, Dumbo, was released on October 23, 1941 at a total production cost of only $800,000. An outstanding success, the film chalked up impressive figures at the box office. Dumbo character merchandise reached shops to the delight of youngsters. Ceramic figurines from the Evan K. Shaw Company, along with an inflatable vinylite doll from the Vanguard Corporation, satisfied buying urges in some quarters. The latter sold for 98 cents. In 1949, a three-record Dumbo album bore handsome illustrations and a narrative by Shirley Temple. A one-shot comic book, *Dumbo,* was issued by the Dell Comic Color Series. Dumbo, who nudged Jumbo in popularity, became a popular insignia for military shoulder patches during World War II. *Value guide: pitcher, figural, $20; toy, stuffed Dumbo, $85.*

Dumbo Tin Toy

DURAND GLASS

Victor Durand (1870-1931), was a French-born American art nouveau glass artist. He emigrated to America with his father, who had been employed by Baccarat. Durand assumed the management of the Vineland Flint Glass Works of Vineland, New Jersey, about 1897. Skilled workers hired from the Quezal Art Glass and Decoration Company began experimenting with various iridescent-glass ornamenting techniques. The iridescent-glass specialties they perfected, known as Durand Art Glass, bore a striking resemblance to Quezal glass. Other pieces were imitative of Tiffany's output, but the shapes were somewhat less inventive. Production of art glass, started in the early 1920s, ceased in 1931. In addition to a paper label, objects were typically marked "Durand," or with the letter "V" in the pontil. *Value guide: cracker jar, iridescent green, black webs, silver top, $450; vase, King Tut, gold over white, 9" tall, $750.*

EAGLE AND EAGLETS BANK

The American Eagle toy savings bank was widely promoted in advertisements from the J. & E. Stevens Company in the 1800s. It was pictured on a colorful advertising card from the firm. The

Eagle & Eaglets Bank

patent, dated 1883, was received by Charles M. Henn of Chicago. The action of the bank was described in this manner: "Place a coin in the Eagle's beak, press the lever and the Eaglets rise from the nest actually crying for food. As the Eagle bends forward to feed them, the coin falls in the nest and disappears." At present this mechanical wonder parades under the title "Eagle & Eaglets." Prices have soared on banks with their original paint. *Value guide: Eagle and Eaglets bank, cast-iron, 6" tall, $450.*

EASTLAKE, CHARLES

Charles Lock Eastlake's *Hints on Household Taste,* published in England in 1868, had a profound influence on designers between 1870 and 1900. An American version appeared in 1872. Eastlake is acknowledged as the chief theorist of the Art Furniture Movement, which suggested holding furniture together by pegged joints rather than glue. Marquetry, shallow carving, and incised gilt lines were recommended to achieve a richness in quality. American furniture makers marketed pieces with straight lines, square or turned tapering legs, spindles, and recessed panels. Ebonized woods were widely favored. Although mass-produced forms abounded, superior examples were fabricated by such respected craftsmen as the Herter Brothers and Kimbel & Claus. *Value guide: chair, side, brass and mother-of-pearl inlay, circa 1875, $1,400; table, library, marble top, black walnut, 29" tall, circa 1880, $750.*

EDISON MAROON GEM

The "Talking Machine" that, in 1909, Americans were listening to

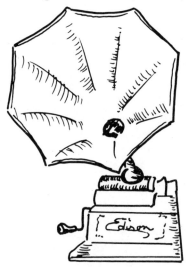

Edison Maroon Gem

and talking about was the Edison Maroon Gem. This Edison Model D bore such distinguishing characteristics as the gold Edison decal, along with Edison's familiar decaled signature. Because its reproducer was equipped with two styluses, the machine played both two- and four-minute cylinders. By far the most pronounced feature was the maroon painted horn and body, which gave rise to the term "Maroon Gem." The machine was bargain-priced at $14, evidence of the fact that phonograph prices were tumbling at this time due to fierce competition. *Value guide: Maroon Gem, $1,000.*

EGYPTIAN REVIVAL PENCILS

Once Tutankhamen's Tomb was opened in 1924, an Egyptian Revival was underway in the United States. People without the means to cruise the Nile sailed into local shops to partake of Egyptian-inspired jewelry, fashions, furniture, and a dizzying array of decorative objects. One of the most intriguing, yet inexpensive, novelties was the retractable Egyptian Revival pencil charm. This "write on" collectible, which measured a mere 1½ inches tall when the bottom half was retracted, had a representation of an Egyptian head at the top. This modestly priced item enabled the masses to participate in the excitement over Egyptian eccentricities. *Value guide: pencil, 1927, $75.*

Egyptian Revival Pencil

ELEPHANT BANKS

Elephants have been prominently featured on over a dozen mechanical banks and numerous stationary banks since the late 1800s. Two early examples, Jumbo and Light of Asia, served as banks as well as pull toys. When a penny was deposited in the elephant's back, it nodded its head in appreciation. Another Stevens bank, Elephant and Three Clowns, was a trifle more intricate. On this version, the elephant swings down his trunk and knocks the coin into the top of a tub, while the clown on his back turns at the waist. His performance certainly would have pleased P. T. Barnum! The Elephant with Howdah, from the Enterprise Manufacturing Company of Philadelphia, features the elephant lowering his trunk to push the coin fully into his mouth while a man pops up from the box on his back. Mechanical and stationary elephant banks have been marching into museum collections. *Value guide: Elephant and Three Clowns, 5¾"tall, $750; Elephant with Howdah, 6¼" tall, $200.*

ELGIN WATCHES

The National Watch Company was incorporated in Elgin, Illinois, in 1864, on a 30-acre site that was a gift from the town's residents. Instant success necessitated additional space; so new buildings and extensions were added to the facility. On May 12, 1874, the company became known as the Elgin National Watch Company, and by the 1880s some 1,200 employees were making 12,000 watch movements daily. Elgin watches were becoming more famous by the hour, the company's sales having exceeded 50 million watches by 1953. *Value guide: Father Time, 17 jewels, nickel plate, open face, Damaskeened, $90; Veritas, 23 jewels, ¾, nickel plate, gold jewel settings, hunter case, gold train, $325.*

THE ENGLISHWOMAN'S DOMESTIC MAGAZINE

What periodical did an English lady consult for fashion tips between 1852 and 1877? None other than *The Englishwoman's Magazine.* This magazine was England's answer to *Godey's Ladies Magazine.* It boasted hand-colored fashion plates by prominent artists. Jules David, one of the foremost fashion-plate artists, had his work shown repeatedly in this publication. Those intent upon uncovering money in old magazines prefer issues having their fashion plates intact, but even framed fashion plates from this periodical are never out of style. *Value guide: single issue, fashion plates intact, 1865, $20.*

EPPELSHEIMER & COMPANY

America's first wholesale ice cream business was founded by Jacob Fussell, of Baltimore, in 1851. Practically overnight, pewter ice cream mold makers sprung up along the eastern seaboard. Eppelsheimer & Company, of New York City, is considered a pioneer in the field. Company catalogs featured everyday and holiday molds depicting animals, birds, patriotic, figural, and fraternal subjects. For that special occasion, a large 31-inch tall Statue of Liberty mold was available on a rental basis. Those inflicted with mold madness seek any example having Eppelsheimer's initials on the flat part of the hinge. *Value guide: dolphin, pewter, $75; Santa Claus, pewter, $70.*

FANCY BUREAUS

The dressing bureau, defined as a chest of drawers with an attached mirror, was an essential piece of furniture in late 19th century

Fancy Bureau

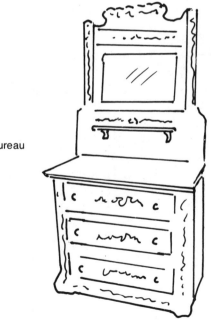

bedrooms. Gaily ornamented "fancy bureaus" were offered separately, or as part of a complete bedroom set. A standard type bore flowers and scrolls against a suitably colored background. A landscape scene was often attempted by an artist blessed with ability. As a general rule, most bureaus bore adaptations of French Revival styles. While cream-colored background found favor, black was also utilized. When fitted with marble tops, the painted dressing bureau evoked the "American French antique style." *Value guide: fancy bureau, flowers, cream background, original decoration, four drawers, circa 1890, $950.*

FAVORITE VEGETABLE BINS

Vegetable bins, dating from the late 1800s and early 1900s, rate as treasured kitchen keepsakes. These essentials held vegetables that did not require refrigeration; thus, potatoes, carrots, onions, and other produce were stored in these open-air stands. Numerous varieties were offered, usually of painted tin. Some bear a maker's name or patent date. One trusty model was the Favorite. Many homemakers during the pre-World War I era favored this stand from the G. B. Porter & Company. Those old vegetable bins have sprouted into choice collectibles. *Value guide: Favorite, circa 1910, $40.*

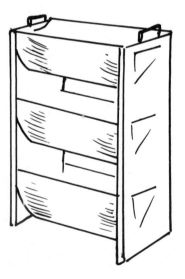

Favorite Fruit Bin

FELIX THE CAT

Feline fanciers were elated when Paul Sullivan, an Australian-born cartoonist, introduced Felix the Cat in an animatd cartoon in 1917.

110

Prior to Sullivan's death in 1933, Felix frolicked in over 100 additional cartoons. The King Features Syndicate had the artist incorporate the character into a comic strip for the Sunday page in 1923. By 1927, a daily strip was in syndication. Felix was reportedly inspired by Rudyard Kipling's "Cat Who Walks by Himself." The black feline's lonely life, in which he stages a battle against alienation and fate, converted him into a super hero. The feature has always been more beloved in Europe than in America; French academician Marcel Brion wrote that "Felix is not a cat, he is the Cat. Or better to say yet, he is a supercat, because he does not fit in any categories of the animal kingdom." *Value guide: doll, jointed, Schoenhut, 1922, 4" tall, $250; doll, leather ears, Sullivan, wood, patent 1925, 9" tall, $135.*

Felix The Cat Toy

FENTON GLASS

Carnival glass aficionados owe a debt of gratitude to Frank Fenton, who designed such beloved patterns as Horse, Medallion, Butterfly and Berry, Butterfly and Fern, Orange Tree, and Dragon and Lotus. This pioneer glass artisan founded the Fenton Art Glass Company of Martin's Ferry, Ohio, in 1905. Initially, they ornamented glass banks from other sources, but two years later following a move to Williamstown, West Virginia, Fenton was producing his own glass. While best known for carnival glass, the company produced diverse offerings such as chocolate glass and pressed glass. Their "off-hand" glass, kept in production for a couple of years in the mid-1920s, is eagerly sought. The Fenton firm, known for fine-quality reproductions of earlier glassware, flourishes to the present. *Value* *guide: carnival glass paperweight, fish, blue, $40; vase, Empress, milk glass, 8" tall, $95.*

FERDINAND THE BULL

When members of the Academy honored Ferdinand the Bull as the best cartoon short subject feature of 1938, they presented Walt Disney with an Academy Award. The sensitive Ferdinand was immediately depicted on insignias, as an emblem of faith during World War II. The animated drawings and celluloids from the feature went on sale at the Couirvoisier Galleries of San Francisco. A glazed fabric/leather bull rendition of Ferdinand was marketed by Richard G. Krueger of New York City. The Knickerbocker Toy Corporation entered the ring with dolls and figures of Ferdinand. One of the finest Ferdinand representations was the Marx wind-up toy. *Value guide: figurine, bisque, 3" tall, $65; stuffed toy, Kreuger, 1940s, $50.*

Ferdinand The Bull Toy

FIESTA WARE

Remember songs like "Boo-Hoo" and "I've Got You Under My Skin?" They were being hummed by Americans in 1936 when the Homer Laughlin Company of Newell, West Virginia, introduced Fiesta Ware. The uncomplicated design was characterized by a band of concentric circles, starting at the rim. Full-circle handles adorned cups until 1969, when partial circle handles appeared. Originally, bright green, red, blue, and yellow tablewares were marketed. As the fame of Fiesta spread, ivory, turquoise, gray, rose, forest green, light green, and chartreuse were added. That incised "Fiesta" mark can be noted on these fortunate finds. *Value guide: coffeepot, red, $35; pitcher, ice lip, yellow, $40.*

Fiesta Ware Cookie Jar

FIRESIDE ROCKER

Late 19th-century fireside rockers always receive a warm reception
from flea market followers. When folding furniture became fashion-

Fireside Rocker

able, the "fireside rocker" took up residence by the hearth in America. It was easy to position these lightweight, portable rockers to a sport near an open fireplace. Furniture makers offered all-wooden versions, along with caned seat and upholstered models. Carpet upholstery, a rage of the late Victorian era, adorned many models. Others were treated to tapestry or needlepoint seats, crafted by ladies swift with the needle. *Value guide: carpet upholstery, carved details, walnut, circa 1890, $225.*

FISHING COLLECTIBLES

A number of collectors are hooked on creels, fly rods, reels, nets, fly boxes, trout rods, and other fishing gear. Fly rods, those long, slim bamboo wands, have been ascribed to such early craftsmen as Edward Payne and Hiram Lewes Leonard. These articles, expensive acquisitions when crafted, remain so today. Decidely more affordable are the pre-1940 production line rods by the South Bend Bait Company and James Heddon & Sons. The reels for holding the fish are also sought, especially early handcrafted types by Julius Von Hofe and Yawman & Erbe. Any pre-World War II reel is considered quite a catch by fishing gear fanciers, particularly the giant salmon types and tiny "midge" trout reels. *Value guide: fly rod, Hirman L. Leonard, 1917, $600; fishing net, wood, Thomas, 1930s, $40.*

FLASH GORDON

Flash Gordon flashed onto American comic pages on Sunday, January 7, 1934. Alex Raymond created this science-fiction hero for King Features. A daily strip, drawn by Raymond's former assistant

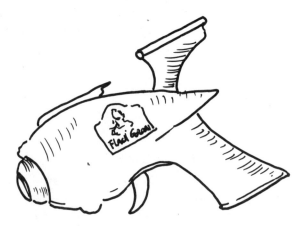

Flash Gordon Signal Pistol

Austin Briggs, appeared on May 27, 1940. Flash Gordon, "renowned polo player and Yale graduate;" his girl companion, Dale Arden; and a scientist, Dr. Hans Zarkov, were introduced in the opening sequence. Over the years, other artists sustained the image of the character. Grosset & Dunlap published an original novel, *Flash Gordon in the Caverns of Mongo*, in 1936. A movie serial starring Buster Crabbe appeared the same year. It became a radio program in the '30s and '40s, followed by a television series in 1953-54. All of which proved that Flash Gordon was no flash in the pan. *Value guide: gun, toy, blue, dated 1935, boxed $385; pistol, radio repeater click, boxed, $165.*

FLASKS

Gentleman, as well as lady, imbibers of the late 1800s and early 1900s had a wide variety of flasks at their disposal. Those with an affinity for alcoholic beverages often preferred the sterling silver or silverplated varieties over the more fragile glass examples. The metal types boasted a wide diversity of exterior decoration, notably embossed and engraved designs. They were produced in various capacities and countless shapes by spirited American silversmiths. Many were lettered with appropriate phrases. One heart-shaped model bore the sentimental working, "Drink Heartily." *Value guide: heart shape, Homan, silverplate, $45; sterling silver, repousse florals, Gorham, circa 1895, $650.*

FLORAL PATTERN

The *Passiflora* (passion flower) was utilized as a decorative device

 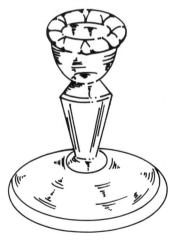

Floral Pattern Candlesticks

on a Jeanette Glass Company depression favorite. Tableware in this pattern had a passion flower motif incorporating leaves and flowers. Between 1931 and 1934, approximately 25 different accessories were available in pink, crystal, emerald green, and jadite. It was a rather extensive line, featuring coasters, ashtrays, refrigerator dishes, and cereal sets. The pitchers were cone shaped. More than one depression enthusiast has developed a passion for Jeanette's floral. *Value guide: cup and saucer, green, $12; salt and pepper shakers, pink, $30.*

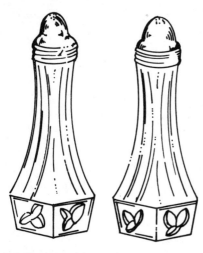

Floral Salt & Pepper Shakers

FLORENTINE PATTERN

Two mold-etched patterns having identical styles but different shapes were made by the Hazel-Atlas Glass Company in the 1930s.

Florentine No. 1 Footed Tumbler

Both featured flower and scroll pinwheel centers, and scrolls and poppylike flowers on the borders. Old Florentine was the earliest, dating from 1932 through 1934, and appearing in green, yellow, pink, crystal, and sometimes dark blue. Florentine made between 1934 and 1936, was produced in similar colors. Old Florentine, however, had hexagonal shapes and serrated edges, while Florentine objects boasted round shapes. Therefore, mixing and matching might be the order of the day with this depression duo. *Value guide: butter, pink, Florentine, $60; tumbler, Old Florentine, yellow, $14.*

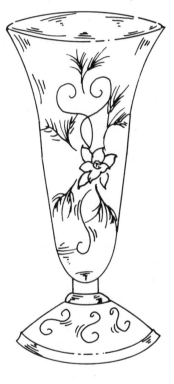

Florentine No. 2 Vase

FLORODORA DOLLS

George Borgfeldt, revered American doll impressario, introduced Florodora in 1901. The trademark was registered in Germany, where the bisque heads were manufactured by the Armand Marseilles works. These dolls had composition ball-jointed or kid bodies. Generally, they ranged between 8 and 24 inches tall. Florodora boasted an open mouth, sleep eyes, and a beautiful wig, and was attired, of course, in a fancy outfit. Attribution problems seldom exist, for the adorable Florodora doll was usually marked "Made in Germany, Florodora, A. 2 M." *Value guide: doll, 22" tall, $425.*

Florodora Doll

FOLDING CAMERAS

After the birth of photography, a need developed for more sophisticated equipment for field work. Manufacturers obliged, introducing

Folding Camera

folding, bellow-type cameras which generally can be divided into two groups: the small hand- held models for family use and the larger tripod versions for professional work. The majority of family cameras accommodated roll film. Their simple operation and compact size made them more desirable than box cameras. Studio equipment has been subjected to only minor changes, with most varieties having fine woods, leather bellows, removable backs, and removable lenses and shutters. At present, folding cameras hold more than sentimental value. *Value guide: No. 3 Folding Kodak Deluxe, circa 1903, $120; Pony Premo, 6" × 8", $90.*

FOSTORIA GLASS COMPANY

The famed Fostoria Glass Company of Fostoria, Ohio, was founded in 1907 by L. B. Martin. When a gas well went dry shortly thereafter, the company relocated to Moundsville, West Virginia. This presently flourishing concern earned nationwide respect with superior quality tablewares, oil lamps, pressed glass, art glass, and other notable accomplishments. Their figurines are fervently collected. Art deco magazines (1920-1940s) featured countless advertisements for Fostoria's clear and colored table settings. Deeply etched, naturalistic forms characterized the firm's output. Discontinued clear and colored glass patterns rate as continuing favorites at markets. *Value guide: cup and saucer, Versailles, $30; figurine, seahorse, $90.*

FOUNTAIN PENS

Do names like Sheaffer, Waterman, Eversharp, and Parker cause your pulse to quicken? Then perhaps you are a fountain pen collector. Historical pen lore heralds the fact that the first pen with an ink reservoir was invented by Bartholomew Folsch, in 1809, while the initial quill pen with a reservoir was perfected by J. H. Lewis in 1819. Following various improvements in the field in the 1890s American and British manufacturers entered into the full-scale production of fountain pens with 14-karat gold nibs tipped with iridium. Self-filling lever action models were introduced during World War I. Examples dating from the 1920s through 1940s are in demand, particularly gold pens or pen and pencil sets. Why are damaged models purchased by collectors? Simply because their worn parts can be used to restore similar versions. *Value guide: Sheaffer pen, Crest Triumph, 1500, $25; Waterman, Ideal Ink View, $15.*

FOXY GRANDPA

Foxy Grandpa made a rather auspicious debut on the front page of the *New York Herald* comic section on January 7, 1900. The strip, by C. E. Schultze, became an overnight sensation. After a few years, the feature began fading, at which time the Hearst Company placed the strip on the back page of the "American Weekly" section. Schultze had joined Hearst's *New York American* in 1902. By the end of the decade, Foxy Grandpa was at home at the *New York Press,* where it continued until 1918. Schultze revived the character in a daily series of animal and nature narratives for children in the early 1920s. Foxy collectors have been hoarding Foxy Grandpa artifacts ever since. *Value guide: match holder, bisque, circa 1915, $75; papier-mache candy container, removable head, circa 1910, $60.*

Foxy Grandpa Game

FRANKART INCORPORATED

During the 1920s, when flappers were kicking up their heels, Frankart Incorporated of New York City initiated a line of green metal accessories. The beautiful people of the period referred to them as "greenies." Those without sufficient funds to purchase "greenies" were understandably green with envy. Frankart's line, which was decidedly art deco, featured figurines, figural creamers, figures holding ashtrays and lamps, stylized birds and animals, and other equally inventive objects. Additionally, the maker marketed a full range of other reminders of the Roaring Twenties. Positive identification poses no problem, for the bulk of their output was marked Frankart, along with a patent date and the year of manufacture. *Value guide: ashtray, nude holding tray, $525; lamp, nude holding lamp, $275.*

Frankart Table Lamp

FRANKOMA POTTERY

Christmas plate collectors are familiar with the wares of the Frankoma Pottery of Sapulpa, Oklahoma. Various utilitarian objects, typically possessing Southwestern themes, were also potted. John Frank, originator of the pottery, relocated from Chicago to Oklahoma in 1929. While working for a geological survey of regional clay he taught art and ceramics at the University of Oklahoma. In the early 1930s, he opened a studio at Norman. He later moved to Sapulpa in 1940, which, geographically speaking, placed him at the source of the red-burning clay so vital to his potting experiments. Eventually, the studio evolved into a factory. Frankoma's glazes and designs attest to his intense interest in the mountains and deserts of Oklahoma. *Value guide: flask, lavendar, thong holder, $38; sugar and creamer, brown, $30.*

FRETWORK

A craze for fretwork cut a path across the United States in the post-Centennial era. Exhibitions at the fairgrounds prompted this fretwork frenzy. Fretwork, Sorrento carving, and jigsaw work were closely allied with woodcarving. Most objects were fabricated with a fretsaw from prepared patterns. The *Art Amateur* and other publications gave impetus to this art recreation with detailed instructions. Oak, walnut, cherry, ash, white holly, and ebony were among the favored woods. Woodworkers demonstrated their adroitness by fashioning objects ranging from birdcages to wallpockets. *Value guide: birdcage, intricate, 20" tall, circa 1895, $450; wallpocket, oak, ornate, $150.*

Fretwork Birdcage

FRUIT CRATE LABELS

When California fruit growers began using colorful lithographed labels to identify their products in the latter 19th century, it prompted a fad so flagrant that by the 1930s over 2,000 different orange brand labels were in use. Early motifs, printed by stone lithography, often bore the word "Love," or sentimental subject matter. As competition escalated, fruit crate art covered every conceivable subject, from Indians to monks. Lithographed labels were supplanted by engraved types by the depression era. When cardboard boxes replaced wooden crates in the mid-1900s, fruit crate labels by the bushel and the peck popped onto flea market tabletops. *Value guide: Big Ben Oranges, tower with clock, $20; First American Lemons, Indian girl, tepee, Los Angeles, $60.*

FRUIT JARS

The fruit, or canning, jar was perfected to provide an airtight storage container for food sterilized by boiling. Food could now be maintained in a sterile state, thereby preventing contamination by airborne bacteria. Nicolas Appert's book, *The Art of Preserving,* was published in France in 1910. Early free-blown cylindrical vessels were supplanted in mid-century by improved wax seal jars. Later, screw top jars occupied cupboard space, the first developed by John Landis Mason. He patented a mold capable of producing a fruit jar with a threaded neck and a corresponding zinc top in 1858. In 1869, Lewis R. Boyd completed the project by patenting an opal glass liner for the lid. Competitors developed a never ending stream of closures and decorative embossings. *Value guide: Atterbury, handmade, tapered stopper, embossed name, aqua, quart, $300; Star, handmade, "Star" embossed above star, aqua, quart, $75.*

Imperial Fruit Jar

FRY, H. C.

The major American business news of 1874 centered around the opening of Bloomingdale's on Third Avenue in New York City. Scant attention was focused on H. C. Fry, who assumed the presidency of the Rochester Tumbler Company of Rochester, Pennsylvania. Was he successful? Who could deny it, for by 1901, the glasshouse was operating as H. C. Fry Glass Company. Their magnificent cut glass brought them fame, and reportedly, fortune. But when the demand slackened by the mid-1920s, the company faced financial hardship. Between 1926 and 1927, Foval or Pearl glass, an art glass, was produced for a few months. Following several attempts at reorganization, Fry faltered in 1934. *Value*

guide: cup and saucer, Foval, jade green handle, $65; water set,
Foval, opalescent, jade base and handle, pitcher, five footed tumblers,
$600.

FULPER POTTERY

Abraham Fulper, a Hollander, became a partner in the Samuel Hill
Pottery of Flemington, New Jersey, in 1847. About 13 years later
he acquired the works, renaming it the Fulper Pottery. Utilitarian
objects, notably drain pipes, stoneware bottles, jars, and churns

Fulper Lamp

were potted. About 1910, when ceramic engineer J. M. Stangle
became associated with the pottery, art wares were introduced.
When restrictions were placed on imports during World War I,
dolls' heads were made, along with Kewpie dolls. Following a
disastrous fire in 1929, the major operation relocated to Trenton.
One year later, J. M. Stangle purchased the pottery. *Value guide:*
box, art deco, woman, 1920s, $100; rose bowl, grey-green, 7" tall,
$150.

GASOLINE ALLEY

The characters in "Gasoline Alley" have always chronicled a pictorial review of middle class life in America. Frank King introduced

Skeezix Nodding Figure

the strip to readers on Sunday, November 24, 1918, in the *Chicago Tribune*. A daily strip started in the *New York Daily News* on August 23, 1919. It soon became apparent that "Gasoline Alley" could go on forever, which is essentially what happened. King was the first to allow a comic character to grow and age like an actual human being, which is precisely what Skeesix Wallet did over the years. The memorable characters in Gasoline Alley appeared on mementos ranging from Big Little Books to nodding figurines. A 1951 Columbia feature, starring Scotty Becket, introduced the characters to another generation of youngsters. *Value guide: bisque nodder, Mr. Wicker, Germany, $135; toothbrush holder, tin, Skeesix, advertising Listerine, $90.*

GENERAL BUTLER BANK

Figural still banks covered depictions ranging from George Washington to Andy Gump. In 1878, the J. & E. Stevens Company introduced a caricature bank depicting General Benjamin Butler. The Greenback Party nominated him for president in 1884, but his economic philosphies failed to enthrall voters. Butler was in favor of issuing sizable amounts of paper money in order to clear the debts incurred by people during the Panic of 1873. The bank featured him as a green-backed frog holding paper money in his left hand. The wording on his right arm read, "For the Masses." "Bonds and Yachts For Me" appeared on his left arm. *Value guide: General Butler, cast-iron, 6¼" tall, $750.*

GENERAL MACARTHUR DOLL

The Freundlich Novelty Company of New York City scored a direct

General MacArthur Doll

hit with this wartime favorite of the early 1940s. The General MacArthur doll, standing a full 18 inches tall, was realistically executed. It was an all-composition doll with a molded hat, painted features, and jointed hips and shoulders. Naturally, the General wore his military uniform. Designers added a bit of detail so one arm could be raised to a saluting position. Doll collectors have been known to form battle lines when the bartering begins on this patriotic plaything. *Value guide: doll, 18" tall, dressed, $165.*

GEORGE AND MARTHA WASHINGTON PITCHERS

Thanks to a working kiln, the American Pavilion drew more than its share of visitors to the 1939 New York World's Fair. One of the six potteries joining forces for this tribute to domestic potters was the Homer Laughlin Company of Newell, West Virginia. The pottery is known to those who fancy Fiesta Ware. They produced 5-inch tall figural representations depicting George and Martha Washington. Undoubtedly, they provided a touch of patriotism to the proceedings. All George and Martha mementos are sought, but none more so than these remarkable remembrances that originally sold for 50 cents. *Value guide: Washington pitchers, $65.*

GEORGE VI TEAPOT

One of the most regal souvenirs issued to commemorate the crowning of George VI and Elizabeth in 1937 was a crown-shaped teapot. English tea drinkers were indebted to the General Household Utilities of Norbury, England, for this regal remembrance, because the teapot represented the ultimate symbol of royalty. Portraits of King George VI and Queen Elizabeth were prominently displayed on the teapot, along with the wording, "To Commemorate the Coronation, May 12, 1937." Coronation collectors deem it a crowning achievement anytime they locate a mint condition example. *Value guide: $75.*

GEORGIAN PATTERN

Georgian deserves the recognition of being the initial mold-etched depression glass pattern issued by the Federal Glass Company. Between 1931 and 1935, green and crystal table settings beguiled beleaguered depression consumers. The design was comprised of lovebirds alternating with baskets joined by festoons in a chain motif. The diminutive birds are almost indiscernible on some specimens, and are, in fact, absent from the 9-ounce tumbler and 13-ounce iced tea glass. Dinner services, and eventually luncheon sets, were marketed by Federal. The latter had smaller creamers and sugars. Georgian, or Lovebirds, has been fairly flying out of flea markets. *Value guide: cup and saucer, green, $8; plate 8½" diameter, green, $10.*

GILBREDS IMPROVED FRUIT JARS

Those who fancy fruit jars often encounter rare specimens that qualify as superior finds. In 1885, the Gilbreds Improved Jar landed on general store countertops. This jar, having a ground lip, appeared in green and aqua. The embossed motif featured a five-pointed star with the word "Improved" lettered across it. The "Gilbreds" name was above the star, and the word "Jar" appeared beneath the central star. Perhaps the most distinguishing characteristic was the fact that wires ran completely around the jar, since few jars were fashioned in this manner. Questers are on the prowl for Gilbreds quart-size fruit jars. *Value guide: aqua, $135.*

GIRL SKIPPING ROPE BANK

Those activated in the direction of mechanical banks prize this James H. Bowen design, manufactured by the J. & E. Stevens Company. It was patented on May 20, 1890. The superb casting depicts a girl jumping rope and a squirrel on the right side of the bank. A penny placed between the paws of the squirrel activates the clockwork mechanism. To wind up the motor, a key is inserted above the squirrel. When a lever next to the girl is pressed, the girl moves up and down, rhythmically jumping rope as her legs swing back and forth. In addition, the girl's head performs the same action. Youngsters enjoyed the action, which continued long after the penny had been deposited. *Value guide: Girl Skipping Rope bank, cast-iron, 8¼" tall, $6,500.*

GLOBE SAVINGS BANK

In the late 1800s, when a penny saved was a penny earned, the Globe Savings Bank was an intriguing inducement to thrift. This bank sold for just 25 cents in 1889. As might be anticipated, the shape of the bank simulated a world globe. The coin slot was ingeniously placed in the side of the globe, directly in front of the eagle finial. (It was that lofty eagle perched atop the bank that provided it with a patriotic flavor.) The prices on these penny banks would indicate that collector interest has been compounding on a daily basis. *Value guide: Globe bank, good condition, $90.*

GOLDEN OAK

The heavy, mass-produced oak furniture used in American factories, offices, and homes between the 1880s and 1920s is known as "Golden Oak." This title encompasses the light-colored and darker oak objects ranging from dining room sets to bedroom sets. There were over 62 furniture factories working in Grand Rapids alone, employing over 9,000 workers by the 1890s. Many tables had carved pedestals, while chairs boasted turnings and carvings along

Golden Oak Ice Box

with curved backs. A three-piece "Chamber Set," including a carved bedstead, sold from $11.85 to $67.50. Both local and outside manufacturers exhibited their wares at semiannual flea markets in Grand Rapids. One commentator noted, "The exhibits were economic and artistic, rather than majestic or magnificent." *Value*

Golden Oak China Cabinet

guide: china closet, curved sides, bowed front, claw feet, oak, medium size, circa 1900, $850; table, oak, square, 48", circa 1900, $285.

GONE WITH THE WIND

A collecting cult has developed around the film *Gone With The Wind*, based on Margaret Mitchell's famed novel, which was published by MacMillan in 1936. Editor John Latham not only changed the name of the heroine from Pansy to Scarlet, but was also responsible for changing the title, which was originally, *Tomorrow Is Another Day*. Within three years, the book chalked up sales of 2 million copies. The release of Victor Fleming's film starring Clark Gable, Vivien Leigh, Olivia de Haviland, and Leslie Howard was anxiously anticipated. It premiered in Atlanta, Georgia, the novelist's home town, in 1939. Because the film ran an unprecedented 222 minutes, its producers decided to interrupt it for an intermission. Collectors seek any item associated with the film, fearing that before long they too might be "Gone With The Wind." *Value guide: book, movie version, $22; paper dolls, uncut, $300.*

GOOFUS GLASS

Goofus glass, originally known as Mexican glass, was a favorite premium item at fairs and carnivals in the early 1900s, thus traveling the same route as carnival glass. Goofus glass had various embossed designs, such as roses, carnations, strawberries, grapes, sunflowers, and peacocks. It was originally painted gold, red, bronze, green, pink, or purple; other bright colors were also used. The stems or leaves were customarily treated to a bronze or metallic paint. Due to oxidation of the paint, some specimens acquire a dull appearance which often can be revived by applying a silver polish. Numerous American glasshouses girded for the onslaught of Goofus glass orders in the pre-World War I era. *Value guide: apothecary bottle, Statue of Liberty, $75; vase, peacock decor, gold and red, 10" tall, $85.*

GOUDA POTTERY

Gouda has been a thriving pottery center, in Holland, since the 17th century. Factories situated there have earned a far-flung reputation, especially in the area of tin-glazed earthenwares. Modern works include the Zenith pottery, established in the 18th century. This still-active factory specializes in faience for everyday use, tiles, tile pictures, and tea services. Another firm, De Zuidhollandische Plateelbakkerij, has developed superior tablewares, vases, and imitations of Rosenburg art nouveau pottery. Blue and white Delftware bearing the "Gouda" mark also generates intense inter-

Gouda Pottery Bowl

est among ceramic seekers. *Value guide: creamer, cow, circa 1900, $75; vase, art nouveau, double gourd shape, 7" tall, circa 1890, $125.*

GRAND RAPIDS

Over 27,000 buyers from around the world attended the semiannual markets held in Grand Rapids, Michigan, in 1913. Many furniture factories in this area employed skilled designers of French, Austrian, or German origin. These mass-produced forms typically displayed Renaissance Revival, Gothic, or Eastlake details. To trim production costs, flatter carving and incised lines were utilized. Oak and walnut were widely favored by most makers. Due to fierce competition, factories were constantly experimenting with faster and more economical procedures. The Grand Rapids style, con-

Grand Rapids High Chair

sisting of flat surface areas and geometric shapes, earned them a "reputation, popularity and goodwill." *Value guide: bookcase, Golden Oak, four shelves, four lifting glass doors, 48" × 58", circa 1910, $550.*

GRANITEWARE

Graniteware objects were introduced to American consumers at the Philadelphia Centennial Exposition of 1876. By the turn of the century, many manufacturers were engaged in producing this ware, which was of sheet iron coated with a porcelainlike substance. Many utilitarian objects were produced, most intended for use in the kitchen or bathroom. A few makers marked their output, some with paper labels that have all but disappeared with time. Graniteware, or agateware, has acquired many admirers, principally due to its swirled, mottled, or marbleized surface. While the background color was usually white, the designs in gray, blue, green, yellow, brown, turquoise, and other colors gave it its distinctive appearance. In the early 1900s, white pieces trimmed in blue became fashionable. Graniteware has developed into the durable collectible that its name implies. *Value guide: butter dish, gray, pewter trim, finial, $250; teapot, gooseneck spout, turquoise, $40.*

Graniteware Dish Pan

GRATERS

American graters, large and small, have appeared in untold numbers over the years. Quite often the small nutmeg graters were pocket size, so that they could be used to flavor beverages while one was visiting. The famous Edgar nutmeg grater made its debut in 1891. When the improved Edgar grater was introduced shortly thereafter, it was described as follows: "It will not clog, tear the fingers nor drop the nutmeg. It grates the nutmeg very fine, distributes it evenly and grates it all up." Some fruit or vegetable graters were hand pierced with artistically arranged dashes, dots, or stars. By the late 19th century, graters were experiencing their greatest acceptance. *Value guide: clamp-on, Schroeter, cast-iron, $40; Edgar, nutmeg, pat. 1891, tin and wood, $55.*

GREENAWAY, KATE

Kate Greenaway (1846-1901), the English artist, executed drawings of quaint children for *Little Folks Magazine* as early as 1873. During the 1880s, her illustrations brightened the pages of *Wide Awake, Every Girl's Annual, The Girl's Own Paper,* and *St. Nicholas.* Collectors concur, some of the most charming drawings appeared in books published by Marcus Ward & Co., Goodall & Sons, and George Routledge & Sons. Somewhat more available are her Valentines and Christmas cards designed for various English publishers. Kate Greenaway children adorned fans, buttons, calico, parasols, wallpapers, ceramics, silverplated tablewares, and calendars. Little girls with muffs and little boys wearing ulsters became her trademark. *Value guide: napkin ring, silverplate, figure with frog after fly, $235; tiles, Four Seasons, set of four, $400.*

Kate Greenaway Napkin Ring

GREENWOOD CHINA

Trenton, New Jersey, was a thriving pottery center in the late 1800s. The Greenwood pottery was one of the most prolific during this period. Between 1861 and 1868, it operated as Stephen Tams & Company. Bone china, graniteware, vitrified china, and translucent wares brought them a far-reaching audience. Art porcelain lines were crafted in limited quantities. Unlike other potters, Greenwood did a healthy business in hotel china, which, presumably, proved too lucrative to abandon. Attribution problems seldom exist, for Greenwood's output typically bore the potter's name and location. *Value guide: bowl, ironstone, green banding, 10" diameter, $20; jar, woman's head handles, cobalt trim, $45.*

GREY IRON CASTING COMPANY

In 1840, the Brady Machine Shop opened in Mount Joy, Pennsylvania. It was operating as the Grey Iron Casting Company 41 years later. By the early 1900s, it became the talk of toydom with a full array of children's playthings; orders rolled in for cap pistols, toy stoves, banks, trains, and variously wheeled vehicles. Their company's numerous toy soldiers always rate a special salute from collectors. As with other metal toys, those possessing original paint are preferred. The Model T Fords dating from the 1920s have been positively speeding out of markets. *Value guide: cap pistol, bulldog, $25; horse drawn wagon, cast-iron, 13" long, $275.*

GRUEBY POTTERY

The Grueby Faience Company, an outgrowth of Atwood & Grueby, was founded in Boston in 1897. It specialized in producing tiles and other pottery mainly for architectual purposes. Eventually, other decorative and utilitarian wares were marketed, many boasting Egyptian forms and matte finishes. The matte-glaze was to become synonymous with the Grueby name. Natural shapes, such as the mullen leaf, tulip, and acanthus leaf, were favored. Grueby furnished lamp bases to such prestigious firms as Tiffany, Duffner, Kimberly & Bigelow, and Kinnard & Company. Art pottery lines were discontinued about 1910. Although varying marks were

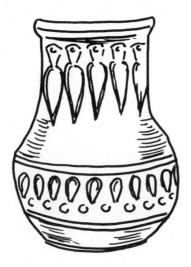

Grueby Pottery Vase

utilized, all had the Grueby name incorporated into the backstamp. *Value guide: tile, impressed and graffito tulip, yellow and green, 6" square, $625; vase, leaves and flowers, green matte, 8" tall, $2,250.*

GUNTHERMANN

In some quarters, S. Gunthermann is regarded as the pioneer of Nuremburg tinplate toy makers. This company was first mentioned in city directories of 1880. Following Gunthermann's death in 1890, his widow married Adolf Weigel, the firm's manager. His initials "A. W." were incorporated into the toy manufacturer's "S. G." trademark. By 1901, approximately 250 workers were actively filling orders for fire engines, horse-drawn vehicles, aeroplanes, and a series of Gordon Bennett racing cars. This respected toy works was purchased by Liemens in 1965, and the production of superior quality tinplate models continues. *Value guide: beetle, tin wind-up, 7½" tall, circa 1911, $175.*

HALL CHINA COMPANY

People intent upon acquiring tomorrow's antiques search for Hall China Company presentations. This presently flourishing American concern was founded by Robert Hall in 1903. Yellow-ware articles dominated early production. Later, a fireproof white body with a colored glaze was perfected. Restaurant wares became factory staples by 1914. Collectors have also fallen for the Autumn Leaf dinnerware services marketed between 1933 and 1977. Their contemporary cookie jars, coffeepots, and kitchenwares of the 1930s and 1940s made Hall a household word. *Value guide: casserole, covered, orange poppy, 8½″ diameter, $30; cookie jar, Puss'n Boots, $35.*

HALL CHINA TEAPOTS

The Hall China company began making a line of teapots in 1920. Each teapot has a special design name, but may be marketed in a variety of colors. Some of the highly collectible models include Airflow, 1940; Albany, 1930; Automobile, 1938; Basket, 1938; Boston, 1920; Globe, 1940; Hollywood, late 1920; Los Angeles, mid-1920s; Philadelphia, 1923; and Streamline, 1940. Other teapot lines included Twin-Tee, 1926; Tea for Two, 1930s; Twinspout, late 1940s; Victoria & Albert, 1940s; and Miss Terry. Collector interest has also perked up recently on Hall Coffeepots, such as Big Boy, Step-down, Armory, Blaine, and Coffee Queen. *Value guide: Aladdin, teapot, cobalt, gold trim, $40; Cleveland, yellow, gold, $35.*

HALL'S EXCELSIOR BANK

The prolific J. & E. Stevens Company of Cromwell, Connecticut, kept its Hall's Excelsior bank in production for a prolonged period of time. It was patented by John Hall on December 21, 1869. The white building, having a "monkey" cashier on the top, was trimmed in red and blue. Pulling the door knob lifts the roof, exposing the "monkey" cashier. The weight of the coin lowers the tray, at which time the roof closes and the cashier disappears; the mechanism is simply a variation of the age-old jack-in-the-box idea. Because the cashier was made of wood, locating one in pristine condition can be a chore. Identification problems seldom exist, for the building bears the wording "Hall's Excelsior Bank." *Value guide: Hall's Excelsior Bank, iron and wood, 5¾" tall, $300.*

HAMPSHIRE POTTERY

The Hampshire Pottery & J. S. Taft & Co., active in Keene, New Hampshire, between the 1870s and 1920s, must be singled out for its many ceramic accomplishments. American cupboards became stocked with their redware, stoneware, and majolica. Art pottery lines, suggestive of Rookwood and Weller, were introduced at the turn of the century; they are noticeably scarce, however, resulting in ever higher prices. When business faltered, hotel china was marketed to bolster sagging profits. Astute collectors have been quietly hoarding Hampshire pottery. *Value guide: plate, Old Witch House, 6½" diameter, $5; teapot, art deco, butterfly finia, $70.*

HANDEL, PHILIP

Adolph Eyden and Philip Handel joined forces as glass decorators in

Handel Lamp

137

the 1880s. Handel acquired full control of the company in 1893, operating as Handel & Company. Although metalwares, ceramics, and glassware originated at the factory, he became best known for his lamps. Handel received a patent in 1904 for a "chipped glass" process, capable of creating a textured surface on the finished glass. Some of his lamps had a chipped surface on the exterior and a painted design on the interior; sometimes glass beads furnished the textured surface effect. Other lamps were made of leaded glass or metal framed glass techniques. Until the firm's closing in 1936, most of their output bore the signed "Handel" mark, either impressed, on a cloth label, painted, or stamped. *Value guide: table lamp, yellow domed shade, poppies, bronze baluster, signed, 21" diameter, $900; table lamp, leaded shade, flowers, signed, 23" diameter, $3,200.*

HANDPAINTED CHINA

The art of china painting, fashionable on the Continent and in England earlier in the century, swept through America in the 1880s. For several decades correspondence courses, books, and publications, including *The China Decorator*, enlightened practioners. Internationally known potters, such as Haviland and Elite, furnished blanks of every description. The quality of workmanship varied, depending on the skill of the artisan. Superior specimens often bore the artist's signature or initials. Many dated pieces exist. The fad persisted into the 20th century, when one source noted that over 20,000 professional china painters were active in the United States. *Value guide: fish set, Coronet, Limoges, gravy boat, under platter, 12 plates, circa 1905, $1,100; vase, asters, circa 1900, $175.*

HAPPY HOOLIGAN

Fred Oper's classic Irish character, Happy Hooligan, was introduced on Hearst's comic pages in New York and San Francisco in 1900. Until 1932 the strip ran under several different names. Hooligan, originally pictured with a ruddy nose and blue can for a hat, became known for impulsive undertakings that brought him into the hands of law enforcement agencies. Despite repeated problems, he optimistically maintained a cheerful smile. This short, rotund figure became leaner and taller over the years. Hooligan's happiness spread beyond the comic pages, for he was the subject of stage productions, animated cartoons, books, and a hit song. Unfortunately, Oper was forced to abandon the strip due to failing eye sight in 1932. *Value guide: toy, Happy Hooligan in cart, pulled by horse, cast-iron, 1905, $400; Happy Hooligan Walker, wind-up, Chein, $250.*

Happy Hooligan Roly Poly

HARLEQUIN

Harlequin, a Fiesta Ware look-alike, was marketed by the Homer Laughlin Company between 1938 and 1964. These tablewares were sold minus any trademark through F. W. Woolworth outlets. Harlequin was available in all standard Fiesta colors, except green and ivory. Color-conscious buyers also found it available in such non-Fiesta colors as maroon, mauve, blue, and spruce green. This inexpensive ware had a concentric ring design, but differed from Fiesta because the rings were separated from the rims by plain margins. The angular cup handles were almost triangular in shape. In 1979, Harlequin staged a comeback, appearing in turquoise, green, yellow, and deep coral. *Value guide: donkey, figurine, yellow, $30; water jug, red, $18.*

HARTMAN FURNITURE COMPANY

At the turn of the century, one Golden Oak furniture maker confidently stated, "We can furnish the home of a mechanic or millionaire." The executives at the Hartman Furniture Company of Chicago, Illinois, abided by this principle; their catalogs featured pieces suitable for any room in the home. Pedestal tables boasting ornate lion legs, suggestive of Empire styles sold for between $16.58 and $21.35. Roman chairs were extensively promoted, most retailing from $4.29 to $13.95. Endeavoring to tempt the rich man as well as the poor man, they offered a solid oak couch covered with imported velour for just $9.95. Golden Oak furniture bearing the Hartman name is being mined by astute flea marketeers. *Value guide: couch, oak, green velour, circa 1910, $350; table, pedestal, lion's leg decor, 48" diameter, $1,800.*

Hartman Roman Chair

H. J. HEINZ COMPANY

The H. J. Heinz Company traces its roots to Sharpsburg, Pennsylvania, where Henry J. Heinz and L. C. Noble began packaging horseradish in green bottles about 1869. Heinz had been supplying Pittsburgh grocers with surplus produce from his garden for about a decade. Although Heinz & Noble suffered financial setbacks about 1875, creditors were paid off eventually. By 1876, Heinz, along with his brother and cousin, founded F. and J. Heinz. The business flourished when Heinz's Tomato Ketchup was introduced. Following a reorganization in 1888, the company functioned as H. J. Heinz. In 1896, upon spotting a streetcar ad while traveling on the New York elevated train advertising 21 shoe styles, he was prompted to adapt "57 Varieties" as his slogan, although he was producing far in excess of that number of products. *Value guide: keg, stoneware, gallon size, circa 1885, $55; toy delivery truck, $60.*

HEISEY GLASS

When George Duncan died, James Duncan, his son, and Augustus Heisey, his son-in-law, became the owners of the George Duncan Glass Company of Pennsylvania. The company merged with the United States Glass Company in 1893, at which time Heisey departed from the glasshouse to start his own factory in Newark,

Ohio. Heisey & Company was founded in 1896. That familiar "H" within a diamond trademark came into existence about 1900. Many early patterns were in the "Colonial" theme. Through the early 1920s, clear, custard, emerald green, cobalt, and milk glass articles dotted company catalogs. Following Heisey's death in 1922, his son, Edgar Wilson Heisey, assumed control. When his brother, T. Clarence Heisey, became president of the firm in 1942, figurines, stemware, and tablewares were marketed until the firm shuttered in 1957. *Value guide: figurine, Goose, wings down, $375; goblet, Victorian, $20.*

Heisey Glass Sugar and Creamer

HEYWOOD-WAKEFIELD

Cyrus Wakefield of Boston, Massachusetts, was crafting furniture from cane as early as the 1840s. A decade later, he expanded to larger quarters in South Reading, Massachusetts. By the 1870s, he was devoting 10 acres of floor space to the production of wicker furniture. He incorporated as the Wakefield-Ratten Company, but the firm floundered during economic hard times. His wife kept the company afloat following his death, at which time a nephew, Cyrus Wakefield II, became the manager. Levi Heywood, of the Heywood Brothers, began buying rattan seats from Wakefield about this time. Mr. Heywood had been in the furniture business from 1861. By the 1870s, he was acknowledged as America's foremost chair maker. The two companies began competing for the wider trade, merging as the still flourishing Heywood-Wakefield in 1897. *Value guide:*

Heywood-Wakefield Sewing Stand

settee, arched back, intricate design, circa 1895, $1,250; tea wagon, removable glass top, 34" diameter, $350.

HIRES ROOT BEER

Charles Elmer Hires developed root beer from a recipe for an herbal tea about 1875. After perfecting the formula, he exhibited Hires Root Beer Extract at the Philadelphia Centennial Exposition of 1876. The name "root beer" was adapted on the suggestion of a friend, on the assumption that hard-working Pennsylvania coal miners would be more attracted to purchase root beer than herbal tea. By 1886, Hires was being sold in bottles, exploiting the advantages of brewing the tea at home from Hires extract. By 1905, it was being sold to soda fountains. The first in a series of advertising mementos was a Mettlach stein. The Hires Boy attire changed over the years. Between 1891 and 1906, he wore a dress, bib, or bolero style jacket; between 1907 and 1914, he was attired in a bathrobe; and between 1915 and 1926, he wore a dinner jacket. *Value guide: sign, man and woman at fountain, cardboard, 35" × 24", $600; thermometer, 40" tall, $55.*

HOBNAIL PATTERN

Throughout the late 19th century, American glasshouses profited from the Hobnail pattern. It was not surprising, therefore, that a depression glass reissue was undertaken by the Hocking Glass Company. Between 1934 and 1936, this faithful adaptation of a traditional design became available in crystal and pink. The pink tableware, utilized as a premium item in 1935, was discontinued just one year later. In 1942, Hobnail accessories surfaced in *Moonstone,* an opalescent glass. Milk white articles abounded in the 1960s. Those graduated raised dots or hobnails make this pattern unmistakable. *Value guide: decanter, stopper, red trim, 32-ounces, $15; vase, footed, pink, 6½" tall, $30.*

Hobnail Pattern Sherbert

HOHNER ACCORDIONS

According to company promotions of the late 1800s and early 1900s, each and every Hohner accordion was "harmoniously tuned." These German imports usually sold for between $2.45 and $23.45. The costliest model, known as the Hohner Organ Accordion, had 16 folds of black leatherette fitted with brass corners. Other standard equipment included 31 invisible keys arranged in three rows fitted with mother-of-pearl buttons and six sets of bronze reeds. Did Mr. Hohner need a publicist on the payroll? Probably not, for his like-

Hohner Accordion

ness appeared 16 times and his name 68 times on this deluxe accordion. *Value guide: Hohner Organ Accordion, 12⅞″ × 12¼″, circa 1910, $150.*

HOLD-TO-LIGHT POSTCARDS

Around the turn of the century, novelty postcards were being posted in sizable numbers. Postcard designers utilized varying techniques in creating hold-to-light varieties. The majority had a thin layer of paper (usually yellow) placed between two pieces of perforated cardboard. The face of the card customarily featured a scene showing windows. This enabled light to shine through the windows when the card was held to the light. American and European publishers added a touch of individuality with varied methods and subject matter. Church windows proved especially popular for Christmas cards. Hold-to-light postcards are held in high esteem by deltiologists. *Value guide: Christmas card, church scene, $10.*

HOLLY AMBER

The public's outcry for artistic glass prompted the Indiana Tumbler & Goblet Company to introduce Holly Amber in 1903. It was produced for a few months between January 1 and June 13. Holly Amber accessories had a characteristic opalescent appearance achieved by means of a reheating process. When first issued, it was

Holly Amber Butter Dish

known as Golden Agate. The pressed design of holly leaves, however, gave rise to the title Holly Amber. Scarcity has prompted prices to hedge perilously close to the prohibitive point on Holly Amber glass. *Value guide: butter dish, covered, $1,300; sugar, open, $550.*

HOME COMFORT RANGE

Cooks throughout America were indebted to the Wrought Iron Range Company of St. Louis, Missouri, in the late 19th century, because the Home Comfort Range made cooking a pleasure, rather than a chore. Company publications noted, "This steel family range was made wholly of malleable iron and wrought steel." Despite its weight and size, each range was delivered free of shipping charges. They were sold "by our traveling salesmen, from our own wagons throughout the country." This works, founded in 1864, stated that over 230,000 of their ranges could be found in American kitchens by the 1890s. *Value guide: Home Comfort Range, $400.*

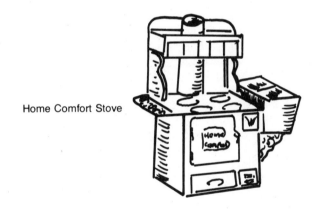

Home Comfort Stove

HOME SAFETY RAZORS

The Eastman & Krauss Razor Company of New York City was the exclusive maker of the Home Safety Razor in the 1890s. Although razors and strops were a specialty of the company, pocket cutlery, shears, and scissors also enabled them to cut a figure, financially speaking. The Home Razor was ballyhooed as being "specially adapted to the young, just beginning to shave; to the old, with trembling hands, and to others with very tender faces." Apparently, advertising paid, for countless users considered this razor just a cut above the rest. *Value guide; Home Safety Razor, circa 1900, $18.*

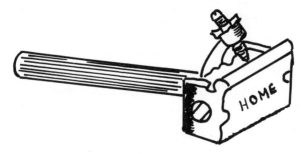

Home Safety Razor

HOMESPUN PATTERN

The Homespun pattern, also known as Fine Ribbed, rates as another fast selling depression glass design from the Jeanette Glass Company. Complete table settings in this pressed pattern became available to consumers between 1938 and 1940. Depression buffs have uncovered pieces in pink, crystal, and blue. Dinner plates had a central waffle design, while rims boasted narrow, vertical ribbing. One rarity in Homespun is the 14-piece child's tea set. Other prized acquisitions include the bulbous water pitcher known as a "tilt jug" and the covered butter dish. *Value guide: butter dish, pink, $45; tea set, child's, 14 pieces, crystal, $220.*

Homespun Pattern Tumbler

HOOKED RUGS

Early hooked rugs display an engaging naivete of design, for the rug maker had to exercise taste at every turn. Form, color, texture, and skilled needlework combined to create the desired pattern. The earlier rugs boasted soft, muted colors. While varied subject matter was attempted, hookers were especially hooked on floral, geometric, and pictorial themes. A design often bore regional characteristics, such as lighthouse views favored by New England makers. In the post-Civil War era, preprinted patterns were commercially marketed. Although lacking the spontaneity of earlier achievements, collectors are nonetheless hooked on these colorful floor coverings. *Value guide: rug, tulip pattern, 3"× 4", circa 1890, $225; rug, whale and ship decor, 52"× 30", circa 1900, $475.*

HOOSIER KITCHEN CABINETS

Prior to the introduction of built-in kitchen cupboards during the 1920s, the extensive Hoosier line was a kitchen staple. These handsomely designed cabinets, made for maximum efficiency, had sufficient storage areas for spices, flour, sugar, and other necessities. Various sizes and styles were available, some with breadboards. Over the years the name became so respected that almost any multisectioned cabinet was called a Hoosier. Once relegated to thrift shop status, these cabinets are being purchased by people with a passion for yesteryear's furniture. *Value guide: Hoosier, oak, copper bins, large size, circa 1910, $475.*

HOPALONG CASSIDY

William Lawrence Boyd, known to millions as Hopalong Cassidy, was born on June 5, 1895, on a farm in Cambridge, Ohio. Dreaming of stardom, he ventured to Hollywood, appearing as an extra in Paramount's *Why Change Your Wife*. Cecil B. De Mille, impressed by his athletic appearance, featured him in several films. By the early 1930s, with the advent of talkies, Bill's popularity began waning. Lady Luck smiled on him once again, however, when Harry "Pop" Sherman offered him the title role in a series based on C. E. Mulford's *Hopalong Cassidy* novels. After 10 years and 44 features, Sherman terminated the series. Between 1946 and 1948, Boyd produced 12 more Westerns. A television series followed, creating Hoppymania for toys, candies, records, magazines, hair tonic, and games. These mementos, avidly collected by members of "Hoppy's Trooper's," fetch premium returns along the flea market trail. *Value guide: bedspread, single size, $200; pocketwatch, 1950s, $275.*

HUBBARD, ELBERT

Elbert Hubbard and John Larkin established the Larkin Soap Company in 1875. Although the business prospered, Hubbard divested himself of it, preferring to devote his energy to writing and publishing *The Philistine Magazine.* Influenced by the English Arts and Crafts Movement, he founded an American community in East Aurora, New York. It was based on the principle "Not How Cheap, But How Good." A print shop opened in 1897, which evolved into a craft center where workshops made diverse offerings such as baskets, copper, silver, leather, rugs, and Mission-style furniture. When Elbert and his wife Alice died aboard the Lusitania in 1915, their son, Elbert III, managed the Roycrofters community through its auction dispersal in 1938. *Value guide: rocker, oak, leather seat, $300; wastebasket, slat sides, 13" tall, $225.*

Roycroft Dresser

HUBLEY TOYS

The Hubley Manufacturing Company of Lancaster, Pennsylvania, was organized in 1894. Almost overnight, their circus wagons, horse drawn vehicles, and cars began filling toy trunks. They also issued a number of cleverly conceived, cast-iron penny banks. By the 1930s, company advertisements noted that small scale cars "looked like the real ones." Many toys had the Hubley name cast into the body; others bore a decal label. At the outbreak of World War II, bomb fuses were made. In 1965, this respected toy concern was acquired by Gabriel Industries, makers of Gilbert erector sets. *Value guide: Monarch tractor, painted, cast-iron, 5½" long, $135; road roller, $120.*

148

Hubley Bell Telephone Truck

HULL POTTERY

Three potters with a purpose, Addis E. Hull, W. A. Watts, and J. D. Young, founded the A. E. Hull Pottery in 1905. From the outset, this Crooksville, Ohio works concentrated on stoneware and utilitarian lines. Striving for diversity, they also imported European pottery, which was sold through American outlets. By 1927, tiles were added to production schedules. Collectors compete for the artwares, dating from 1930 to 1950. After 1950, all matte-glazed wares were discontinued. Following a disastrous fire, the reorganized Hull Pottery opened in 1952. *Value guide: basket, dogwood, beige and pink, 7½" tall, $40; tea set, parchment and pine, three pieces, $65.*

Hull Pottery Teapot

HUMMEL FIGURINES

The first Hummel figurines were issued by W. Goebel Company, of Germany, in 1935. They were based on the drawings of Berta Hummel, who became a Franciscan nun. Born on May 21, 1909, at Massing, near Munich, Berta possessed a vivid imagination as a child, painting cards and printing verses for family celebrations. In 1927, she moved to Munich to enter the Academy of Fine Arts, where she met two Franciscan sisters. Seven years later she en-

149

tered the Convent of Siessen, becoming Sister Maria Innocentia. Within the confines of the convent, she made sketches for Hummel cards and figurines that were destined to make her, as well as the convent, internationally known. Following a lengthy illness, she died on November 6, 1946. *Value guide: Be Patient, #197/2/0, 1952, $125; Soloist, #135, 1955, $90.*

Hummel Rubber Doll

HUMPTY DUMPTY BANK

Peter Adams and Charles G. Shephard first patented the colorful Humpty Dumpty mechanical bank in 1882, and again in 1884 as a design patent. It was manufactured by the Shephard Hardware Company of Buffalo, New York. This bust bank depicted a character attributed to the renowned 19th century pantominist George

Washington Fox. Because of Fox's ingenuity, Humpty Dumpty became the most celebrated clown of the era. The simple, yet effective, action is triggered by pressing a lever behind the clown's left shoulder. As he deposits a penny in his mouth, his eyes roll about in wide-eyed merriment. *Value guide: Humpty Dumpty bank, cast-iron, 7" tall, $350.*

Humpty Dumpty Bank

HUMPTY DUMPTY CIRCUS

P. T. Barnum would have approved of Schoenhut's Humpty Dumpty Circus, introduced in 1903. The original jointed clowns were named Humpty, Dumpty, and Cracker Jack. As the crowd cheered, various characters and animals were added to the troupe. They included a Ringmaster, Lion Tamer, Gent Acrobat, Lady Acrobat, and Lady Circus Rider. These characters had wooden or bisque heads. The latter are particularly prized. Animal figures, issued in sufficient numbers to fill a zoo, initially boasted glass eyes and woolly manes. Later, painted eyes and carved manes were employed. Additional flavor was provided with a collapsible tent and sawdust ring. Youngsters were advised that the Humpty Dumpty circus clan could perform 1,001 tricks. *Value guide; alligator, glass eyes, $250; lady acrobat, bisque, $260.*

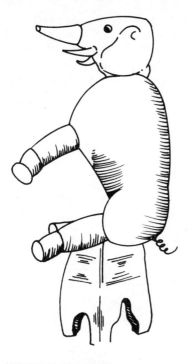

Humpty Dumpty Circus Elephant

HUNTLEY & PALMER

The Huntley & Palmer firm had its beginnings in 1822, when Joseph Huntley founded a bakery in Reading, England. In 1841, he was joined by George Palmer, under whose leadership they succeeded. Their tin boxes were made by Huntley, Boorne, & Stevens. In 1879, these tin manufacturers received a license to print "directly" onto tin by offset lithography, a development that revolutionized the

Huntley & Palmer Biscuit Tin

industry. Huntley & Palmers immediately saw the potential, and packaged their products in decorative tins, which were introduced each year at Christmas. Over the years, surfaces have been covered with topical events, scenes of British life, fashions, geometric forms, and various other pictorial representations. Some containers such as the Cannon, Grandfather's Clock, and Windmill had moving parts. Between 1900 and 1924, over 10 variations of Huntley & Palmers "book" theme circulated about. *Value guide: Marble Column, $64; Palace of Westminister, $50.*

HUNZINGER, GEORGE

George Hunzinger was among the numerous furniture designers of German origin who prospered in New York City during the second half of the 19th century. Hunzinger departed from the middle stream by focusing his efforts on chairs, specifically the reclining or folding

Hunzinger Chair

variety. Over 10 different chair designs were illustrated and described in a catalog of the 1870s, all of his chairs displaying a touch of inventiveness and imagination. Hunzinger received a number of patents for his folding forms. These chairs, often inspired by Renaissance Revival styles, attest to the influence of the machine age. The turned wooden parts on Hunzinger's models conjure up visions of iron piping or the components of an engine. *Value guide: side chair, folding, turned elements, walnut, circa 1880, $375.*

153

ICE WATER PITCHERS

The silverplated, multi-walled ice water pitcher furnished a source of cool drinking water in the premechanical refrigeration era. A number of late 19th century patents were granted, the first in the name of James Stimpson in 1854. Early metal linings were supplanted by porcelain ones to "facilitate cleaning chores." Their heavy weight led to patents being issued for tilting arrangements. The ice water pitcher, often presented to a distinguished community figure, was typically ornamented with Victorian designs. Over

Silverplated Ice Water Pitcher

57 varieties were listed in silver company catalogs by the late 1860s but by the 1890s, they were receiving only lukewarm public response, and the number of styles dwindled to 14. *Value guide: silverplated pitcher, Reed & Barton, chased moss rose decor, circa 1885, $200.*

IDEAL TOY COMPANY

Morris Michton had already won the hearts of the American public with his Teddy Bears, prior to founding the Ideal Novelty & Toy corporation of Brooklyn, New York, in 1907. Baby Mine, Dandy Kid, and other character dolls brought him additional attention. Some dolls in this line sold for 25 cents and up. By 1914, over 100 new numbers were in production, many with sleep eyes. One year later, over 200 employees were actively creating 150 different dolls. Through the 1920s, Ideal's crying dolls, walking dolls, and composition-headed dolls were deemed ideal by customers. Shirley Temple dolls were the rage in 1934, followed three years later by Betsy Wetsy. Early productions bore the Ideal name within a diamond; later, however, the diamond device was omitted. *Value guide: Deanna Durbin, composition, dressed, 20″ tall, $375; Mortimer Snerd, composition, 12″ tall, dressed, $300.*

Deanna Durbin Ideal Doll

ILLINOIS WATCH COMPANY

In 1869, with a capital investment of $100,000, John Adams established the Illinois Springfield Watch Company. One year later, 25 watches were being produced each day by 125 employees. Growing competition, however, the foe of many watch makers of the era, caused financial hardship by the mid-1870s. Between 1885 and 1927, operating under the title Illinois Watch Company, over 5½ million watches were sold. The company was later purchased by the Hamilton Watch Company. Watches having a trademark from this firm seem to become more valuable by the minute. *Value guide: railroad watch, 21 jewels, 14K gold, circa 1890, $275.*

IMARI

Bold and beautiful Imari derived its name from the Japanese port from which it was exported. Although manufactured as far back as the 17th century, the later 19th century specimens are more plentiful. Initially, the wares were quite simply decorated. Later, the heavily brocaded patterns, often in underglaze blue and overglaze "seal wax" red, reached American shores. Pieces typically had touches of gold, or secondary colors such as yellow or turquoise. Chinese versions abounded, usually possessing a grayer clay, thicker glaze, and darker colors. Some designs were based on textiles. Imari wares were chiefly made for export. The patterns and colors gained such attention in Europe that many English potters endeavored to market similar productions. *Value guide: cup and saucer, basket of flowers decor, circa 1885, $60; umbrella stand, birds and butterflies, 23½" tall, circa 1890, $400.*

Imari Plate

IMPERIAL JEWELS

The presently flourishing Imperial Glass Company of Bellaire, Ohio, had consumers jumping for joy over Jewels art glass in 1916. Reportedly, the line was inspired from antique models. This pressed and blown glassware was enhanced with gem-like colors; thus the name "Jewels" seems quite natural. The colors were vividly described in advertisements as "shimmering pearl green," "delicate pearl white," "glowing pearl ruby," and "deep rich tones of amethyst." Jewels has developed into a glistening collectible, especially those objects that possess Imperial's name and German cross symbol. *Value guide: plate, Jewels, green, 7¾" diameter, $45; vase, Jewels, amethyst, 5½" tall, $150.*

INGRAHAM COMPANY, E.

Elias Ingraham (1805-1885) had been involved in various clockmaking ventures prior to the establishment of his own works in 1852. Such innovative designs as the Sharp Gothic shelf clock have

Ingraham Shelf Clock

been ascribed to this craftsman. As the company flourished into the 20th century, a decision was reached to purchase the Bannatyne Watch Company about 1911, signalling the Ingraham firm's entry into the pocket watch field. In 1931, the first Ingraham wristwatches were marketed, retailing for about $5.00. Within one year, over 2,000 were being manufactured daily. When the company stopped producing its own watches in 1967, over 65 million pocket watches and over 15 million wristwatches had been marketed. *Value guide: Alliance, 8-day, oak case, 38¼", $500.*

IRIS PATTERN

Between 1928 and 1932, the Iris depression glass pattern originated at the Jeanette Glass Company. It had been a decorative device several decades earlier on art nouveau presentations. Buyers acquired complete table settings in crystal, pink, and green. During the 1950s and 1960s, an Iris reissue in an "amber sprayed on carnival" enjoyed widespread acceptance. Crystal reproductions reached the marketplace in 1969, followed the ensuing year by milk white renditions. *Value guide: cup and saucer, marigold, $9; sugar and creamer, crystal, $18.*

Iris Pattern Vase

IRVING CUT GLASS COMPANY

Six adventuresome and skilled glass cutters founded the Irving Cut Glass Company of Honesdale, Pennsylvania, in 1900. Widely promoting their "American Rich Cut Glass," they produced figured blanks furnished by Fry. Their cut glass was exported by the boatload to ports in China, Japan, South Africa, and Spain. William Hawkens, one of the original owners, designed many patterns including White Rose, patented in 1900. Interest intensifies on specimens bearing the lightly etched "Irving" name in script. *Value guide: plate, Victrola pattern, 10" diameter, signed, $375.*

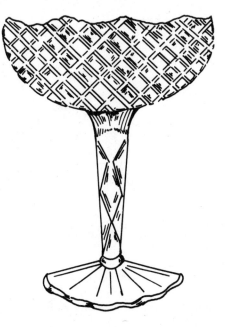

Irving Cut Glass Compote

IVES, EDWARD RILEY

Edward Riley Ives set up a factory in Bridgeport, Connecticut, in 1870. Two years later it was operating as Ives and Blakeslee. Their production was centered around mechanical figures for window displays and automata. Despite a succession of partnerships, the Ives name was retained. For an advertising slogan, the company chose the positive approach; their motto was, "Ives toys make happy boys." Brightly painted tin locomotives, some powered by clockwork, were among their earliest toys. In the 1880s and 1890s, cast-iron toys were widely distributed. By the early 1900s, when floor runners became outdated, clockwork trains and tracks in U.S. gauge 0 were introduced. These were followed in 1912 by gauge 1 trains. Ives became a respected name, known especially for excellent replacement service. Following a bankruptcy in 1931, Ives was absorbed by Lionel. *Value guide: walking horse dray, cast-iron, 10½" long, $475.*

JACK ARMSTRONG

Robert Hardy Andrews, the creator of Jack Armstrong, felt that his character was "larger than life because you only heard his voice, you couldn't see him and so you were free to think, 'that could be me.' " When the first episode aired in 1933, millions of American children began identifying with this true-to-life character. "Jack Armstrong . . . the All American Boy" brought lasting fame to "Wheaties, Breakfast of Champions." By 1934-35, premiums such as photographs of the cast, stamp-collecting kits, and the first of several Hike-O-Meters were being offered. The list grew lengthier through the years as a vast amount of premiums became available. One of the most coveted is the 1942 Secret Bombsight. Time and television took its toll on the kid from Hudson High by July of 1951, when the last adventure aired. *Value guide: cereal bowl, white milk glass, $20; Sky Ranger Plane, $50.*

JACK-IN-THE-PULPIT VASES

Jack-in-the-pulpit vases sprung up as favorites around the turn of the century. Although variations abound, all resemble the plant for which they were named. American and European glassmakers employed the latest glass techniques; opalescent, amberina, cranberry, satin, and vaseline glass methods were utilized by various makers. Iridescent varieties emerged from such glasshouses as Tiffany, Quezal, and Loetz. These uniquely shaped vases were made in many sizes. Nowadays it requires more than a green thumb to locate a bargain priced jack-in-the-pulpit vase. *Value guide: Am-*

Jack-In-The-Pulpit Vase

berina, signed Libbey, 7" tall, 375; opalescent cranberry, 10" tall, $100.

JEP

After undergoing several name changes, this famous French toy-maker operated as Jouets en Paris (JEP) from the early 1930s on. They competed admirably against Citröen cars, creating toys that were of an impressive size. Their large-scale racing cars, fitted with steering mechanisms, were introduced about 1930. That same year brought about the marketing of two of their most prized cars, the Rolls Royce and Jispano Suiza. These two cars had similar chassis, body, and wheels. Other models, including the 40 HP Renault and Talbot Lago 6 Coupe, had bonnets that opened to reveal the engines, lights, and opening side doors. Dedicated toy collectors appreciate their attention to detail. *Value guide: Renault Touring Car, tin, clockwork, 13½" length, circa 1930, $1,250.*

JOE PALOOKA

Hal Fisher's Joe Palooka began knocking out readers of the comic pages in 1928; however, he failed to score a "TKO," with youngsters until the strip appeared in the *New York Mirror* on January 1, 1931. Fisher surrounded his naive prize fighter with a troupe of amusing characters, including Senator Weidebottom, the French-Canadian Bateese, and Humphrey and Jerry Leemy. Joe's long-running relationship with Anne How culminated in a celebrated marriage in 1949, which positively floored readers. Joe Palooka became a feature film in 1933, a radio program in the '30s, and later a television series. He was also featured in a long-running comic book series in the 1940s. Mementos pertaining to this beloved prize fighter are prized by collectors. *Value guide: Joe Palooka lunch box, 1946, $30; punching bag, $50.*

JUKEBOXES

The jukebox, that large, complex machine introduced in the 1930s, has kept American feet tapping ever since. These music makers could accommodate a varying number of records, which could be played singly or in a series. Considered oversized for home use, jukeboxes were intended for places of amusement. To entice listeners, most sported eye-catching art deco plastic and metal cases. Colorful neon tubing made them as memorable as Vaughn Monroe's "Racing with the Moon." Packard, Rock Ola, Seeburg,, and Wurlitzer models have been selling at record prices. *Value guide: Rock Ola Model 1426, $1,800; Wurlitzer, Model 71, countertop, $2,250.*

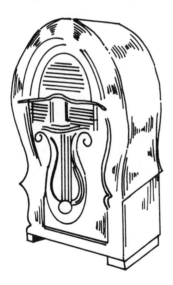

Wurlitzer Jukebox

JUST ME DOLL

Armand Marseilles Jr. won a Grand Prize for his doll exhibit at the St. Louis Exposition of 1904. The Armand Marseilles factory of Germany, founded in the mid-1860s, had already established a worldwide reputation for bisque dolls' heads at that time. The Just Me doll was added to their lengthy list of accomplishments about 1925. This bisque, socket-head doll was available in several sizes. Just Me had beautiful glass eyes that glanced to the side, along with a closed mouth and curly wig. In addition, she was dressed in

162

Just Me Doll

fashionable attire. Dolls having the "Just Me, A.M. 310, Germany" trademark can easily be converted into dollars. *Value guide: Just Me, bisque socket-head, closed mouth, curly wig, composition body, dressed, 9" tall, $775.*

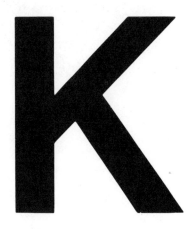

KEMPLE GLASS

Prior to establishing his own glassworks at East Palantine, Ohio, in 1945, John E. Kemple had been in the employ of the Fostoria Glass Company. When a fire disrupted production, Kemple Glass moved to Kenova, West Virginia, in 1957. Obviously, Kemple loved early glass techniques, for he marketed renditions of many 19th century favorites such as End-of-Day, amber, cobalt blue, red, green, black, amethyst, and slag glass. These pieces were generally made from earlier molds utilized by the McKee Glass Company, the American Glass Company, Indiana Tumbler and Goblet Company, the Phoenix Glass Company, or the Mannington Art Glass Company. To avoid unnecessary confusion, however, Kemple used the letter "K" to identify his output, which terminated upon his death in 1970. *Value guide: goblet, Lace and Dewdrop, amber, $25; plate, milk glass, 8" diameter, $15.*

KENTON HARDWARE COMPANY

All minors' merrymakers stamped "Kenton" are avidly sought by toy collectors. Originally, when founded in 1890, the firm operated as the Kenton Lock Company. By the early 1900s, officials tapped the profitable toy market with notable success. For several decades their cast-iron horse-drawn vehicles were regarded as winners. Reproductions derived from original models abounded during the 1940s and 1950s. Throughout the years, Kenton vehicles exhibited tremendous detail, as noted on the Double Decker bus. Their cast-iron banks, which appeared in a multitude of motifs, also earn

Kenton Toy Road Grader

collector interest. *Value guide: fire engine, horse-drawn, cast-iron, 13½" long, 1920s, $450; surrey, cast-iron, 1920s, $85.*

KEWPIES

Rose O'Neill created the unforgettable Kewpie in the early 20th century. This impish character was introduced through the pages of the *Ladies Home Journal Magazine.* In 1913, the Kewpie doll was designed by O'Neill, complete with pug nose, slight smile, tiny wings, and topknot. Dolls of various materials have been made by such firms as Borgfeldt, Kestner, Fulper Pottery, Mutual Doll Company, Karl Standfuss, Rex Doll Company, and Cameo Doll Company. Although company trademarks were used, most had the Rose O'Neill and/or Kewpie name either incised or on a paper label. As Kewpiemania gripped the public, bells, bottles, calendars,

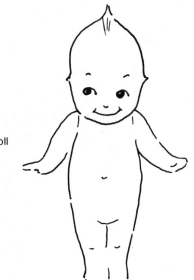

Bisque Kewpie Doll

Christmas cards, postcards, clocks, flannels, napkin rings, jewelry, ceramics, and other Kewpie keepsakes flooded the marketplace. *Value guide: doll, composition, 14" tall, $165; tray, advertising ice cream, tin, $150.*

KIDDIEJOY DOLLS

Kiddiejoy infant dolls could be spotted under many Christmas trees in the mid-1920s. The Armand Marseilles factory produced these bisque-headed dolls for Jacob Kassler of New York City. Kiddiejoy dolls had molded hair, sleep eyes, closed mouths, cloth bodies, and composition arms and legs. Most measured between 9½" to 12" in height. Originally, these dolls came with their own boxes, complete with several dresses. Marked examples bearing the "Germany, Kiddiejoy A. 1. M" trademark bring joy to dedicated doll buffs. *Value guide: doll, original box, 12" tall, $450.*

KNOBLOCK PYRAMID TOASTER

The Knoblock Pyramid Toaster, capable of toasting four slices of bread in a few minutes on its slanted sides, was patented in 1909. Its flat top provided an ideal spot for brewing a cup of coffee or tea. Advertisements mentioned that it was suitable for use on any gas,

Knoblock Toaster

166

gasoline, or oil stove. The toaster was aptly named, for it did resemble a pyramid. Collectors who scour the marketplace for kitchen keepsakes acquire any model possessing a maker's name or trademark. *Value guide: Knoblock Pyramid Toaster, good condition, circa 1912, $50.*

LACE EDGE PATTERN

A pierced or open border gave Lace Edge an edge over other depression-glass patterns. Radial lined sunbursts combined with large and small alternating circles on this Hocking Glass Company design. Scalloped rims adorned many accessories. Between 1935 and 1938, pink and crystal table settings were sold through major outlets. The crystal items are in short supply. Similar lace edge designs were made by the Lancaster Glass Company, the Imperial Glass Company, and the Westmoreland Glass Company. *Value guide: butter dish, pink, $60; sugar and creamer, $35.*

Lace Edge Candle Holders

LALANCE & GROSJEAN MANUFACTURING COMPANY

"Keep Poison out of the kitchen" warned Lalance & Grosjean, graniteware makers of Boston, Massachusetts, in the early 20th century. Of the 17 American graniteware makers, few advertised their products as extensively. Consumers were advised to look for the "Agate Nickel-Steel-Ware, L. & G. Mfg. Co." trademark on every piece. Their pasted-on blue label showing a chemist's certificate was even copied by rival concerns. Their full line of graniteware cooking accessories appeared in a variety of colors. Other advertisements officially noted that their agateware had the approval and recognition of the U. S. Health reports. *Value guide: coffeepot, turquoise, $45; covered bucket with handle, blue, $40.*

LALIQUE, RENE

Rene Lalique (1860-1945) was a multi-talented French jeweler, silversmith, artist, and glassmaker. One of his first important patrons was Sarah Bernhardt, for whom he designed jewelry. Following several showings, he opened a combination studio and workshop in Paris in 1902. Lalique abandoned jewelry designing, favoring glass experiments. A commission was received from Coty to design a range of molded glass scent bottles in 1908. Many new varieties of glass originated at his factory. By the 1920s and 1930s, many objects incorporated in relief the human form, usually nude, or animals and insects, often with foliage. His opalescent glass specialities earned him the respect of his peers. The mark "R.

Lalique Hood Ornament

Lalique" was used through his death in 1945, when the title was altered to "Lalique." *Value guide: figurine, sparrow, frosted, thorny bramble, 4" tall, 1930s, $300; perfume bottle, clear and frosted, 4¼" tall, $235.*

LEHMANN, ERNST

Ernst Paul Lehmann formed a Brandenburg, Germany, factory for the production of tins and containers in 1881. Shortly thereafter, toys were being manufactured, some fitted with flywheel mechanisms; later, identical toys boasted clockwork motors. Prior to World War I, some toys were hand colored. Fortunately, their toys were always clearly marked, generally including patent specifications. By the mid-1930s, over 400 workers were busy filling orders for their colorful tin toys. Highly imaginative designs won them international acclaim. The factory was sequestered by the Russians in 1949; original heirs reestablished the works near Nuremburg, in 1951. *Value guide: acrobat, tin, wind-up, 10" tall, $300; sea lion, tin, wind-up, 7½" tall, $225.*

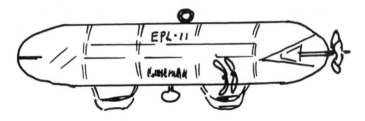

Lehmann Toy Dirgible

LENCI DOLLS

Enrico and Elena de E. Scavini established a dollmaking concern at Turin, the felt center of Italy, just prior to World War I. "Lenci" was Elena's nickname. Utilizing locally made felt, their doll's faces were made by steaming and stiffening fabric in a mold to form a three-dimensional face. The dolls' faces surrendered to hand-painted details; they measured from 4 to 48 inches in height and had jointed felt or felt and muslin bodies. Lenci creations had the third and fourth fingers stitched together, while the remaining ones were separated. Ink signatures, metal tags, cardboard tags, and ribbon labels offer identifying guides to this still active doll dynasty. *Value guide: girl, sundress and bonnet, 17" tall, circa 1930, $400; Russian boy, 17" tall, circa 1932, $1,400.*

Lenci Doll

LETTER RACKS

With the advent of the postal system, mail volume escalated dramatically. Letters required a safe repository, thereby creating the need for the letter, or card, rack. Originally, they were known as envelope racks, desk racks, or letter-paper racks. Regardless of the size, shape, or materials, all had sufficient space between the front and back for storing correspondence. Silver and silverplated versions in varying designs won the stamp of approval in the 1880s and 1890s. Other metals were also used, often enlivened by engraved or embossed themes, and guaranteed to beautify any desk top. *Value guide: brass, pierced motif, circa 1900, $35; silverplate, openwork florals, $45.*

LIBERTY BELLE DOLL

The Liberty Belle cloth doll, created for the Philadelphia Sesquecentennial Exposition of 1926, has made the transition from rags to riches. It was patented by Annin & Company, of New York City, on March 23, 1926. This red, white, and blue doll bore printed features. Her hat was decorated with stars and stripes and the inscription "Liberty Belle." Across the bell-shaped dress were the words "150 years of American Independence, 1776-1926." A reissue marked "1776-1976" circulated about during Bicentennial activities. The Liberty Belle cloth doll, it cannot be denied, has an authentic American ring. *Value guide: Liberty Belle doll, 1926, $125.*

Liberty Belle Doll

LI'L ABNER

Al Capp's Li'l Abner became "must" reading for comic page devotees upon its introduction in 1934. Even sophisticated urban readers chuckled over the antics of the hillbilly characters. This situation comedy, tinged with satire, made names like Daisy Mae, Sadie Hawkins Day, the Schmoo, Lord Cesspool, Kickapoo Juice, Pansy Yokum, and others household favorites. Li'l Abner and his sidekicks were soon occupying the front pages of comic sections throughout the nation. A film prompted by the strip was released by RKO in 1940. In 1957, it became a smash Broadway musical, followed by a technicolor film version. Over the years the folks from Dogpatch have been honored with paperbacks, comic books, and even one hardback publication. *Value guide: toy, Li'l Abner Dogpatch band, wind-up, $375; wristwatch, boxed, $200.*

LION AND TWO MONKEYS BANK

Louis Kyser and Alfred C. Rex, owners of a Philadelphia hardware concern, patented the Lion and Two Monkeys bank in 1883. This mechanical bank features two little monkeys at the top of a tree, staring straight into a lion's face. When a penny is placed in the larger monkey's hand, a lever at the base of the tree is pressed. As the larger monkey drops the coin into the lion's mouth, the smaller one climbs over his shoulder to view the action. This bit of monkey business was colored with a tan lion and two brown monkeys. *Value guide: Lion and Two Monkeys banks, 9¼" tall, $450.*

LIONEL TRAINS

Joshua Lionel Cowen (1881-1965), born in New York City, opened a small electrical shop business about 1901. Fine quality miniature trains were made under the title of the Lionel Manufacturing Company. Smaller, somewhat more affordable models appeared about 1906. He patented his own gauge for trains, described as "standard gauge." Trains were made in standard gauge, 2 1/8 inches between the rails; O gauge, half as big as standard gauge; and HO gauge, half the size of O gauge. They also sold OO gauge, about 3/4 inches; and S gauge, 7/8 inches between the rails. As the fame of the trains grew, a move to larger quarters was deemed a necessity, and the acquisition of Ives was also executed. By the late 1930s, his staff exceeded 1,000 workers. Following a decline in sales, the railway department was sold to Gilbert in 1968. *Value guide: car, 12 cattle,*

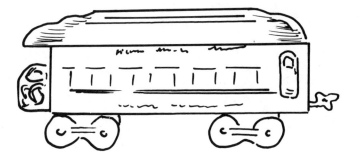

Lionel Train Car

green, S gauge, 1906, $75; locomotive, 384, steam, eight-wheel, 384T, tender, S gauge, $350.

LITHOPANES

Although lithopanes reportedly originated in France, they were quickly copied by other European potters. A *lithopane* is a porcelain transparency having an impressed design brought to fullest visual detection when held to artificial light or sunlight. Lithopane pictures were employed on various porcelain objects, notably teacups, plaques, lampshades, night lights, steins, and mugs. Their production was undertaken by such ceramic giants as Meissen, Sevres, Royal Copenhagen, Copeland, Minton, and Wedgwood. Lithopanes became closely associated with the Berlin state porcelain factory, giving rise to the term "Berlin transparency." *Value guide: lamp, five panels, mother and child, iron frame, $950; plaque, rural scene, 4½" × 5½", $130.*

LITTLE ORPHAN ANNIE

The classic American comic strip featuring a little red-haired girl named Little Orphan Annie originated in 1924. As this curly-haired blank-eyed heroine, defended herself against bratty playmates and overzealous protectors through trials and tribulations, she realized that her doll Emily and her dog Sandy were her only true friends.

Little Orphan Annie & Sandy Toy

Combining realistic characters along with effective drawings made the strip a huge success. Between 1935 and 1940, Orphan Annie was sponsored on the radio by Ovaltine, which initiated numerous premium items. Apparently there is a tomorrow for Annie for she has triumphed in movies, radio, and Broadway without ever aging! *Value guide: doll, cloth, mohair hair, dressed, 18" tall, $150; wristwatch, Ingersoll, boxed, $185.*

LITTLE SHAVER DOLL

Those razor-sharp officials at the Alexander Doll Company, of New York City, introduced the cloth Little Shaver doll in 1937. It had a pink stocking body that curved to a tiny waist. Little Shaver had a mask face with large, painted eyes that glanced to the side, a tiny mouth, and a glued-on floss wig. The doll appeared in several sizes, the largest measuring 16 inches in height. Apparently Little Shaver was an avid party-goer, for she wore a sheer dress. The original doll bore a cloth dress tag which read, "Little Shaver/Madame Alexander/New York/All Rights Reserved." *Value guide: doll, good condition, 16" tall, $190.*

Little Shaver Doll

LOCKS AND KEYS

Locks and keys, known for centuries, represent outstanding collectibles for the curious. They have been uncovered in many materials, notably brass, steel, bronze, and cast or wrought iron. The main categories are rim locks, fitted to the surface of the door; mortise locks, fitted within the body of the door; cabinet locks, found on furniture; safelocks, for maximum security; and padlocks. Of course, locks with original keys are preferred. Two important 19th century developments were Jeremiah Chubb's detector safe lock of 1818, and Linus Yale's cylinder rim lock of 1848. A discarded lock and key could open the path to unexpected profits! *Value guide: brass, figural dog lock, with key, $80; iron, turn handle with key, 4"× 6", circa 1840, $125.*

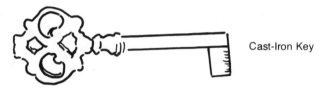

Cast-Iron Key

LOETZ GLASS

Johann Loetz assumed control of an existing glasshouse in Bohemia about 1840. By the 1880s, cameo, stone, colored, and handpainted milk glass specialties had garnered an international reputation. Under the supervision of M. R. von Spaun, iridescent glass articles, imitative of Tiffany's won world-wide approval. All production ceased at the outbreak of World War II. Over the years the firm used a variety of trademarks including two crossed arrows with a star in each intersection; Loetz, Austria, crossed arrows within a circle; and Loetz, sometimes accompanied by Klostermuhle. *Value guide: inkwell, feather motif, iridescent blue, 5¼" tall, $325; vase, iridescent gold, metal holder, 10" tall, $450.*

Loetz Vase

LONE RANGER

Frank Striker's hit radio program, "The Lone Ranger," became a comic strip in 1938. The Lone Ranger, whose identity always remained a secret, was the sole survivor of a band of Texas Rangers gunned down in ambush by a mob of outlaws in the 1890s. Donning a mask, he fought alone against crime. Perhaps not quite alone, for he had his trusty horse Silver and his Indian companion Tonto. The strip rode off into the sunset in 1971 making it the longest running Western series to cavort through the comic pages. Over the years, the public has been treated to Lone Ranger comic books, movies, novels, and a television series. Sufficient Lone Ranger mementos have appeared to fill more than one saddle bag. *Value guide; doll, chaps, hat, boxed, $175; wristwatch, boxed, 1939, $350.*

Lone Ranger Tin Wind-Up Toy

LONHUDA POTTERY

W. A. Long, W. H. Hunter, and Alfred Day established the Lonhuda Pottery of Steubenville, Ohio, in 1892. Long, a former druggist, had experimented with pottery glazes for several years. His Lonhuda customarily featured underglaze decorations on a blended brown background. Motifs included Indians, birds, flowers, dogs, seascapes, fish, and famous people. When Lonhuda was exhibited at the Chicago World's Fair in 1893, it came to the attention of Samuel Weller, who convinced Long to produce the pottery at his plant in Zanesville. Together they formed the Lonhuda Faience Company. Long severed their relationship in about a year, moving on to work for J. B. Owens. Weller marketed a similar ware, calling it "Louwelsa," while Owen's interpretation became known as "Utopian." As for Long, he founded the Denver China and Pottery Company and subsequently the Clifton Art Pottery prior to returning to work with Weller between 1909 and 1912. *Value guide: vase, Lonhuda, light brown, white florals, 7" tall, $250.*

Lonhuda Pottery Vase

LORAIN PATTERN

The Lorain depression design, originally known as Indiana's Number 615 pattern, was sold from 1929 to 1932. Table services were available in yellow, green, and crystal. The snack sets typically had fired-on blue, red, yellow, green, and crystal. Indented cups and saucers were another distinguishing feature on snack sets. The plates had central motifs composed of scrolls and garlands enclosed by an eight-sided swag terminating in finials and scrolls. The most recognizable motif, however, was the basket of flowers which dominated each corner between scrolls and garlands, which explains why some collectors prefer the more descriptive name "Basket." *Value guide: bowl, green, 10" diameter, $35; plate, yellow, 7" diameter, $9.*

LOTUS WARE

Between 1891 and 1898, luscious Lotus Ware was potted by the Knowles, Taylor, & Knowles Company of East Liverpool, Ohio. Several beautiful pieces won attention when exhibited at the Columbian Exposition of 1893. Colonel John N. Taylor, president of the pottery, named it Lotus Ware. This Belleek-like porcelain was so named because it emulated the petals of a lotus blossom. The ornamentation, often figure work, was enameled over the glaze in the *pate-sur-pate* technique. Blanks were available to artisans swept up in the craze for china painting. Ceramic connoisseurs prize pieces bearing the letters KTK Co., with a star and crescent, and Lotus Ware printed below in overglaze green. *Value guide: biscuit jar, flowers, leaves, $350; vase, bulbous, florals, 7" tall, $650.*

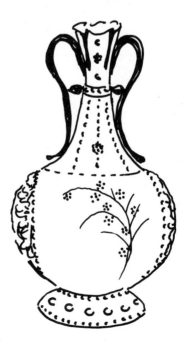

Lotus Ware Vase

LOW TILES

Those who trek after old tiles hold the Low name in high esteem. John Gardner Low developed an interest in ceramics while working for the Chelsea Ceramic Art works. In 1878, he formed a partnership with his father, the Honorable John Low. When John's grandson replaced him as an active partner in 1883, the Massachusetts pottery operated as the J. G. and J. F. Low Art Tile Works. Hundreds of relief tiles, some hand modeled, brought them distinguished honors. Various sizes of tiles were produced. In addition to standard shapes, many narrow and round types were marketed. John Low's tile soda fountains were sold subsequent to 1889. Despite chalking up triumphs in the tile field, the company faced liquidation in 1907. *Value guide: Grecian man's head, 1880s, $40; Oriental figure with instrument, 6" diameter, $165.*

Low Art Portrait Tile

MADAME ALEXANDER

Maurice Alexander of Russia, moved to New York City in 1891.
There he not only founded a doll shop and hospital, but also married

Madame Alexander Carmen Doll

a girl from Austria. The Alexander's eldest daughter, Beatrice, designed dolls to be sold in her father's shop. In 1923, following her marriage to Philip Berman, she established the Alexander Doll Company. Beatrice, who became known as "Madame Alexander," made dolls based on book characters. These were cloth dolls having mask-type faces and pressed, handpainted features. Many composition-headed dolls appeared in the 1930s and 1940s, including the Dionne quintuplets, Jane Withers, and Snow White. A number of highly coveted stuffed animals were introduced in the mid-1930s. Age is not the determining factor in assessing the worth of an Alexander doll, for even recent issues from this still active dollmaker can be easily converted into dollars. *Value guide: First Ladies, Abigail Adams, $185; Jacqueline Kennedy, dressed, 10" tall, $650.*

MADRID PATTERN

Over 40 different tablewares in the Madrid pattern were made by the Federal Glass Company between 1932 and 1938. Even a gelatin mold is known to exist in this depression glass design. Initially, Springtime Green was produced, followed by Golden Glow (amber) one year later. Subsequently, Madonna Blue and pink objects received a limited run. Crystal tablewares were executed, along with a flashed iridescent yellow. At present, dated reissues from the late 1970s have been circulating about. *Value guide: butter dish, green, $65; sugar and creamer, amber, $30.*

Madrid Pattern Cookie Jar

MAGAZINE CYCLONE CAMERAS

The Western Camera Company of Chicago reminded photographers in the late 1890s that "The Cyclone Camera has always been and will always be the best for the money." Despite this claim, they did advertise "Improved Models." The smaller No. 4 version sold for $8.00, while the larger version fetched $10.00. They were capable of taking 12 pictures in 12 seconds. Other selling features included a "pneumatic bulb release, automatic shutter, automatic regular, shutter lock and the quickest and best lens ever made." One must assume that the officials at Kodak did a double take when this model reached local outlets. *Value guide: Improved Magazine Cyclone No. 4, 1899, $120.*

MAGIC BANK

The Magic building bank was patented by H. W. Prouty of Boston, Massachusetts, in 1873 and 1876. This fancy gray structure boasting blue and red trim was added to production schedules at the J. & E. Stevens Company. When a coin is placed on the cashier's tray and a lever pressed at the side of the building, the cashier, along with the door to which he is attached, begins revolving. The cashier stages a disappearing act, depositing the coin in the bank. Then the outside of the door appears, and the bank is closed again. To deposit another coin the door could be opened by hand. At present, Magic banks have been staging their own disappearing act. *Value guide: Magic bank, cast-iron, 5¼" tall, circa 1884, $650.*

Magic Mechanical Bank

MAGIC LANTERNS

The magic lantern was invented by Athansaius Kircher in the mid-17th century. It was mainly regarded as a form of adult entertainment, until August Lapierre, a French tinsmith, introduced a toy version in 1843. Through the early 1900s, many European makers, especially German manufacturers, produced a variety of magic lanterns. Early lanterns were lit by lamp or candlelight. The less expensive versions were often made of black painted tin or polished Russian iron. As for the slides, they illustrated a vast array of subjects; religious and educational themes were widely favored. Long narrow slides painted in soft colors were used in the early 19th century. After 1860, most slides were reproduced photographically and hand colored. *Value guide: kerosene type, brass wooden base, 10 slides, 10" tall, $150; "Lanterna Magica," Germany, original box, $80.*

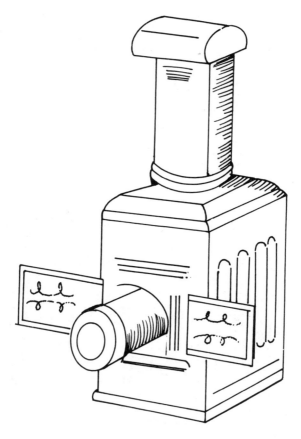

Magic Lantern

MAGICIAN BANK

This bit of "now you see it, now you don't" whimsy was patented by bank designer William C. Ball in 1901. The J & E. Stevens Company was the maker of this rarity. The top-hatted magician, attired in black, stands in front of a small red table with a blue base. The base bears the wording "Magician Bank." After placing a penny on the table, a lever is pressed behind the steps. The magician's hat covers the coin as he lowers his head; thus the traditional magician's hat was pressed into service for maximum results. The coin travels down the chute into the magician's legs, and then onward toward the base of the bank. *Value guide: Magician bank, cast-iron, 8¼" tall, $650.*

MAJESTIC CUT GLASS

Wolf M. Spiegel and his son, Saul, organized the Majestic Cut Glass Company of Elmira, New York, in 1900. Previously, the father and son team had served as owners of a salvage and metal works. Through World War I they produced light, cut glassware in a spectrum of sparkling patterns. This enterprising duo also imported heavy, cut-glass blanks from European sources. At the height of business activities, they employed more than 25 glass cutters. Majestic's high caliber cut glass was sold through leading retail outlets. Specimens having the "M" within a circle trademark mesmerize glass connoisseurs. *Value guide: bowl, hobstars, signed, 8" diameter, $200; decanter, hobstars, 8" tall, $250.*

MANHATTAN PATTERN

When the Manhattan depression glass pattern was introduced in 1939, New Yorkers were agog over the opening of La Guardia Airport. Manhattan was aptly named, for it is as art deco as Radio City Music Hall. This wide horizontal ribbed design appeared in crystal, green, and pink. In fact, some flea market shoppers have adopted the more descriptive name of Horizontal Ribbed. By 1941, when the design was discontinued, over 20 different shapes had rolled out of Anchor Hocking headquarters. It requires the services of an energetic excavator to locate a Manhattan Lazy Susan relish server. *Value guide: bowl, crystal, 9" diameter, $12; salt and pepper shakers, pink, $25.*

MARBLEHEAD POTTERY

Dr. Herbert J. Hall, a Marblehead, Massachusetts, physician, began a pottery project as therapy for his patients in 1905. Installed in the sanitorium, the pottery became a commercial success. Arthur E. Baggs, artist and designer, assumed ownership of the pottery in 1915. It flourished through 1936 after its relocation to 111 Front

Street, Marblehead. Conventional designs and marine forms, including seaweed, sea horses, and fish, were favored. Later, conventionalized flowers, fruit, herbs, and animals ranked as decorative subjects. Their most celebrated glaze was the Marblehead blue, which resembled turquoise. Other shades included yellow, green, brown, and lavender. Marblehead pottery was characteristically marked with a stylized ship flanked by the letters "M.P." *Value guide: tile, sailing ship, 6½" square, $300; wall pocket, blue, 4" × 5", $75.*

MARBLE-TOP FURNITURE

Furniture designers active in America during the Empire period (1815-1840) introduced marble tops to American audiences. It was during the lengthy Victorian era (1837-1901), however, that the masses fell under the spell of marble. Tables, commodes, bureaus, sideboards, and other functional finds typically bore marble tops. Marble in white, pink, chocolate, and other shades topped Rococo, Renaissance, and Eastlake pieces. In fact, Abraham Lincoln had a turtle top center table in his home in Springfield, Illinois. Marble tops rate as flea market heavyweights. *Value guide: library table, marble top, 28" tall, 48" diameter, $750; chest of drawers, Eastlake, walnut, three-drawers, mirror, white marble top, 32" width, circa 1885, $575.*

Marble-Top Eastlake Table

MARGARET O'BRIEN DOLL

The Alexander Doll Corporation of New York City, gladdened the hearts of "Little Women" everywhere in 1946, with its Margaret

O'Brien doll. Famous child stars of the 1930s and 1940s were often honored in this manner. The doll had a swivel neck, jointed shoulders and hips, a dark mohair wig, and, of course, pigtails. It was marketed in 14-, 18-, and 21-inch tall sizes. The Alexander name was embossed on the head and torso, while the dress tag read "Madame Alexander, Margaret O'Brien." Dedicated doll seekers are on constant "Journey for Margaret." *Value guide: doll, dressed, 14" tall, $450.*

Margaret O'Brien Doll

MARGIE DOLLS

The almost indestructible Margie doll was introduced by the Cameo Doll Company of New York City, in 1929. Designed for durability, it featured a composition head and wood-segmented body. Joseph Kallus, the designer, provided the doll with a smiling face, molded hair, painted teeth, and a closed mouth. Originally, each doll bore a red triangle chest label reading "Margie, Des. and Copyright by Jos. Kallus." Most dolls measured between 9½ and 10 inches high. Marked and unmarked Margie dolls are being adopted on a regular basis by flea marketeers. *Value guide: doll, original label, 10" tall, $150.*

Margie Doll

MARKLIN

When Marklin of Goppingen, Germany, was found in 1859, Theodore Friedrich Wilheim and Caroline Marklin specialized in tin kitchenware. Following her husband's death in 1866, Caroline struggled to keep the venture solvent. When her sons assumed control the firm flourished, and by 1888, they operated as Marklin Brothers. After E. Fritz became active in the toy works about 1892, the title was altered to Gerbruder Marklin & Company. Another name change was instituted in 1907 when the name became Gerbruder Marklin et Cie. During World War II, munitions were made at the factory. High quality toys have been the hallmark of the company, which by 1959 employed over 2,000 workers. *Value guide: train station, 12" × 7" × 10", circa 1915, $275.*

MARTELE SILVER

Under the guidance of English artist, W. J. Codman, the Gorham Manufacturing Company undertook the creation of Martele silver in the late 1890s. When the line reached the marketplace it was expensive, being crafted of 950/100 fine silver which is softer and purer than the sterling standard. Each piece was meticulously hammered into ornamental shapes. Workmen were trained to craft designs from prepared patterns. Art nouveau female forms, undulating curves, florals, sea serpents, and foliage were executed. Every piece bore the Martele stamp on this painstakingly beautiful wrought silver. *Value guide: fish platter, 23½" long, $4,750.*

Martele Silver Bread Tray

MARTIN, FERNAND

Fernand Martin, the famed French toymaker, began experimenting with mechanical toys from an early age. By the mid-1870s, he was engaged in designing activities for various manufacturers and making some toys of his own. He founded his Paris factory in 1878. At the height of production, close to 800,000 mechanical toys were being marketed annually, and over 200 people were employed at his factory by 1880. Martin won numerous medals for his inventive toys at European exhibitions. Eventually, Martin was honored as president of the French toy industry. Through 1908, elastic bands were used to drive simple models. Clockwork toys, including the Dutch servant girl and red-nosed drunkard, attest to this maker's ingenuity. In 1912, Bonnet et Cie acquired the Martin works. *Value guide: rabbit, standing, mechanical, 8½" tall, circa 1900, $350.*

MARX, LOUIS

Louis Marx, born in 1894, began his illustrious toymaking career as an office boy for Ferdinand Strauss. After forming a partnership with his brother, this New Yorker took over many successful Strauss toy lines. Upon acquiring several other factories, he blossomed into a millionaire at the age of 30. Why? Because his delightfully designed toys, electric trains, and wind-up toys had mass appeal. They were constantly whimsical, but never expensive. Theatrical, movie, radio, and comic characters served as sources of inspiration, including Charlie McCarthy, Fred Flintstone, and Pinocchio. Marx's creations had widespread marketing, often being sold through mail order outlets or major chain stores. This still-active concern has become a recognized name with those who treasure old toys. *Value guide: Busy-bridge, wind-up, $125; Dagwood in the Airplane, tin, wind-up, $650.*

Marx World War I Soldier

MASSIER, CLEMENT

Clement Massier, French artist-potter, followed in the family tradition and opened a pottery at Golfe-Juan in 1883, placing him within

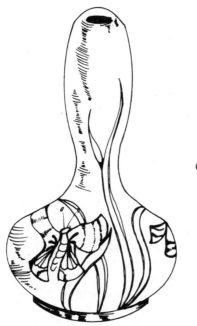

Clement Massier Vase

190

close proximity to his father's works at Vallauris. Massier showed a preoccupation for iridescent glazes. His earthenwares were enlivened with colored luster decorations based on art nouveau concepts. Plant and naturalistic motifs were painted in luster, giving his presentations a distinctive effect. The Massier name, initials, and location furnish positive identification. Upon his death in 1917, Massier's son Jerome kept the family's name alive in potting society. *Value guide: vase, florals, iridescent, 6" tall, $225.*

MAYFAIR PATTERN

Between 1931 and 1936, buyers were beguiled by Hocking Glass Company's Mayfair depression design. Truckloads departed from the factory's headquarters in pink, topaz, green, blue, and crystal. Striving for originality, some articles had a "satin finish." They often submitted to handpainted florals. Square dinner plates with cut-off diagonal corners had a center circle of roses with widely spaced lines radiating to the inner rims. Each scalloped edge corner featured a garland of roses, which explains why some people prefer

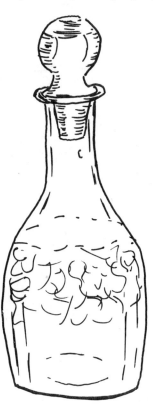

Mayfair Pattern Decanter

the name "Open Rose." The covered candy jar, cookie jar, and large size water pitcher are difficult to snare in Mayfair. *Value guide: bowl, flared, pink, 12" diameter, $30; candy dish, covered, blue, $150.*

McKEE GLASS

The mere mention of the name of McKee brings fine quality American glassware to the forefront. Samuel and James McKee were busy making window glass and bottles at their Pittsburgh factory from the 1830s. In 1850, James and Frederick McKee began operating a flint glass works known as J. and F. McKee. Two years later it was functioning as McKee & Brother. When Steward McKee became active in the family enterprise, the name was changed to McKee & Brothers. About 1889, the entire works moved to Jeanette, Pennsylvania. The McKee's, along with several other glassmakers, formed the National Glass Company, but the brothers parted company with the group in 1903 to form the McKee Glass Company. Pieces marked "pres-cut" or "McK" indicate prize acquisitions from the mighty McKee clan of glass artisans. *Value guide; figurine, Chow Dog, milk glass, $185; tumbler, jade, bottoms up, $20.*

MEAT CHOPPERS

Commenting on meat choppers, the *Treasure House of Knowledge* informed its readers in 1890, "This little machine is indispensable

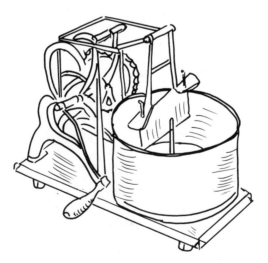

Meat Chopper

192

in every family where sausage and mince pies are favorite dishes." These cast-iron, crank-handled machines with revolving wheels or teeth were also capable of cutting or chopping scrapple, chicken croquettes, hamburg steak, or other family favorites. Most machines were touted as doing their work "perfectly and with great rapidity." The Thol Machine Company patented one of the most cherished choppers in the late 19th century, having marvelous coordination between the descending and ascending blades and revolving hopper. *Value guide: Athol Machine model, $140; The Little Giant, No. 205, $35.*

MERIDIENNE

The meridienne, that alluring lounging chair, was a favorite with furniture factories throughout the late 19th century. They were typically crafted to blend with prevailing styles. When Eastlake's "sincere forms of construction" influenced American designers in the closing decades of the century, the soft or day bed, known as the *meridienne*, surrendered to subtle changes. Suddenly, they had straight lines, stamped patterns, incised motifs, and applied balls. Some were upholstered in haircloth. Most makers favored walnut or black walnut, adhering to other Eastlake designs. These new details gave meridiennes the opportunity of gliding right into the 20th century as choice lolling spots. *Value guide: Eastlake meridienne, walnut circa 1885, $800.*

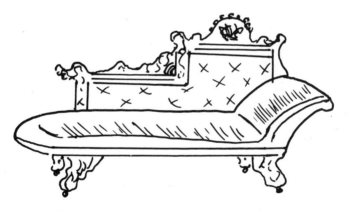

Eastlake Meridienne

MERRY WIDOW HAT POSTCARDS

The popular operetta "The Merry Widow" played to standing room audiences throughout the United States in 1908. Overnight, the wide, flat-brimmed Merry Widow hat became a fashion must. It became the object of satirical sketches on several postcard sets. In

1908, I. Grollam copyrighted a series of 16 black and white photographs of women wearing the hat, accompanied by humorous quotations. Commenting on the craze, one observer noted, "In cities where sidewalks are narrow, the men have taken to the roadways for fear of having their throats cut." *Value guide: postcard, Gollman, $4.*

MICKEY MOUSE

America's favorite mouse, Mickey, made his film debut in Walt Disney's "Steamboat Willie" on November 18, 1928. A comic strip was introduced in 1930. The first character merchandise authorized by Disney featured Mickey Mouse. When Disney offered a free autographed picture of his new star to young readers, within two weeks 8 to 10 sacks of mail were being received daily. In 1933, over 10 million Mickey Mouse ice cream cones were consumed. The 25 millionth Mickey Mouse watch was presented to Disney in 1957. By 1931 no one could deny that it was a Mickey Mouse world, when a writer wryly observed, "Shoppers carry Mickey Mouse satchels and briefcases, bursting with Mickey Mouse soap, candy, playing cards, bridge favors, hair brushes, chinaware, alarm clocks, and hot water bottles wrapped in Mickey Mouse paper, tied and paid for out of Mickey Mouse purses with savings hoarded in Mickey Mouse banks." *Value guide: bank, tin, Mickey's First Step, 1935, $275; doll, Knickerbocker, dressed, 11" tall, $250.*

Mickey Mouse Bisque Toothbrush Holder

MIGNOT

Model soldier collectors snap to attention at the sight of a Mignot creation. This company ranked as France's foremost maker of flats, solids, and hollow-cast figures. Founded in 1825, they entered the toy soldier field in 1838, marking their wares "C.B.G." in honor of the three founders. Designers focused their skills on French armies. The more expensive soldiers are far less plentiful than the flats. Some figures had detachable bodies, removable saddles, and saddle cloths. Mignot produced a number of historical figures, including Joan of Arc, Abraham Lincoln, George V, and Queen Mary. Napoleon III evidently held their productions in high esteem, because he commissioned a large army for the Prince Imperial. *Value guide: French Army Zouaves, original box, 1914, $125; French Infantry of the line, original box, 1916, $120.*

MILK BOTTLES

The Warren milk bottle, issued under a patent granted to the Warren Glass Works in 1880, was in use by 1881. Three years later, the so-called Whiteman Milk Jar was introduced. In that same year Dr. Henry D. Thatcher, a Pottsdam, New York, druggist, invented an embossed milk bottle with a bail-type fastener. The figure of a farmer milking a cow was followed by other motifs including flags,

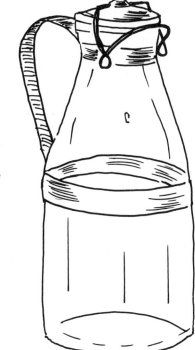

Early Milk Bottle

stars, buildings, animals, and human figures. Thatcher developed a glass closure for his design in 1886, followed three years later by the Common Sense Milk Jar, which had a waxed paper cap resting on the groove inside the bottle. Collectors enjoy fortifying their collections with heavily embossed or unusually colored bottles in sizes ranging from 1 inch up to 1 gallon. *Value guide: Challenge Milk Company, elk, amber, $30; Shawsheen Dairy, embossed Indian head, quart, $14.*

MILLER, EDWARD

While Tiffany, Handel, Jefferson, and Pairpoint are regarded as giants in the art nouveau lighting field, other lesser known factories

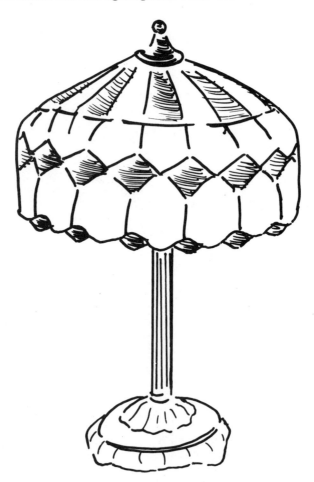

Miller Table Lamp

also produced wares. In the early 1900s, Edward Miller & Company of Meriden, Connecticut, was inundated with orders for metal bases for kerosene lamps. As electricity gained widespread use, however, they switched to manufacturing lighting fixtures. Table lamps, desk lamps, and hanging fixtures boasted colorful shades and pierced metalwork motifs. Collectors are plugging into Miller lamps while the supply remains plentiful. *Value guide: table lamp, green and white, pierced metalwork, 22" tall, $350.*

MINNEAPOLIS SEWING MACHINES

In the early 1900s, Minnesota Sewing Machines were the pride and joy of Sears, Roebuck, & Company. These tailormade collectibles possessed many of the features associated with costlier machines. They had richly carved and embossed oak cases, many with drop leaf covers. The drawers were large and roomy, with the center one conveniently partitioned off for storage. Most machines sold for between $10 and $14. One turn of the century critic observed, "every contrivance upon which a description of the sewing machine can be printed, pasted, or hung, has been pressed into service." *Value guide: Model D, $75.*

Minneapolis Sewing Machine

MINNIE MOUSE

Minnie Mouse became the world's most famous female mouse upon her introduction in 1930 by Disney. Renditions of Minnie dolls were marketed by Charlotte Clark, Magarete Steiff, Dean's Rag Book Company of England, and the Knickerbocker Doll Corporation. Even examples made from Clark's *McCall's* patterns are prized. Handkerchiefs from the Waldenburger, Tanner, & Co. of Switzerland, were marked "Mickey & Minnie Mouse, Cpr., 1928, 1930, by Walt Disney." Manufacturers also baited the trap for young consumers with a Mickey and Minnie Handcar, silverware, purses, marionettes, figurines, and books. *Value guide: doll, Steiff, early 1930s, $375; pop-up books, Minnie Mouse, $125.*

Minnie Mouse Figurine

MISS AMERICA PATTERN

That winning Hocking Glass Company pattern, Miss America, reigned supreme on American tabletops between 1933 and 1936. Distinctive shapes and fine pointed edges dominated the design of this Old English Hobnail revival. The dinner plates had a large central sunburst of radial lines, accompanied by hobnail rims terminating in points. Table settings were available in various colors, including pink, crystal, amber, and green. The latter rate as rarities. Some pieces were treated to a "satin finish." Over 30 different objects in the Miss America pattern have paraded onto flea market runways. *Value guide: butter dish, green, $475; candy dish, covered, crystal, $50.*

Miss America Pattern Pitcher

198

MISSION FURNITURE

Elaborate Victorian eclectic styles were being shunned by furniture patrons by about 1900. Gustav Stickley, that man with a mission, began crafting straight-lined furniture, devoid of any ornamentation except for the prominent mortise and tenon joints. Stickley's simple, functional forms, usually of oak, were instantly copied by fellow furniture crafters. The name Mission was supposedly derived from pieces used at the Franciscan missions of California. Since Stickley's mission in life was to promote a return to honest craftsmanship, the term could not be more fitting. Mission furniture flourished briefly in the United States, but by 1916, mass-produced versions appeared in Sears, Roebuck catalogs. *Value guide: bookcase, two-door style, Gustav Stickley, red decal mark, 56" tall, $2,000; rocker, arms, vertical slats on side and back, L. & J.G. Stickley, clamp decal mark, circa 1909, $575.*

Mission Side Chair

MIX, TOM

Tom Mix debuted on the silver screen in the semidocumentary Western *Ranch Life in the Great Southwest* in 1909. A series of silent shorts followed, culminating in a lucrative contract with the William Fox Studios. By 1922, his salary had risen to $17,000 per week. After 11 years and 80 action packed films, he departed from the Fox studio. Mix ranked as the number one cowboy of the silent screen.

With the advent of sound, his career floundered until Universal Studios offered him the film *Destry Rides Again* in 1932. Tom never appeared on The Ralston Tom Mix Radio Show that originated in 1933, but he was impersonated by other actors. The show, however, was still offering premiums in 1950. This legendary movie cowboy died in an automobile accident in 1940. *Value guide: arcade cards, set of 17, $125; ring, periscope, $60.*

MODERNTONE PATTERN

In its day, Moderntone depression glass was as modern as "Thoroughly Modern Millie." Designers at the Hazel-Atlas Glass Company cast tradition aside with this pattern, preferring to capitalize on art deco themes. Angular patterns and shapes grace it in a decidedly '50s appearance. Widely spaced concentric rings were used to evoke a modern look. Table settings in blue and burgundy were widely offered. Amethyst, opaque white with fired-on blue, red, and yellow were made, but in limited quantities. Mass-produced Moderntone, like cloche hats, short-cropped hair, and cupid's bow mouths evoke memories of the deco decades. *Value guide: cup and saucer, pink, $7; salt and pepper shakers, blue, $25.*

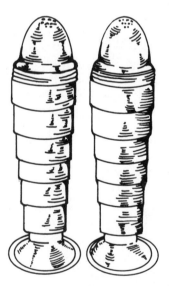

Moderntone Pattern Salt and Pepper Shakers

MONARCH COFFEE VACUUM BOTTLE

Aviation addicts compete with advertising addicts over this treasured vacuum bottle. The Monarch Coffee Company promoted its products with this quart-size, mercury-lined container. Originally, it came complete with four nesting cups. The lithographed tin container boasted the following wording: "Airline Pilots Deserve Good Coffee, Keep This Bottle Filled With Monarch Coffee—It Will Add Pleasure to Every Flight." With such a testimonial, is it any wonder that prices have soared on the "Monarch Coffee Airline Pilot" bottle? *Value guide: vacuum bottle, $250.*

MONKEY AND COCONUT BANK

The mechanical banks conceived by designer James A. Bowen of Philadelphia, always displayed superb timing. All of his banks were made by the J. & E. Stevens Company. One of Bowen's most imaginative designs was the brown and tan Monkey and Coconut bank patented in 1886. This bit of monkey business involved placing a penny in the monkey's right hand and pressing a lever on the back of the bank. As his left hand lifts the top of the coconut to await the penny, his right hand releases the coin. At this point, his mouth opens and his eyes look down after the penny. Needless to say, this money-saving monkey brought shrieks of joy from penny savers. *Value guide: Monkey and Coconut bank, cast-iron, 8¼" tall, $525.*

MONROE, C. F.

Around the turn of the century, the C. F. Monroe Company of Meriden, Connecticut, became known for opal-decorated glass articles. They specialized in dressing table items such as jewelry boxes, powder boxes, and collar and cuff boxes. They also marketed vases, jardinieres, and selected tablewares and household articles. The blanks were purchased from European sources, or from the Pairpoint Corporation of Massachusetts. Many objects, often ribbed, were hand painted with florals. Wave Crest Ware, Kelva, and Nakara were the three trademarks Monroe used through 1916, when the factory ceased operating. *Value guide: biscuit jar, Wave Crest Ware, florals, silver lid, $500; box, puffy, florals, Kelva, 6½" diameter, $550.*

Monroe Jewel Box

MONROE, MARILYN

Two minor parts in two major films of 1950 launched starlet Marilyn Monroe on the road to stardom. The former Norma Jean Mortensen tapped fame on the shoulder in *All About Eve* and *The Asphalt Jungle*. 20th Century Fox groomed the luscious lady into a box office bonanza with *How To Marry a Millionaire, Bus Stop,* and *Gentlemen Prefer Blondes.* It soon became apparent that the public preferred Marilyn. When *Playboy Magazine* began publication in 1954, Marilyn was on the cover. Not content with being just another pretty face, she perfected her comedic talents in films like *The Seven Year Itch* and *Some Like It Hot.* In 1961, she co-starred with Clark Gable in *The Misfits.* Her death silenced her screen career but awakened the public's interest in Marilyn's loves, life, and legendary looks. *Value guide: "Playboy Magazine," December, 1954, $475; playing cards, complete, $50.*

MOON MULLINS

Frank Willard's "Moon Mullins," along with his crony, Mushmouth, made their first appearance in the *Chicago Tribune* on June 19, 1923. Following Willard's death in 1958, Fred Johnson took over the long-running Mullins strip. Originally, a boxing theme was planned, but this was abandoned, for Moon felt more comfortable at the

Moon Mullins & Kayo Handcar Toy

circus, in a pool parlor, or at a ritzy mansion. He became adept at bluffing his way into a meal or more. Little Egypt, Emmy Schmaltz, Kayo, and Mamie were the supporting players in the Moon Mullins entourage. Louis Marx manufactured two different versions of the Moon Mullins and Kayo on a Hand Car in the 1930s. Both featured the twosome holding their hats awaiting impending disaster. *Value guide: hand car, 1930s, $400; figure, wood jointed, signed Willard, 5½" tall, $75.*

MOORCROFT, WILLIAM

William Moorcroft garnered the attention of his peers while apprenticing for James MacIntyre of Burslem, England, from 1897. After developing a distinctive style—primarily stylized flowers and unusual glazes—he founded a pottery in 1913. His unique flambe glazes brought him many honors in potting circles. It represents true hand work, for each piece was thrown on a potter's wheel and then decorated. Following his appointment as Potter to Her Majesty, Queen Mary, an advertising pamphlet noted the tablewares "were found in Royal households and many of the finest homes in the world." His son, Walter, continues operating the pottery at present. While varying backstamps were used, the presence of the Moorcroft name or signature furnished positive identification. *Value guide: cache pot, pomegranates, signed, 7¼" tall, $325; vase, poppy, pewter base, 6½" tall, $475.*

MOORISH TABLES

The Turkish Bazaar and Cafe proved to be one of the most exotic attractions at the Philadelphia Centennial Exposition of 1876. It

Moorish Table

triggered a trend for Turkish, Moorish, Syrian, and East Indian life styles. The inlaid Moorish or Damascus side table became a mainstay of the "cozy corner." These low-sided tables generally had inlaid tops and side panels extending downward between the legs. Various interpretations were presented by American furniture makers. By 1900, Moorish tables, hookahs, incense burners, brass trays, and Turkish carpets became little more than dust collectors. *Value guide: Moorish table, eight-sided, inlaid top, circa 1890, $185.*

MORIAGE

Moriage is a name associated with the exquisitely beautifully applied clay relief ornamentations attributed to Japanese artisans. Pottery and porcelain objects ranging from vases to teapots were skillfully decorated by several varying methods. A hand-rolling or shaping procedure involved applying one or more layers to the biscuit in different thicknesses. A second technique, known as tubing or sliptrailing, was accomplished by decoration applied from a tube. It was comparable to decorating a cake. Another process, *hakeme,* reduced the slip to liquid form, and the piece was ornamented with a brush. Color could be applied before or after this step. Moriage pieces have been prompting ever higher prices. *Value guide: chocolate pot, florals, multi-colored enamels, $175; teapot, pink, florals, beaded decor, $160.*

MORRIS CHAIR

The adjustable armchair, known as the Morris chair out of deference to English designer William Morris, was introduced in the 1860s. A

Morris Chair

standard form evolved having a rectangular seat and high back fitted with loose cushions. Early models often had padded arms, with the space between the arms and side seat filled in with turned spindles. The front legs were usually square or shaped. Most chairs were supported on socket castors. In America, versions of black walnut or cherry were supplanted in popularity by oak and mahogany chairs in the 1880s and 1890s. Mass-produced Morris chairs marched out of many factories, especially those centered around Grand Rapids, Michigan. When Mission styles proliferated in the early 1900s, Morris chairs were designed accordingly. *Value guide: oak, pierced wide stretchers, Limbert, circa 1910, $550; oak, reclining back, lion's paw feet, circa 1885, $300.*

MORTON SALT

Joy Morton had been working for the E. L. Wheeler & Company for about six years prior to establishing her own factory in 1885. This 30-year-old entrepreneur founded the Joy Morton & Company, which ranked as the only nationwide marketer of salt. The company's familiar Morton girl with an umbrella and package of salt first appeared in advertisements about 1911. The slogan "When It Rains It Pours," was introduced simultaneously. A round blue salt box was the first package to feature the trademark in 1914. Over the years the girl, umbrella, and her attire have been updated to maintain a contemporary appearance. Reportedly, the words "Morton's Salt" became "Morton Salt" sometime prior to 1941. The company, now a part of Morton/Norwich, became Morton International, Inc., about 1965. *Value guide: salt box, early 1915, $18.*

MOSAIC TILE COMPANY

The Mosaic Tile Company of Zanesville, Ohio, began operating in 1894. Karl Langenbeck and Hermann Mueller, founding partners,

Mosaic Tile

earned respect for their imaginative floor and wall tiles. Although quite inexpensive, their tiles imitated mosaics. As might be expected, many earthenware presentations were deemed ideal for architectural use. Eventually, matte-glazed tiles were widely distributed. Tiles with the company's name or MTC monogram practically floor collectors. *Value guide: Abraham Lincoln portrait, blue, 3½" diameter, $60; Woodrow Wilson, blue and white, $55.*

MOSER, LUDWIG

Ludwig Moser, Bohemian glass craftsman, founded the still-flourishing glasshouse bearing his name in 1857. Within several decades, Moser glass had gained international acclaim. Cameo glass, along with molded and crystal glass objects, won praise from peers and public alike. Quite often a single object submitted to a variety of techniques, such as engraving, enameling, etching, or faceting. Around the turn of the century, iridescent glass specialties of unsurpassed beauty brought Moser additional fame. In the pre-World War I era, Ludwig Moser & Sohne emerged as Czechoslovakia's foremost glasshouse. *Value guide: bowl, amethyst, gold engraved border, footed, 4" diameter, $225; vase, enameled decor, cranberry, gold trim, 6" tall, $300.*

MOSS MAJOLICA

Domestic and European potters participated in the majolica madness of the late 19th century. Striving for variation, some makers

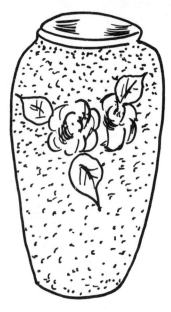

Moss Majolica Vase

experimented with sanded effects. These objects were known as sanded or moss majolica. A typical specimen had a sanded surface; raised, applied flowers; and a smooth interior. Frequently, the applied floral areas have been subjected to chipping over the years. Various colored backgrounds were selected for standard treatments, as potters attempted to attract consumers. In 1879, extra large Moss rose vases were affordably priced at $1.75. *Value guide: vase, maroon, applied flowers, 10" tall, $50.*

MOXIE

Dr. Augustin Thompson, a Lowell, Massachusetts, physician, developed a liquid as a concentrated nerve food suitable to be taken by the teaspoon in the 1870s. By the mid-1880s, Moxie Nerve Food was being served with carbonated soda. Over the years this soft drink has been sold in bottles with crown tops, Hutchinson's stoppers, and glass-labels. Between about 1900 and the 1920s, the promotionally minded company issued numerous advertising items and premium articles. Moxie toys, trays, signs, thermometers, bottles, and glasses serve as refreshing finds by those who admire advertising mementos. *Value guide: sign, horse and girl driving car, tin, 27" × 16", $350; tip tray, girl holding glass, 6" diameter, circa 1900, $125.*

MUFFINEERS

Homemakers of the 1800s pressed muffineers into daily use. They were used in sprinkling sugar or a mixture of sugar and cinnamon on muffins. The more affluent muffin lovers preferred sprinkling from silver or Sheffield versions, while those of humbler means relied upon glass containers, in clear and colored variations. Many had enameled motifs. The majority of muffineers were fitted with silverplated tops. They were usually two or three times larger than salt and pepper shakers. Muffineers have disappeared from every tabletop, save the flea market tabletop. *Value guide: cut glass, sterling top, $100; milk glass, acorn, blue, $135.*

MY DREAM BABY DOLL

Grace Storey Putnam's Bye-Lo Baby was the doll sensation of the mid-1920s. In an attempt to compete against this fast seller, various doll companies marketed very similar variations. My Dream Baby, registered in 1924, was the Arranbee Doll Company's answer to the Bye-Lo Baby. Company officials had the bisque heads made in Germany by the Armand Marseilles works. This infant doll appeared in several sizes; both flange and socket necks were available. These dolls have moving glass eyes that provide them with a touch of realism. The smallest size My Dream Baby was dream priced at just $1.25. *Value guide: bisque, cloth body, 16" tall, $500.*

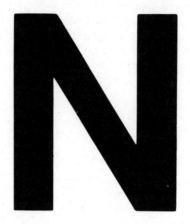

NANCY DOLLS

Dolls ascribed to the Arranbee Doll Company, of New York City, practically sell on sight. Nancy dolls reached toy shops in 1930, at the height of the depression. They were made in sizes ranging from

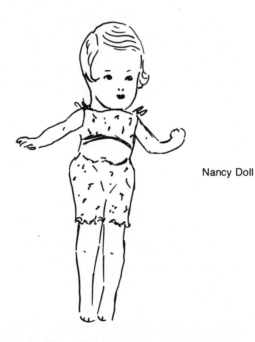

Nancy Doll

208

12 to 20 inches. Youngsters had a choice of all-composition models, or composition swivel head and limbs on a cloth torso. Originally, each doll had a dress tag that read "Nancy/An Arranbee Doll." The company's trademark appeared on the head of each doll. Thus, Nancy dolls have no identity problems, even for beginning collectors. *Value guide: Nancy doll, composition swivel shoulder head, sleep eyes, open mouth with teeth, dressed, 18" tall, $165.*

NAPKIN RINGS

The napkin ring appeared on American tabletops in the mid-19th century. By 1860, three different styles were listed in Meriden Britannia Company catalogs. These examples bore beaded, engine-turned, engraved, or applied medallions. In the post-Centennial era, figural napkin rings with round, rectangular, or triangular bands held napkins neatly in place. They were originally designed for children. From a collector's standpoint, these figural forms in dog, chicken, bird, rabbit, goat, turtle, dolphin, and countless other varieties are eagerly sought. Napkin rings, plain or figural, were made and marked by most of America's foremost silver concerns. *Value guide: figural, dog pulling cart, moveable wheels, silverplate, $240; Kate Greenaway children, girl pushes ring, silverplate, $175.*

Silverplated Napkin Ring

NEWCOMBE POTTERY

A pottery at Newcombe College, New Orleans, which is the women's division of Tulane University, was founded in 1895. Functional objects, generally based on traditional folk pottery rather than contemporary themes, were crafted on a commercial basis. The concept was to teach pottery-making techniques to art students.

Designers were primarily influenced by their surroundings, favoring such motifs as the Louisiana oakleaf. Their wares reflected honest functional themes, with total disregard for mass marketing. The Newcombe College mark "N" within a "C" was utilized, frequently with the decorator's initials. *Value guide: bowl, blue flowers, cream ground, 5" diameter, $850; vase, purple, shiny glaze, 4¾" tall, $400.*

Newcombe Pottery Mug

NEW MARTINSVILLE GLASS COMPANY

Glass specialties from the New Martinsville Glass Company of Ohio, began occupying space on American tabletops in 1900. Initially, restaurant glass and lamps were produced. Art Glass was also conceived, including opaque articles in various colors, and peachblow glass. Ruby-stained glass objects in a parade of patterns brought them additional attention. Although the glasshouse underwent a change of ownership in 1937, basic lines remained in production. From 1944, fine quality glass echoing Swedish traditions has been marketed under the Viking Glass Company title. *Value guide: bookends, seal, $140; bride's bowl, peachblow, ribbed edge, 10" diameter, $175.*

NILOAK POTTERY

Marbleized art pottery became the mainstay of the Niloak Pottery of

Benton, Arkansas, active between 1909 and 1946. How did the pottery get that unusual name? Simply by spelling *kaolin* backwards. Charles Dean "Bullet" Hyden saw potential in the varicolored clays of Saline County's hills. The mixture of clay was thrown on a potter's wheel, forming a multi-colored spiral design of natural color clays. Therefore, no two pieces were exactly alike. Niloak was introduced by Hyden in 1910. Most objects bore only an exterior glaze. Was it successful? During its production peak over 75,000 pieces were made annually. When sales slackened during the depression, Hyden marketed a cast line of pottery stamped "Hywood/Niloak." Following its closing in 1946, marked Niloak pieces entered the choice collectible realm. *Value guide: figurine, Southern Belle, 11" tall, $125; vase, swirl, browns and blues, 8" tall, $90.*

Niloak Pottery Vase

NIPPON

Nippon, which appears as a backstamp on Japanese ceramics between 1891 and 1921, denotes Japan as the country of origin. The mark was initiated in 1891, when it became obligatory to include the country of export with the passage of the McKinley Tariff Act. The word "Nippon" was used with or without the manufacturer's trademark. Bold and beautiful porcelain objects, including chocolate sets, hatpin holders, cups and saucers, tea sets, nut dishes, and dresser top accessories were produced by a score of potters. The subject matter, which ranged from flowers to birds and landscapes, incorporated gold highlights or beaded effects for maximum showiness. While imitative of German and Austrian porcelain these lavish productions exhibited the Japanese mode of decoration. *Value guide: chocolate pot, swimming swans, $100; cracker jar, hand painted butterflies, gold trim, $125.*

Nippon Vase

NODDERS

Nodding figurines were the rage of the late 19th century. A *nodder* is a figurine with a head and/or arms attached to the body by wires,

Bisque Nodder

which enabled them to move. German manufacturers almost had an exclusive on these novelties. They were made of various materials, notably bisque, celluloid, porcelain, and wood. Animals and figures served as a source of inspiration for designers, all capable of nodding their heads affirmatively. American-made versions were often based on cartoon characters or Walt Disney favorites. Oriental types abounded, as the nodding fever encompassed potters on a worldwide basis. Marked examples have always received a nod of approval from antiquers. *Value guide: elephant, composition, head and tail moves, $125; Santa Claus, papier-mache, 9½" tall, $185.*

NORITAKE

Noritake china has been produced by Nippon Toki Kaisha of Nagoya, Japan, since 1904. The still-flourishing concern excels in fashioning popularly priced dinnerware services and decorative objects. One of the most sought after discontinued patterns is Azalea, utilized as a Larkin Soap premium item for many years. This pattern was also sold through selected outlets. Other notable Noritake designs bore typically American names such as Sandra, Colby, and Rose Lace. Their porcelain pieces incorporated the Noritake trademark along with the country of origin, "Nippon" or "Japan." The Morimura Brothers were the exclusive American import agents. Many objects bore their "M" within a wreath mark through 1941, when the company ceased operating. Noritake's Royal Ceramic Line (marked "R.C.") and Orura Art line (marked "O. A. C.") rank as choice acquisitions. *Value guide: pitcher, milk, Azalea, 6" tall, $165; teapot, Valiere, $40.*

NORMANDIE

Normandie mold-etched table settings sailed onto American table tops from the Federal Glass Company in 1933. Shoppers have discovered items in pink, amber, iridescent orange, green, and crystal. The major decorative elements included floral bouquets, wreaths, and ribbons. Alternating lattice and florals dominated borders. In fact, some collectors have adapted the more descriptive name "Bouquet and Lattice." Those iridescent carnival-like pieces were used as premiums by the Great Northern Products Company. Federal dropped anchor on Normandie in 1939, when the line was discontinued. *Value guide: plate, pink, 11" diameter, $25; tumbler, iced tea, iridescent, $25.*

NORTHERN AMERICAN IRON WORKS

Between 1877 and 1897, The Northern American Iron Works located at 88 Beekman Street, New York City, became known for its cast-iron confections. Various functional forms submitted to prevailing styles, notably the Renaissance Revival influence. Leafy S-curves and scrolls derived from rococo themes as well as Moorish-inspired designs proliferated. A fringed effect could also be noted on Moorish styles. Cast-iron chairs, settees, tables, planters, and other forms bearing "The Northern American Iron Works, N.Y." trademark rate as flea market heavyweights. *Value guide: armchair, rococo, $375; settee, Moorish, ornate, circa 1890, $465.*

Cast-Iron Settee

NORTH STAR STOVE

One of the hottest selling stoves of the late 19th century was the North star. The W. C. Davis & Company of Cincinnati, Ohio, introduced the stove about 1876. The designer was apparently smitten with Gothic Revival styles, for the center part of the top was designed in imitation of a mansard roof with two small Gothic windows. These windows had isinglass panes on each side. To protect the floors from the intense heat of stoves like the North Star, many stood on pottery tiles, or more often, bricks. *Value guide: North Star stove, circa 1885, $800.*

North Star Stove

NOVELTY BANK

The Novelty Bank was patented by Charles C. Johnson in 1872 and 1873. This 6½-inch tall mechanical bank was manufactured by the J. & E. Stevens Company of Connecticut. The cast-iron creation was

Novelty Bank

in the form of an imposing structure, complete with two chimneys and eight dormers. When the door opens, a cashier moves forward with his tray. The depositor places a penny on the tray, closes the door, and the cashier deposits the coin in the "bank." Novelty building banks were ornamented in yellow with a red and blue trim. Were they novel enough to entice young savers? Apparently so, for they enjoyed great popularity. *Value guide: novelty bank, cast-iron, 6½" tall, circa 1880, $375.*

NUTTING FURNITURE COMPANY

The carriage trade, and others as well, purchased wicker carriages from the W. B. Nutting Furniture and Carriage Company of Boston, Massachusetts, in the closing decades of the 19th century. Babies were wheeled around the block in over 40 different styles of Nutting carriages. They bore price tags ranging from $4.75 to $27.00. The famous Eureka gear and tapered spoke wheels were standard equipment on most models. Superior versions had plush upholstery, with silk lace-edged parasols. As an added inducement, carriages were delivered freight free to any destination within the United States. *Value guide: carriage, large wheels, wooden handle grip, green upholstery, circa 1895, $300.*

Nutting Baby Carriage

NUTTING, WALLACE

Wallace Nutting was one of the most influential pioneers in the reproduction of American antiques. Nutting's philosophy was, "Copy and avoid bad taste. Not all the old is good but all the new is bad." This multi-talented collector was a preacher, photographer, publisher, and promoter of "old houses." Between 1917 and the late 1930s, he produced American reproductions of 17th and 18th cen-

Wallace Nutting Windsor Chair

tury furniture styles. His book, *Furniture Treasury*, has been acknowledged as the foremost reference work on American furniture. The quaint cottages and picturesque lanes he loved to photograph live on for collectors who purchase Nutting prints. Insiders believe that the interior prints are more valuable than the exterior views. *Value guide: print, The Chimney Corner, 8" × 10", $80; Windsor side chair, bow back, signed Nutting, 1930s, $575.*

OCCUPIED JAPAN

Collectors preferring easily dated acquisitions are attracted to "Occupied Japan" or "Made in Occupied Japan" articles. These marks indicate a date of production between 1945 and 1952, when Allied troops were occupying Japan. Various factories issued toys, metal work, porcelain, glass, clocks, and an army of other mementos. Individual factory trademarks appeared on many items. Some ceramic figurines were imitative of Hummels or Royal Doulton. Even the famed Blue Willow dinner service experienced a revival in the hands of Japanese potters. Flea marketeers occupy their time seeking Occupied Japan oddities. *Value guide: creamer, figural cow, $20; toby, MacArthur, $80.*

OLD CAFE PATTERN

Setting a table for two with the Old Cafe depression design can be a difficult task because it was produced in such limited quantities by the Hocking Glass Company between 1936 and 1940. Approximately 14 shapes appeared in pink, crystal, and ruby red. The latter surfaced in 1940. This simply conceived design boasted a center sunburst on plates, surrounded by a circle of amply spaced radial lines. Three narrow lined panels alternated with a series of plain panels around the rims. Flea market shoppers intent upon collecting Old Cafe have found it a challenging experience. *Value guide: cup and saucer, pink, $7; vase, crystal, 7¼" tall, $8.*

OLD MR. BOSTON CLOCKS

Those addicted to American advertising mementos hold the old Mr.

Boston clock in high esteem. Around the turn of the century, timepieces were considered a suitable vehicle for promoting a business or service. This novelty has been ascribed to the William Gilbert clockworks of Connecticut. Gilbert flourished under several partnerships in the second half of the 19th century. Each bottle-shaped clock bore the inscription "Old Mr. Boston/Fine Liquors." They were made in several sizes, customarily with eight-day movements. A check of prices can offer proof positive that these liquor advertising clocks qualify as choice collectibles. *Value guide: Old Mr. Boston, 10⅜" tall, circa 1900, $235.*

Old Mr. Boston Clock

OLD SLEEPY EYE

The Sleepy Eye name has been associated with a town in Minnesota, an Indian chief, and a well-known brand of flour. Thus, it seems appropriate that The Sleepy Eye Flour Mill, which flourished in Sleepy Eye, Minnesota, from the 1880s, would utilize an Indian on their advertising souvenirs. Stoneware articles were freely distributed or sold by the flour company through 1937. Old Sleepy Eye pottery was produced by several potters. One of the earliest items was a mug with the Indian printed in blue from the Minnesota Stoneware Company. The Weir Pottery of Monmouth, Illinois, and later The Western Stoneware Company of Monmouth, Illinois, also made Old Sleepy Eye premiums. The pitchers were made in five different sizes. While the blue decorated pieces are most frequently encountered, other colors have also been discovered by wide-eyed antiquarians. *Value guide: pitcher, cobalt blue, pint, $250; stein, yellow and brown, $600.*

Old Sleepy Eye Pitcher

OPHIR PATTERN

Bourne & Leigh, Staffordshire potters, marketed this semi-porcelain flow blue dinner service in the 1890s. Flow Blue tablewares were enjoying a revival during this period. Later wares generally lacked the dark cobalt blue blurring found on pieces dating from the 1840s and 1850s. Ophir has embossed scrolling around the rim which is almost white, with floral sprays in blue against a background of small Vs. The gold highlights originally ornamenting the scrolled and floral areas have usually been washed away over the years. Members of the Flow Blue collecting fraternity look for the pattern name and potter's trademark that are printed in blue on the underside of the pieces. *Value guide: creamer, $30; vegetable dish, covered, $50.*

ORIENTAL MUD FIGURES

Despite the rather down-to-earth name, Oriental mud figures are outstanding oddities. They were originally used in fish tanks and planters; thus the term mud figure seems somewhat appropriate. Oriental potters favored unglazed faces and hands and glazed clothing. Scholars, workmen, merchants, and farmers proved continualy popular. Occasionally, landscape scenes involving trees and houses were attempted. The current rage for Orientalia causes early 20th century mud figures to whet collectors' appetites. *Value guide: lady, blue dress, 1920s, 5" tall, $30; man, standing, yellow, green, and blue, 6" tall, $65.*

OSTRICH FANS

Ostrich fans fluttered into fashion in the late 19th century, and their popularity persisted into the Edwardian era. While various sizes were on display at local emporiums, most were modestly priced between $2.50 and $3.50. Conservative ladies selected soft shades, but a more daring belle often chose one that had been tinted a vibrant green or red. The majority had wooden sticks, although mother-of-pearl, tortoise shell, and ivory sticks were available. With the vogue for vintage clothing, the once-neglected ostrich fan is now respected. *Value guide: ostrich, ivory sticks, circa 1910, $85.*

OVER YONDER WHERE THE LILIES GROW

Sheet music seekers enter into combat over any titles relating to World War I. "Over Yonder Where the Lilies Grow" is one of the lesser known titles by Geoffery O'Hara, the man responsible for "K-K-K-Katy." The cover design, however, which features a young Dutch girl presenting a flower to an American soldier, was most endearing, making this touching illustration the sole reason this sheet music is so avidly sought. The artist? None other than Norman Rockwell. *Value guide: "Over Yonder Where the Lilies Grow," circa 1919, $30.*

OWENS POTTERY

J. B. Owens started making stoneware in Zanesville, Ohio, in 1891. Five years later he undertook the production of art pottery,

Owens Pottery Vase

emulating Rockwood. By 1904, his Utopian and Lotus lines were earning him high praise in potting quarters. Other lines followed, including Cyrano, with white clay designs, and Henri Deux, bearing incised motifs filled in with color. Feroza art wares had a metallic luster, somewhat similar to Weller's Sicardo. Other Zanesville potters did a double take at his Mission line, which sported a matte glaze with church or landscape views. Red Flame was aptly named, for it bore an embossed flower design covered with a red glaze. Art pottery was discontinued in 1906, when Owens decided to produce only tiles. *Value guide: ewer, Utopian, 6" tall, $235; vase, Mission, 12" tall, $350.*

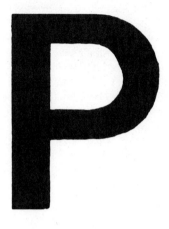

PADDY AND THE PIG BANK

When this J. & E. Stevens Company mechanical bank appeared in
1882, it was called the "Shamrock Bank." This clever bit of whimsy,
based on topical events, was designed by James H. Bowen. Paddy
was depicted with a bottle in his pocket and a white pig with pink
ears on his lap. He was bedecked in a gray hat, blue jacket, yellow
pants, and orange socks. After placing a penny in the pig's mouth, a
lever is pressed behind Paddy. At this point the pig raises his left
leg, kicking the penny in the direction of Paddy's mouth. How does
Paddy respond? He opens his mouth, sticks out his tongue, and rolls
his eyes! *Value guide: Paddy and the Pig Bank, 8" tall, $650.*

PADLOCKS

Padlocks have joined the lengthy list of off-beat collectibles currently enjoying a lively vogue. Some acquire them for nostalgic
purposes, while others delight in their intricate movements. They
varied considerably in shape. Major manufacturers frequently issued hundreds of different styles, some quite simple, others more
complex. As is true of other collecting categories, the unusual
fetches the fanciest returns. Those bearing a maker's name or
trademark can open the path to unexpected profits. Names like A.
E. Deitz, Sargent, Yale, W. A. Harrison, Dayton Manufacturing
Company, Davenport, and Mallory & Company each provide the
key to padlock practitioners. *Value guide: brass tumbler, Winchester, 3" $55; Yale, PRR, brass, signal, $36.*

PAIRPOINT LAMPS

Between 1890 and 1929, the Pairpoint Corporation of New Bedford, Massachusetts, electrified the nation with its lighting fixtures. In addition, glass and silver accessories brought them fame and fortune. Art nouveau lighting manufacturers did a double take over Pairpoint's cut, pressed, and decorated shades in a multitude of motifs. Three basic types of shades were crafted: vertically ribbed ones generally decorated with florals, glass shades with scenic designs, and the highly coveted "blown-out," or "puffy shades." The majority measured between 3 and 22 inches in diameter. Most had complementary bases of glass, wood, or metal. *Value guide: table lamp, puffy, pansy, yellow, white, green, and purple, $1,250; table lamp, reverse painted shade, urn base, scenic, 16" diameter, $2,750.*

Pairpoint Puffy Table Lamp

PANAMA CANAL MANDOLIN HARP

Oscar Schmidt's "Panama Canal" mandolin harp strummed into popularity in the pre-World War I era. It was aptly named, for a depiction of a battleship in the Panama Canal could be seen on its side. As was true of other musical instruments of the period, the mandolin harp came in a handsome box along with an instruction sheet. Sellers offered complete units comprised of a mandolin, case, instruction course, finger chart, and (of course) a tuning pipe. Panama Canal harps in working order and having a fair amount of original ornamentation are always "sailable." *Value guide: Panama Canal mandolin harp, circa 1910, $165.*

PAN-AMERICAN WASHING MACHINES

The Blackstone Manufacturing Company of Jamestown, New York, cleaned up with its line of improved washing machines in the early 1900s. This company was responsible for such super sellers as the Western Defender, The Imperial, and the Western Washer. The New Pan-American was widely heralded as being crafted from "the best selected stock, nicely finished." Its large lid allowed the entire top of the washer to open up. Even repeated shaking failed to foil this machine, for the four legs were bolted to the tub and braced together with steel rods. Best of all, this Monday morning lifesaver was affordably priced at $6.50. *Value guide: Pan-American, circa 1910, $325.*

Pan-American Washing Machine

PAPER CLIPS

From the mid-19th century, spring-loaded clips for gripping a sheaf of papers sprung up on American desks. Overnight, European and American makers produced paper clips of sterling silver, silverplate, copper, brass, and gold. Prominent designs included a duck's head with spring-loaded beak, clam, boar's head, clasped hands, or a single hand. They were offered in a bewildering variety. The more fanciful the clip, the fancier the price. Ornamental versions had staged a disappearing act by World War I, when mainly utilitarian versions found favor. *Value guide: copper, duck's head, glass eyes, circa 1900, $60; silverplate, woman's head, circa 1895, $55.*

PAPER KNIVES

The spread of literacy in the 17th century prompted an increase in European mail to this country and gave birth to the paper knife. Most makers based their designs on daggers. A typical version had a slender blade, sharp point, and an edge capable of slitting, but not cutting, the paper. By the Victorian era, exotic cast silver and gold handles supported blades of horn, ivory, and other nonmetallic substances. Oriental, novelty, and advertising varieties landed on late-19th-century desks. They were relegated to lower drawers when highly spirited art nouveau versions appeared in the 1890s in "scores of styles, shapes, sizes, and prices." *Value guide: cloisonne handle, florals, brass, circa 1900, $35; Royal Typewriter advertisement, cast-iron, $30.*

Sterling Silver Paper Knife

PARROT PATTERN

In 1932 Federal Glass Company's Parrot pattern was regarded as the talk of the town. Reportedly, this tropical triumph depicting parrots and palm trees was designed by an artisan fresh from a vacation in the Bahamas. His preoccupation with tropical scenery, however, was not shared with company executives who discontinued the line after a brief period. Before its demise, green and amber table settings had already flown out of factory headquarters. Sylvan is another acceptable name for this mold-etched design. Cagey antiquers are hoarding Parrot pieces while the supply is still plentiful. *Value guide: butter dish, covered, green, $225; pitcher, 80-ounce size, amber, $425.*

PATRICIAN PATTERN

According to Federal Glass Company reports, the Patrician depression glass design was conceived in 1932. One year later Golden Glow (amber), Springtime Green, pink, and crystal tablewares were being shipped to retail outlets. One must assume that the Golden Glow accessories poured in the profits, for it was the only color still in production by 1935. The round dinner plates with irregular edges were enlivened with an eight-spoked design in the center enclosed by a ten-pointed star. Patrician hexagonal water pitchers and cookie jars rate as formidable finds. *Value guide: butter dish, amber, $60; sherbert, crystal, $9.*

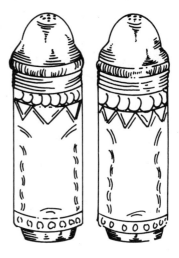

Patrician Pattern Salt and Pepper Shakers

PEDAL CARS

The American National Company, Garten, Kirk-Latty Manufacturing Company, and Sideway National Company were among the prominent pre-1930s makers pedaling pedal cars. These cars, modeled after authentic models, became fashionable in the first decade of the 20th century. One or two children could sit in these realistic cars and pedal down a sidewalk. To furnish a touch of realism, many were equipped with side doors, trim, nickel plated lamps, rubber tires, and imitation tool boxes. Although plastic pedal cars still glide along American sidewalks, the pre-Depression versions have collectors steering in their direction. *Value guide: fire engine, 1930, $375.*

PEPSI-COLA

Pepsi-Cola was introduced in 1898, in New Bern, North Carolina, by pharmacist Caleb Bradham. He developed a formula for a soft drink after mixing fountain drinks for several years. Four years later he abandoned his pharmaceutical career, establishing The Pepsi-Cola Company. By 1903, he was selling approximately 7,968 gallons of syrup annually. He had over 40 bottling plants in operation by 1907. Financial problems began plaguing the company about 1920. When Loft Candy Store executive Edward Guth acquired Pepsi-Cola in 1933, he introduced 12-ounce bottles. These bottles were widely promoted by Walter Mack, who purchased the corporation just one year later. In 1939, Pepsi-Cola challenged Coca-Cola with that unforgettable radio jingle: "Pepsi-Cola hits the spot/Twelve full ounces, that's a lot/Twice as much for a nickel, too/Pepsi-Cola is the drink for you." *Value guide: dispenser, radio shape, $145; sign, three dimensional bottle cap shape, 28" diameter, $65.*

PETALWARE PATTERN

Throughout the 1930s, MacBeth Evans kept retail outlets stocked with Petalware table settings. During the decade it was marketed in

Petalware Pattern
Creamer & Sugar

blue, cobalt, crystal, Cremax, Monax, green, pink, and fired-on blue, green, red, or yellow. Some of the later production had painted bands or florals. The design featured concentric circles from the center and finely scalloped edges. When MacBeth Evans became a division of the Corning Glass Corporation, variations of Petalware appeared. These Petalware offshoots were an effort on the part of glasshouses to manufacture tablewares that resembled ceramics, an indication of their sensitivity to the fact that the public was tiring of depression glass services by the end of the decade. *Value guide: bowl, Cremax, 8¾" diameter, $10; Monax, platter, oval, 13" diameter, $16.*

PET-NAME DOLLS

The "Pet Name" dolls—Dorothy, Agnes, Bertha, Marion, Helen, and Ethel—were distributed by the Butler Brothers of New York City, about 1905. Each had the name molded and painted in gold across her chest. These blonde- and black-haired beauties appeared in heights of 7½ through 21 inches. Some bore educational type cloth bodies printed with letters, illustrations, and names. Parents approved of the informative content of these bodies. Pet-Name dolls are easy to adopt, for a collar and a bow were molded along with the heads, accompanied by the wording "Patent App'd. For, Germany" on the back of the shoulder. *Value guide: Dorothy, china head, 10¼" tall, $165.*

PETTICOATS

Despite cries of protest from some quarters, the petticoat witnessed widespread acceptance in America during the 19th century. In the 1840s, ladies wore several at one time, the undermost usually being of flannel. The crinoline, a petticoat that was corded and lined with horsehair, was generally finished with straw braid at the hem. It developed into the "cage petticoat," which evolved into the "crinolette" by the 1860s. Lavishly designed silk and satin petticoats were fashionable by the turn of the century. Their elaborate borders, frilled or flounced with ribbon or lace, made the Gay Nineties even gayer. *Value guide: petticoat, 30 rows of tucking, circa 1885, $40.*

PEWABIC POTTERY

Mary Chase Perry, along with her neighbor, Horace James Caulkins, formed the Pewabic Pottery of Detroit, Michigan, in 1903. (Pewabic was an Indian name for a nearby river.) Their tiles, including fireplace, bathroom, and floor tiles, brought them untold triumphs. They also made fountains, friezes, and church altars, as well as some vases and lamps. Their tiles beautified such landmarks as St. Paul's Cathedral in Detroit, and the Oberlin College Art Gallery in Oberlin, Ohio. Miss Chase married William Buck Stratton in 1918. Following the death of Caulkins in 1923, she proceeded to operate the pottery. After her demise in 1961, the pottery became the property of Michigan State University. *Value guide: cigarette box, art deco bird, metallic glaze, $325; vase, gold drip over turquoise, 3½" tall, $250.*

PHOENIX BIRD PATTERN

The Phoenix, a mythological bird who was consumed by fire and rose again renewed from the ashes after nine days, surfaced as a decorative device on dinnerware services. Over 30 different varieties, notably of Japanese origin, were issued in blue and white Phoenix Bird tablewares. Local five- and ten-cent stores stocked the pattern in the early 1900s, when it was also freely distributed as a premium item. Over seven different variations have been soaring into collections, the most familiar being the Flying Phoenix (usually looking over his left wing) and the Flying Turkey (looking straight ahead.) The varying backstamps, "Nippon," "Made in Japan," and "Made in Occupied Japan" indicated that the Flying Phoenix was still winging its way onto tabletops into the 1950s. *Value guide: chocolate pot, Flying Turkey, circa 1920, $250; tea set, Flying Phoenix, three pieces, circa 1930, $100.*

PHOENIX GLASS COMPANY

When the Phoenix Glass Company of Pennsylvania, was founded in 1880, company officials concentrated on commercial lines such as kerosene lamp chimneys, tubular glass insulation, and electric

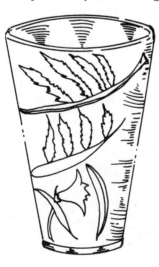

Phoenix Glass Vase

lighting adjuncts. By the mid-1880s, colored glass suitable for lighting accessories became a factory mainstay. From a collector's viewpoint, their colored line of molded sculptured glass offers choice rewards. Ornamental and utilitarian objects in this line date from the 1930s through 1950s. Sculptured glass is regarded as a scrumptious find by flea market shoppers. *Value guide: bowl, frosted and clear lily decor, 14" diameter, circa 1940, $185; vase, lovebirds, blue, 10" tall, $150.*

PHOTOGRAPHIC CHINA

From the 1860s, advertisements mentioned that photographs could be "faultlessly reproduced on china." These ceramic novelties were a welcome source of revenue for the souvenir trade. Practically overnight, famous landmarks were pictured on mugs, vases, plates, pitchers, cups, and saucers. These pictorial ceramic productions resembled travel guides, featuring famous locations from Mt. Vernon to Niagara Falls. Although numerous entrepreneurs tested the field, the American Photographic Company of New York City, outdistanced rivals in a photo finish for customers. Once relegated to thrift shop status, collectors are taking a positive approach toward photographic china. *Value guide: mug, Monticello, circa 1890, $40; plate, Mt. Vernon, 8" diameter, circa 1900, $50.*

PIANO BABIES

The bisque piano baby took up residence atop American pianos in the late 19th century. These bisque beauties, which appeared in positions ranging from playful to provocative, were made in various stages of dress and undress. Miniature types were modeled, along

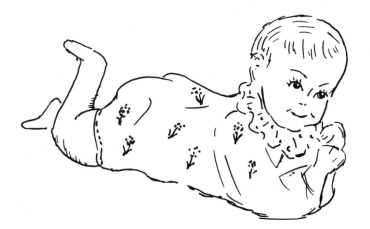

Piano Baby

231

with others that approached life size. Particularly prized are the fine-grained, superbly executed babies made and marked by the Gerbruder Heubach Works of Germany. The function of the piano baby, in addition to furnishing an elegant touch, was to lessen the tedium of piano practice for minor family members. *Value guide: bisque, lying on back, blue trim, Heubach, 7" long, circa 1895, $325; bisque, seated, holding feet, white nightie, 8" long, circa 1900, $190.*

PIANO STOOLS

Around the turn of the century, when piano playing included every age group, the adjustable height revolving stool came into widespread acceptance. More affluent students revolved about on richly carved walnut or mahogany stools with a velvet or tapestry seat. Fringed borders adorned many models, while others incorporated beaded designs. The all wooden types, however, supported the bulk of piano players. They were typically crafted of oak or mahogany, with turned legs terminating in claw and ball feet. Many tickled the ivories on stools that originated at factories scattered around Grand Rapids, Michigan. *Value guide: walnut, velvet seat, circa 1890, $165; wooden, oak, claw and ball feet, circa 1900, $85.*

Piano Stool

PINCUSHION DOLLS

A pincushion doll is a half figure of china or bisque made with holes around the bottom edge for sewing on the bodies. The bodies were usually made of fabric, many having full-brimmed skirts. Dressel, Kister & Co., Ernst Bohne & Sons, Gerbruder Heubach, W. Goebel Porzellanfabrik, and other German potters made them in various sizes. Somewhat elusive are those depicting famous women, Garden Girls, animals, children, men, and flappers. Unusual hairdos, outstretched arms, fancy hats, and dolls holding objects rate as rarities. Although many bore the country of origin as "Germany," few makers bothered to include a factory trademark. *Value guide:*

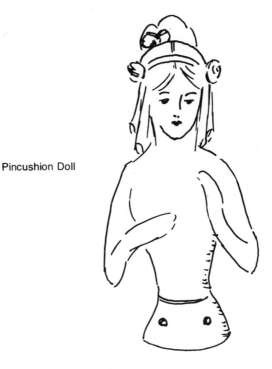

Pincushion Doll

flapper, red hair, green dress, Germany, 4" tall, $90; Spanish queen, arms away, beaded gown, holding fan, 6" tall, $350.

PINEAPPLE AND FLORAL PATTERN

The Pineapple and Floral pattern presently parades under such descriptive names as Windflowers and Many Flowers. They seem appropriate, for the dominant decorative theme is comprised of

Pineapple & Floral Pattern Creamer

flowers surrounded by a pineapple-type decor. Originally, it was referred to as Indiana Glass Company's Number 618 pattern. Between 1932 and 1937, it was produced in crystal, sometimes fired on red and amber. As for the olive green and milk white specimens, it is assumed that they are of more recent vintage. Those diamond-shaped sugars, creamers, and compotes add sparkle to any depression glass display. *Value guide: cream soup, crystal, $15; vase, cone shaped, amber, large, $30.*

PINOCCHIO

Pinocchio's debut on the silver screen prompted a preponderance of character merchandise in 1940. This marionette and his troupe of cohorts were depicted on rubber balls and figures from the Seiberling Latex Products Company. Fountain pens, bookends, brush sets, figurines, and plaques of molded wood fiber circulated about from the Multi-Products Company. George Borgfeldt and the Ideal Toy Corporation cashed in on the Pinocchio doll trade with several different depictions. Collectors have been known to pull a few strings attempting to snag Pinocchio storybooks, cut-out books, banks, statuettes, records, ring-toss games, handkerchiefs, jewelry, and wristwatches. *Value guide: doll, cloth, $85; game, board, complete, $55.*

Pinocchio Doll

PITMAN, BEN

A fretwork frenzy hit the American populace in the closing decades of the 19th century. One of the powerful forces behind this art recreation movement was Ben Pitman. Under his tutelage at the Cincinnati School of Design, pupils were encouraged to participate in a variety of highly ambitious projects. Pitman's geometric and floral patterns were published in the *Art Amateur* in 1880. Would-be woodcarvers, under the eye of this facile artist, crafted cabinets, chairs, church lecterns, mirror frames, screens, tables, doors, and mantels. In 1873, at Pitman's first woodcarving class, over 100 women were enrolled as woodworkers. *Value guide: wallpocket, ornate, circa 1885, $175.*

Pitman Wall Pocket

PLANTERS PEANUTS

Amedeo Obice, Italian-American businessman, came to America at the age of 11. In partnership with his future brother-in-law, Mario Piruzzi, he founded Planters Nut & Chocolate Company in Wilkes Barre, Pennsylvania, 1906. Business prospered, and by 1912 Obici was operating his own shelling plant. To avoid a middle man, he purchased the raw peanuts directly from farmers. He developed a novel selling approach, selling peanuts in bags or in blue tin cans and vacuum jars. After relocating to the heart of the peanut-growing country in Suffolk, Virginia, Mr. Peanut was introduced in 1916. Through the years, this advertising symbol, sporting a monocle and top hat, was featured on a bounty of advertising souvenirs. The company was acquired by Standard Brands in 1961. *Value guide: jar, embossed peanut, four-sided, $275; sign, Planters Peanuts, pennant, tin, 9½" × 8½" diameter, $55.*

Mr. Peanut Doll

PLUTO

Pluto, yet unnamed, was introduced in Walt Disney's 1930 feature "The Chain Gang." He became "Rover" the same year in "The

Pluto Cloth Toy

Picnic," and one year later he achieved his well-earned identity as "Pluto" in "The Moose Hunt." His heart belonged to just one, Fifi, who made her debut in the 1933 film "Puppy Love." Pluto's popularity persisted until 1956, when Disney discontinued cartoons. The cavorting canine was afforded the honor of being depicted on a considerable amount of character merchandise. Early marionettes from the Alexander Doll Company, as well as hand puppets from the Gund Manufacturing Company, are prized. Dolls from the Richard G. Krueger, Inc. of New York City, wholesaled at $14.40 per dozen in the '30s. Collectors also get a howl from Pluto watches, figurines, rubber toys, and pitchers. *Value guide: planter, Pluto and cart, 6½" tall, $18; handcar, Donald and Pluto, boxed, $1,750.*

POCKET KNIVES

Collectors on the prowl for pocket knives are familiar with such names as Alcas, Colonial, Case, Ka-Bar, Queen, and Schrade. They are among the outstanding of the modern pocket-knife manufacturers. Knives by Winchester and Remington, two companies no longer in production, also cut a fancy figure with knife buffs. In this collecting category, form is most important. Some of the most desirable options are folding hunters (one and two blades), peanuts, trappers, Barlows, canoes, elephant toes, Coke bottles, gun stocks, Texas toothpick holders, and Daddy Barlows. Decorative elements also play an important part in determining the worth of a find. In addition to the better-known makers, scores of other manufacturers have made significant contributions in the field of pocket knives. *Value guide: Ka-Bar, #21107, Grizzly, $2,000; Remington, #3333, scout, $120.*

POCKET MIRRORS

Celluloid-backed pocket mirrors were among the popular giveaway items of yesteryear. They promoted every conceivable enterprise from Coca-Cola to vaudeville shows. These round, oval, or rectangular mirrors generally measured under 3 inches in diameter. Principal American makers included Whitehead & Hoag, American Artworks, St. Louis Button Company, and the Culver Manufacturing Company. A maker's name often appears at the rim of a mirror's edge, although some are half hidden under the mirror. Despite rapidly escalating prices, flea marketeers are taking a second look at advertising mirrors. *Value guide: Ballard's Graham Flour, $45: Pittsburgh National League Champions, 1909, $125.*

POCKET PRESTO CAMERAS

The Pocket Presto camera was an exclusive with the Scovill & Adams Company in the late 1890s. Shutter bugs were informed that it was "a midget in size, a giant in capacity." This lightweight camera, measuring 1¼× 2½× 3¼ inches, weighed a mere 5 ounces. The Pocket Presto was sold with a "handsomely finished and loaded case for 25 exposures, together with one film magazine and one glass plate magazine and primer, with instructions, securely packed." The uninitiated were advised that film and glass plates "could be used at will." Best of all, it retailed for $2.50. *Value guide: Pocket Presto Camera, circa 1900, $900.*

PONTIAC INDIAN CHIEF MASCOTS

Early car or company mascots continue to keep collectors all revved up. One of the best known is the Pontiac Indian Chief, which has appeared in numerous variations throughout the years. The original running Indian figure was supplanted by an Indian Chief's head. A plastic rendition suggests a date of production into the 1930s or 1940s. Aware antiquers, ever with an ear to the ground for investment opportunities, pay premium prices for the earlier bronze-faced interpretations. *Value guide: Indian Chief, plastic, 1930s, $40; bronze, faced, 1920s, $85.*

POPE-GOSSER POTTERY

Charles Gosser and I. Bently formed the Pope-Gosser China Company of Coshocton, Ohio, in 1902. Early productions bore the trademark "Clarus-Ware." By 1908, the pottery name was typically incorporated into the backstamp. They followed a traditional path, preferring to market utilitarian articles for home use. A merger with other potteries was undertaken in the late 1920s. By 1933 however, the original owners had regained control. All production ceased in 1958, at which time Pope-Gosser wares entered the collectible realm. *Value guide: mayonnaise set, florals, three pieces, circa 1935, $20.*

POPEYE

On January 17, 1929, the fabled Popeye was introduced into the Thimble Theater strip. The appearance of this fighting, wise-cracking sailor made Thimble Theater one of the famous strips of the '30s. Max Fleischer's animated cartoons originated at the Paramount Studios in 1932, and they are still enjoying worldwide success. Popeye's spinach-eating-for-strength image boosted spinach sales during the Depression. Amidst all this acclaim, his creator, Elzie Crisler, passed away in 1938. He had designed Popeye watches and toys. Popeye, Olive Oyl, and Wimpy have been depicted on games, timepieces, chalkware figurines, wind-up toys, and various other collectibles. *Value guide: cycle, Spinach, Hubley, 5½" tall, $375; toy punching bag, floor type, Marx, $450.*

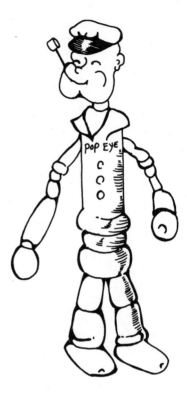

Popeye Wooden Jointed Doll

POSTCARDS

The first postcard to travel legally through the mail was posted in Austria, in 1869. One year later, they were being sent in England, with America following suit in 1873. While paper postcards proliferated, other materials such as birchbark, leather, fabrics, wood, mother-of-pearl, woven silk, and celluloid were utilized. Some had accents of fur, feathers, human hair, peat moss, jewels, and tinsel. Some makers attempted mechanical variations. Foldout cards, hold-to-light cards, and puzzle cards are also held in high esteem by dedicated deltiologists. The coveted Raphael Tuck cards were originally made at the request of Queen Victoria. Members of the postcard fraternity often prefer specializing in a particular artist, publisher, subject, or type of postcard. Early cards picturing disasters, planes, automobiles, or world's fairs are eagerly acquired. The first colored photographic postcard made its debut in 1939. *Value guide: Billiken, 1908, $12; Santa Claus, standing, Tuck, $18.*

POTTER, BEATRIX

Tales of Peter Rabbit, by Beatrix Potter, became a juvenile best seller in 1901. It was followed at regular intervals by 20 other "hare-raising" fables. All of the books bore illustrations by the author. Frederick Warne & Company of London and New York, has continued publishing the titles complete with original illustrations. Beatrix Potter's parade of characters, including Jemima Puddleduck, Squirrel Nutkin, and Tom Kitten have adorned various ceramic collectibles over the years. Children's bowls, plates, mugs, and other accessories may be located bearing the famed Wedgwood backstamp. Although currently in production, the early bone china figurines from Beswick & Company are begining to fetch fabled returns. *Value guide: book, "Tale of Benjamin Bunny," Potter, $40.*

Beatrix Potter Figurine

POUYAT, J.

From the 18th century, Pouyat has been a respected name in French potting circles. Following in the family tradition, Jean Pouyat and Associates opened a porcelain works in the Limoges district in 1842. Pouyat tapped untold profits by concentrating on the American export market. Boatloads of beautiful porcelains satisfied the late 19th century craving for "civilized, refined, and evaulated *objets d' arts.*" Ceramic collectors delight in discovering objects bearing one of the varying Pouyat trademarks. *Value guide: chocolate pot, violets, circa 1890, $65; teapot, roses, circa 1900, $55.*

POWDER FLASKS

American and English factories engaged in manufacturing die-stamped and metal flasks shot into prominence during the 19th century. Flasks of copper and pewter were fabricated in various sizes and shapes. Generally speaking, they fall into three categories: patriotic, sporting, and pocket-pistol. Domestic makers issued them in a string of star-spangled designs, such as eagles, flags, anchors, crossed rifles, and cannons. Hunting motifs abounded, with dogs, deer, horses, squirrels, and various animals leading the pack. Any marked powder flask is certain to trigger collector response. *Value guide: brass, hunting scene, $65; copper, flags and cannons, America, circa 1885, $135.*

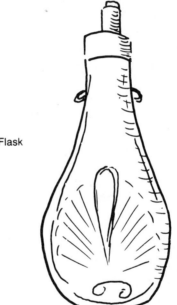

Powder Flask

PRESLEY, ELVIS

Elvis Presley made his first commercial recording, at the age of 19, in 1954. "That's All Right, Mama" and "Blue Moon of Kentucky" brought him only mild success. He moved on to sign an agreement with RCA-Victor one year later. Billed as "Elvis the Pelvis," he gained fame through television appearances. By 1956, when his "Love Me Tender" and "Heartbreak Hotel" were topping the charts, Elvis started his lengthy film career. From the late '50s through '60s, he was a dominant factor in the rock and roll music scene. Following his untimely death, a collecting mania for his memorabilia swept through the country. Items pertaining to "The King," ranging from buttons to calendars, reign supreme at flea markets. *Value guide: hat, 1957, $50; pillow case, $20.*

241

PRESSED-BACK CHAIRS

Around the turn of the century, American furniture factories were inundated with orders for pressed-back chairs. Various woods were used, notably oak, walnut, birch, and elm. In fact, almost any hardwood could be pressed into the desired design. At the top of the line price-wise, were the all-wood versions with intricate carved effects. As numerous factories participated in the pressed-back profit picture, variations abounded with upholstered, caned, or leather seats. Furniture forms, including rockers, desk chairs, dining chairs, armchairs, and children's chairs, were widely distributed and priced between $2.25 and $13. *Value guide: armchair, oak, ornate, circa 1900, $135; rocker, pressed-back, circa 1910, $160.*

Pressed Back Rocker

PRINCESS PATTERN

The Princess pattern normally receives a royal reception from depression glass devotees. Between 1931 and 1935, financially troubled Americans found this Hocking Glass triumph both attractive and affordable. After all, the octagonal shapes did blend perfectly with art deco accents. The central motif resembled a snowflake flanked by eight spokes. Table settings were sold in blue, pink, crystal, green, and topaz. Completing a service in the Princess design qualifies as a crowning achievement for any flea market follower. *Value guide: cookie jar, green, $40; sugar and creamer, pink, $20.*

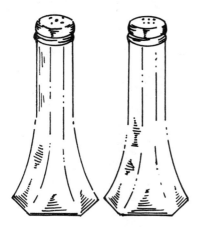

Princess Pattern Salt & Pepper Shakers

PUNCH AND JUDY BANK

The Shephard Manufacturing Company of Buffalo, New York, was an early manufacturer of American mechanical banks. They were active from the early 1880s. Their Punch and Judy bank, featuring the figures in a yellow booth with red and blue trim, was patented by Peter Adams and Charles Shephard on July 15, 1884, and July 22, 1884. The top lever sets the figures in position. Judy turns forward with a tray, while Punch raises the club he is holding. When a coin is placed in the tray, and the lower lever pressed, Judy attempts to deposit the coin by turning backwards, and Punch tries unsuccessfully to hit her with his club. *Value guide: Punch and Judy bank, cast-iron front, tin back, 7¼" tall, circa 1890, $950.*

QUAKER OATS

In 1877, Henry D. Seymour and William Heston formed The Quaker Mill Company of Ravenna, Ohio. The trademark registered for their oatmeal depicted the "figure of a man in Quaker garb." By the mid-1880s, Quaker Oats became one of the first cereals to be sold in cardboard canisters. Three years later, all seven American oatmeal producers merged to form the American Cereal Company. Quaker's dietetic pastry flour, an advance over self-rising flour, won awards at the Chicago World's Fair of 1893. H. P. Crowell and Robert Stuart organized the Quaker Oats Company in 1901, selling brands under the Quaker Oats title. In 1911, they acquired the rival Mother's Oats brand. Quaker Puffed Rice and Quaker Puffed Wheat came on the market in 1913, and was advertised as "The grains that are shot from guns." Further expansion occured in 1926 when they acquired Aunt Jemina Mills. *Value guide: cookie jar, Quaker Oats, $40; mug, Quaker Oats, $12.*

QUEEN MARY PATTERN

The Hocking Glass Company launched its Queen Mary depression glass pattern in 1936. Almost overnight it seems, 36 different pink tableware items floated from assembly lines; several years later, crystal accessories made their debut. Some antiquers prefer the more descriptive name, Vertical Ribbed. This title seems fitting, for plates have a sunburst of radial lines surrounded by a circular band and another, even wider, circle of radial lines. Those with a knowledge of depression patterns realize that it bears a resemblance to Heisey's "Ridgeleigh" line. With nostalgia buffs, Queen Mary ranks as a first class collectible. *Value guide: cup and saucer, pink, $10.*

QUEZAL GLASS

Collectors break into a quickstep at the sight of Quezal glass. Between 1901 and 1925, the Quezal Art Glass and Decorating Company of Brooklyn, New York, produced iridescent glass specialities. Martin Bach, who had worked for Louis Comfort Tiffany, founded the factory with an associate. Naturally, their creations bore a resemblance to Tiffany's productions. Reportedly, when the first Quezal articles reached American outlets, Mr. Tiffany flew into a temper tantrum. It is, therefore, understandable why glass connoisseurs have deemed Quezal Tiffany's major imitator. Glass collectors seldom quibble over the price of a signed Quezal speciman. *Value guide: bowl, King Tut, 7½" diameter, $1,000; vase, pulled feather, 7" tall, $900.*

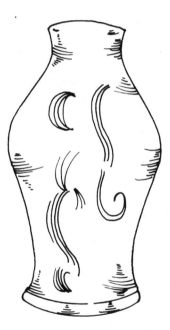

Quezal Vase

QUIMPER POTTERY

Enchanting earthenwares have originated in the town of Quimper, France, for centuries. Typical motifs included Breton peasant themes, animals, and folklore representations. Although recurring motifs were used, standardization was impossible because the

Quimper Quintal

pieces were hand decorated. For almost 300 years, the principal factories were Jules Henriot et Fils and Fraicenceries Bretonne De la Grande Mason. The initials "H B" signify the two families, Hubaudiere and Bouquet, who have long been identified with the works. Both utilized systematic markings that included "Henriot" or "H B" in underglaze blue, along with the name "Quimper." After 1892, the country of origin, "France," was typically incorporated into the backstamp. *Value guide: bank, peasant decor, all over yellow, signed, $200; teapot, Dutch girl, tulips, 6%" tall, $225.*

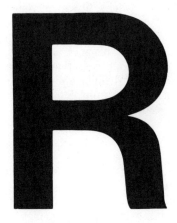

RADIOS

When Pittsburgh's KDKA took to the airways in 1920, it became America's first commercial radio station. Seemingly overnight, manufacturers such as Atwater-Kent, RCA, Radiola, and Magnavox answered the public's plea for receivers. Early battery-operated types had wood or hard rubber receivers. Tube sets came into general use by 1927, and table models and consoles were made to blend with existing art deco furniture styles. Collectors are truly turned on by the small cathedral styles, originally known as midgets or depression models. Other finds for the dialing-for-dollars set include original plastic models, portables, and automobile radios. *Value guide: Atwater Kent, cathedral, $85; Stromberg-Carlson, table model, 125, $200.*

Philco Cathedral Radio

RAILROAD BADGES

Prior to the introduction of badges and uniforms for railroad employees, the workers were almost indistinguishable from passengers. Cap and breast badges, however, quickly eliminated this dilemma. Badges and buttons of brass, nickel plate, and enamel were worn by watchmen, brakemen, station agents, and other railway personnel. Railroad buffs seek any badge bearing the name of a particular railroad, or one having an unusual job designation. Badges from unknown railroad lines or mentioning unusual job titles never fail to make a collector stop, look, and listen. *Value guide: badge, baggage man, PRR, brass, $35; police, C. & N.Y., brass, 3¼" diameter, $180.*

RAILROAD WATCHES

People with a passion for timepieces spend time tracking down old railroad or railway watches. In the second half of the 19th century, numerous American watchmakers manufactured them to meet the stringent requirements of railroad companies. Therefore, names such as Elgin, Waltham, and Hamilton can be spotted on models. These watches gained respect for their amazing accuracy. European attempts, notably by Swiss and German makers, to erode the American market failed. Their versions, often inscribed "Railway Timekeeper," suggested superior performance but proved incapable of delivering it. High-grade domestic railroad watches, in working condition have been growing more valuable with time. *Value guide: Elgin, railroad pocket, 23 jewels, 5 position, 10K gold case, $175; Waltham, Riverside movement, pocket, 18K gold case, circa 1880, $500.*

RAISIN SEEDERS

Although raisins were purchased year round, many pounds were sold during holiday festivities. Homemakers used them for such

Raisin Seeder

treats as mince pie, raisin buns, puddings, and plum cakes. Cast-iron seeders, generally with crank handles, worked efficiently and rapidly. Raisins were seeded the second they dropped into the hopper. Some bore the inscription "wet the raisins" molded into the machine. Various clamp-on models proved popular, although manufacturers continued to offer newly improved versions on a regular basis. The Enterprise No. 36 model, patented in 1895, seeded "a pound in five minutes." *Value guide: Enterprise No. 36, $40; Lightning, Pat. 1898, clamp-on style, $35.*

RAVCA, BERNARD

Those who rummage after dolls hold Ravca dolls in high esteem. Bernard Ravca of Paris, France, began making dolls' heads in 1924. Marguerite from *Faust*, Maurice Chevalier, and Mistinquette were among his earliest works. Some of his original heads depicted young people or French peasants. This French dollmaker produced dolls' heads of cloth with stockinette faces. When Ravca met Frances Diecks, a New York artist and dollmaker, they fell in love, married, and continued making dolls together. Ravca's life-sized "Real People Dolls," American Presidents, World War II historic leaders, "Portrait Dolls," and "French Province" dolls are sought. Frances is famous for the "Ballet Dolls," President's Wives," and "Spirites, Pixies and Fairies." Ravca's playthings typically bore a separate cloth label bearing the maker's name. *Value guide: French peasant, all original, stockinette face, 23" tall, $350.*

RECLINING CHINAMAN BANK

The Chinese were caricatured on this J. & E. Stevens Company mechanical bank dating from the 1800s. The Reclining Chinaman, clad in a black kimono and blue pants, was patented by James H.

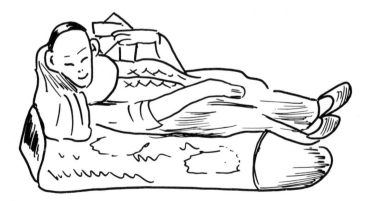

Reclining Chinaman Bank

Bowen in 1882. The bank, based on topical events, suggested the Chinaman held the aces, thus winning the hand over American labor. (Americans feared for their jobs during this era when large numbers of Chinese immigrants worked for minimal wages.) After placing a coin in the Chinaman's left hand, a lever is pressed at the right end of the log on which he is reclining. At this point, his right hand moves down to reveal four aces. At the same time, he left hand moves up to his face, while the coin falls into the bank, and a rat emerges from the left side of the log. *Value guide: Reclining Chinaman, 4¼" tall, cast-iron, $1,200.*

RED BLOCK PATTERN

Mention ruby-stained glass and the Red Block pattern instantly springs to mind. Around the turn of the century, this design practically outdistanced others in popularity. The ruby-stained blocks provided it with an unmistakable appearance. (Some glass companies, however, also produced clear glass variations.) Many pieces surrendered to inscriptions and dates, because souvenir items were the rage of the moment. Who marketed it? Such respected American glasshouses as Doyle & Company, Fostoria Glass Company, and the Model Flint Glass Company. Ruby-stained rummagers have been known to walk a block or more attempting to complete a Red Block table setting. *Value guide: butter dish, covered, $80; pitcher, water, $110.*

RED WING POTTERY

The Red Wing Stoneware Company of Red Wing, Minnesota, began operating in 1878. After repeated mergers, they surfaced as the Red Wing Union Stoneware Company in the 1920s. Initially, flower pots and vases bore a green stain over a tan background. Many were decorated with cattails, leaves, flowers, and cranes. As orders increased, cookie jars, ashtrays, jardinieres, mugs, trays, bowls, and candlesticks were offered. Dinnerware services reached the marketplace in the 1930s. By the mid-1930s, the factory operated as the Red Wing Potteries, Inc. Since Red Wing closed in 1967, their articles have been winging their way into private collections. *Value guide: cookie jar, Bobwhite, $55; vase, cobalt blue, flowers, 13" tall, $65.*

REGISTERING BANKS

The registering bank, unlike still or mechanical banks, automatically adds up the amount of money deposited in it. In addition, it also provides the saver with the total amount at a glance. Various mechanisms were used to operate these banks. While the cash register form was most favored, beehives, trunks, and beanpots also stimulated thrift-minded youngsters. Perhaps the Uncle Sam's 3 Coin Registering Bank has had the lengthiest duration of acceptance in this category. Originally marketed by the Durable Toy & Novelty Company about 1907, it is now being made by their successors, the Western Stamping Company of Jackson, Michigan. The bank has submitted to some subtle changes over the years. Since some registering banks have a minimal action, they are of interest to those mesmerized by mechanical banks. *Value guide: Self Accounting Keene Registering Bank, lithographed tin, building form, 6-¼" tall, $125; registering bank, cast-iron, Gem, pat. 1893, $375.*

RHEINISCHE GUMMI UND FABRIK

Celluloid toys, new to playrooms of the late 1800s, had to fight for existence, because parents feared they would prove flammable. Major advancements were scored by American and European manufacturers that resulted in unflammable celluloid by the first decade of the 20th century. A leader in this field was the Rheinische Gummi and Fabrik of Germany, founded in 1873. By the early 1900s they ranked as a foremost creator of celluloid dolls' heads. Their turtle trademark supposedly represented the long life and durability of the company's playthings. Numerous technical achievements were scored, such as the introduction of glass eyes for celluloid heads in 1905. Dolls having the turtle trademark, singly or within a diamond, are anything but slow movers. *Value guide: doll, dressed, 13" tall, $125.*

RIBBON PATTERN

Those who rummage after the Ribbon depression glass design have uncovered pieces in green and black. The pattern is in short supply, because Hazel-Atlas kept it in production only during 1930-1931. Approximately ten different luncheon accessories reached retail shops. Ribbon does boast a decidedly art deco appearance. This was achieved by furnishing plates with a center sunburst of radial lines, with similar border effects joined together in a hairpin design. No one can deny it; ribbon creamers and sugars do bear a striking resemblance to two other Hazel-Atlas patterns, namely Cloverleaf and New Century. *Value guide: candy dish, green, $20; sugar and creamer, green, miniature, $30.*

RING PATTERN

When the Ring depression glass design made its debut in 1927, it was called Circle. The name was befitting, for most pieces had from four to eight horizontal rings. By 1929, the number of rings had been reduced to two. The ring design provided the green and crystal accessories with an art deco flair. Some crystal pieces sported platinum rings. Later, black, yellow, orange, red, and pink rings enlivened tablewares. Ring, a pressed and thin-blown pattern, was discontinued in 1932. Decanters, cocktail shakers, and ice buckets made Ring the thing for cocktail parties of the era. *Value guide: decanter set, blue, $30; ice bucket, green, $6.*

RIVIERA PATTERN

Seekers of American dinnerware place Riviera on the Fiesta family tree. Between 1938 and 1950, Riviera services rolled off Homer-Laughlin assembly lines. This Fiesta look-alike was sold exclusively through Murphy Company stores. They differed from Fiesta and Harlequin, as the plates were square. Cups bore similar shapes. Cupboard cleaning chores may well unearth a piece in mauve blue, dark blue, ivory, red, yellow, or light green. If so, chalk it up as a flea market find. *Value guide: mug, handled, light green, $40; tumbler, juice, yellow, $35.*

ROBJ

The porcelain bibelots executed for Paris dealer Robj during the 1920s and 1930s form a fascinating collecting category. Basically,

Robj Bottle

they fall into two types; amusing utilitarian enameled porcelain figures, and cream-colored porcelain decorative statuettes influenced by modern Cubist themes. Ten or more liquor bottles included a monk, policeman, three-faced sailor, and Scotsman. Robj ceramics spanned other avenues because inkwells, ashtrays, cocktail shakers, and incense burners were among this Parisian's stock in trade. Renowned artists submitted designs for these offerings at regular competitive exhibitions held by Robj. The "Robj" mark accompanied by "Made in France," denotes a ceramic conquest from this French outlet. *Value guide: liquor bottle, Turk, $85; lamp, Cowboy, 1930s, $225.*

ROGERS SOUVENIR SPOON

Practically every major American silversmith exhibited at the Chicago World's Fair of 1893. The Wm. Rogers Manufacturing Company had an ebony-black pavilion with an anchor, the trademark of the company, borne aloft in a conspicuous manner. Visitors to their display were presented with a souvenir spoon with an anchor handle. It was made and distributed free of charge as an advertising device for the firm's "Anchor Rogers" silverplate. The 25 patterns in this line were exhibited in a case. Prominently featured was their Columbia pattern, designed specifically for this event. One commentator noted, "They had the most attractive line of novelties and useful articles for the smaller class." *Value guide: souvenir spoon, 1893, $20.*

Roger's Anchor Souvenir Spoon

ROLL-TOP DESKS

The roll-top desk, known for its ample space and convenience, became an American favorite in the late 1800s. A typical example had a flat top with a tambour front that rolled back into the desk. Black walnut was heavily preferred, although cherry, mahogany, and later oak versions enjoyed popularity. Many of the Golden Oak desks originated at furniture factories centered in or around Grand Rapids, Michigan. Some manufacturers utilized various woods. Initially, the roll-top desk was produced for office or store use. The

Eastlake types, fashionable in the closing decades of the century, frequently had solid roll-back tops. Long a thrift shop staple, the roll-top desk has made the transition to antique status. *Value guide: roll-top desk, oak, S-curve, oak, 50" × 54", circa 1910, $2,000; roll-top, S-curve, upper letter boxes, oak, 60", circa 1900, $3,800.*

Roll Top Desk

ROOKWOOD POTTERY

The renowned Rookwood Pottery of Cincinnati, Ohio, was founded by Maria Longworth Storer in 1880. The familiar "RP" monogram of this pioneer American art pottery producer was instituted in 1886. each year thereafter, one flame mark was added about the monogram, until 14 flames appeared by 1900. Subsequently, a Roman numeral under the symbol furnished the year of manufacture. Many objects also bore shape marks, process marks, clay marks, or decorator's marks. Throughout its productive period, pottery officials attempted to keep abreast of changing styles, utilizing various clays, designs, and glazes. Recent forgeries have been uncovered, therefore caution is advised for those about to embark on a search for Rookwood remembrances. *Value guide: mug, running antelope, Onkapapa, 1898, signed, 5" tall, $950; vase, primroses, brown ground, signed, 1903, 6½" tall, $475.*

Rookwood Pottery Vase

ROSEMARY PATTERN

Rosemary depression glass articles bounced onto store shelves from the Federal Glass Company between 1935-1936. This chip-mold design was patterned from Federal's short-lived Mayfair molds. Place settings were available in Rose Glow (pink), Golden Glow (amber), Springtime Green, and crystal. (Some collectors prefer the descriptive name Dutch Rose.) Roses provide the major decorative element, while rims featured them between overlapping loops. Sugar bowls were made without handles or lids, thus they are sometimes mistaken for sherbets. *Value guide: bowl, oval, 10" diameter, $12; plate, grill, green, $7.*

Rosemary Pattern
Creamer & Sugar

ROSEVILLE POTTERY

When the Roseville Pottery was organized in 1892, flower pots, stoneware jars, and cuspidors were marketed. George F. Young

Roseville Pottery Teapot

256

decided to initiate art pottery lines in the tradition of Rookwood and Weller. Under the supervision of R. C. Purdy, an underglaze, slip-decorated ware known as Rozane was potted. The name was derived from the pottery's two locations in Roseville and Zanesville, Ohio. By 1910, the entire operation was centered in Roseville. Variations followed, including Rozane Mongol, Rozane Fugi, and Rozane Mara. Frederick H. Rhead, art director between 1904 and 1908, introduced Della Robbia, Aztec, Olympia, Mostique, Carnelian, and Pauleo. His Donatello line was hugely successful by World War I. The trademark "Roseville U.S.A." was adapted in 1918. Subsequently, embossed designs dominated the pottery's output through its closing in 1954. *Value guide: Donatello cuspidor, $100; vase, Blackberry, 8" tall, $165.*

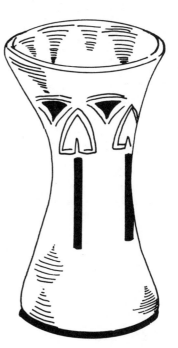

Roseville Mostique Vase

ROULETTE PATTERN

In early Hocking Glass Company advertisements for Roulette depression glass, it was described as a "winning pattern." The name was befitting, for the radial lines on plates conjured up images of roulette wheels. Some collectors prefer the title Many Windows. Luncheon sets appeared in 1936. Pieces have been uncovered in crystal, green, and pink. Approximately six different size tumblers were marketed, the smallest being 2½-inch tall whiskey glass.

Roulette ceased spinning out of the factory about 1938, when production was abandoned. *Value guide: measuring cup, green, $8; tumbler, pink, 12-ounce, $9.*

ROWLAND & MARSELLUS

Around the turn of the century, blue printed historical wares marked Rowland & Marsellus became fast sellers in American shops. The ware, ascribed to the British Anchor Pottery Company of Longton, England, has attracted a loyal following of antiquarians. Various American landmarks were featured when cities from coast to coast were honored by the potters. One plate was executed in honor of Theodore Roosevelt. Quite frequently, the name of the retailer was incorporated into the backstamp. One specialty of the company was the rolled edge plate with a central building or scene and related views in cartouche on the rolled-over edge. *Value guide: plate, historic Kalamazoo, $85; plate, Theodore Roosevelt, $65.*

ROYAL BAYREUTH

The presently active Royal Bayreuth porcelain factory was established in Tettau, Bavaria, in 1794. Through the years many marks incorporated the founding date of the works. Collecting interest centers around the imaginative lines marketed by the company between the 1880s and World War I. Their inexpensive figural souvenir lines encompassed such forms as animals, fruits, vegetables, and people. Numerous tableware articles were conceived. They also produced floral, scenic, and portrait wares. Articles featuring the Card and Devil motif, Sunbonnet Babies, Sand Babies, and Snow Babies fetch premium prices. The Scenic and Rose tapestry pieces, created by covering the porcelain with a piece of tightly stretched fabric prior to decorating and glazing, sell on sight. Although unmarked specimens exist, items bearing the Royal Bayreuth crest mark in varying colors and designs delight porcelain pursuers. *Value guide: Devil and Cards water pitcher, 7¼" tall, $425; Rose tapestry powder box, covered, $240.*

ROYAL CROWN COLA

Claude A. Hatcher, a Columbus, Georgia wholesale grocer, began bottling soft drinks under the Royal Crown name in 1905. Eventually, he organized the Union Bottling Works. By 1912, Royal Crown Cola and Chero-Cola were being bottled by the works. After reorganization, the company operated as the Chero-Cola Company. Franchises were issued to other Georgia bottlers. By 1914, Chero-Cola sales topped the 611,000 mark. Six years later the figure jumped to over 4 million. The drink, Nehi, was introduced in 1924. It proved so popular that the company was renamed Nehi

Corporation in 1928. Royal Crown Cola was introduced in 1934, but that name was not adapted by the company until 1959. *Value guide: thermometer, 25" tall, $35.*

ROYAL LACE PATTERN

Between 1934 and 1941, the Hazel-Atlas Glass Company had competitors doing a double take with its mold-etched Royal Lace depression design. Table settings were available in pink, green, amethyst, crystal, burgundy, and deep blue. (The latter appeared during the final production years.) Royal Lace earned its name; pieces had lacy scrolls, leaves, and flowers almost covering the entire surface. The round dinner plates bore scalloped edges. Why is Royal Lace so plentiful? Because throughout its lengthy reign, it was a Sears, Roebuck, & Company staple. *Value guide: butter dish, green, $325; plate, blue, 10" diameter, $18.*

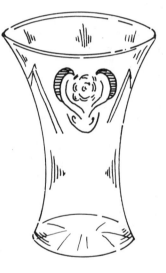

Royal Lace Pattern Tumbler

RUBY-STAINED GLASS

A number of important American glasshouses participated in the vogue for ruby-stained articles around the turn of the century. Many noteworthy patterns submitted to staining, including Red Block, Ruby Thumbprint, Plume, and Button Arches. Dozens of other patterns appeared in complete table settings. Regardless of the design, all had sufficient space for etched or engraved inscriptions, dates, and names. Souvenir lovers acquired pieces from famous spots such as Asbury Park, Atlantic City, or Gettysburg. Others were inscribed at fairs or expositions. Dated examples suggest that the ruby-stained fad was in high gear between the 1890s and 1910.

Ruby Stained Bowl

Value guide; mug, Atlantic City, 1901, $35; tumbler, World's Fair, 1893, plume pattern, $40.

RUSTIC FURNITURE

As early as the 1840s, A. J. Downing noted that "rustic seats, placed here and there in most inviting spots, heighten the charm of any interior." Rustic furnishings had their roots in the Western movement in America. Wood crafters joined branches together to fabricate chairs, settees, tables, footstools, and other accessories. Personalized touches were undertaken that resulted in many one-of-a-kind renditions. Those having a way with woods frequently achieved mosaic effects by blending vari-colored woods. In recent years, rustic furniture has branched out, capturing collectors' im-

Rustic Table

260

aginations. *Value guide: armchair, circa 1890, $250; rocking chair, circa 1900, $265.*

RUTH, GEORGE HERMAN "BABE"

In 1920, Jacob Ruppert, owner of the New York Yankees, signed George Herman Ruth for $25,000. Also included were promises of a large loan. Thus, the former Boston Red Sox pitcher began a memorable 14-year career with the Yankees. Overflow crowds came to Yankee Stadium over the years to view the "Sultan of Swat." As for that record-breaking 60th home run, it was hit by Ruth in 1927, off a pitch by Washington's Tom Zachary, thus establishing a record that was to stand for 30 years. Babe Ruth wristwatches, watch fobs, watch cases, medals, plaques, books, buttons, belt buckles, and other mementos rate as big league finds. *Value guide: book, "The Babe and I," Clare Ruth, $15; Babe Ruth plaque, oval, plaster-of-Paris, copper colored, $135.*

S PATTERN

The unnamed S pattern from the MacBeth Evans Glass Company
has been dubbed the Stippled Rose pattern by depression buffs. The
rather complicated design, composed of a small circular center
surrounded by leaves and fine stippling, also has leaf, or stippled
effects on the outer rims. When combined with scroll motifs, they

S Pattern Tumbler

provide the S pattern with its descriptive name. This mold-etched marvel was marketed in pink, topaz, crystal, Monax, and crystal with blue, green, amber, or platinum trim. A few pieces have been reported in cobalt blue and cherry. Between 1930 and 1933, the S pattern became a five-and-ten-cent store sensation. *Value guide: plate, crystal, 9¼" diameter, $7; sugar and creamer, amber handle, $12.*

SAFE BANKS

Safe banks were considered safe repositories for coins of the late 19th century. Several hundred different varieties were made by such bank manufacturers as the J. & E. Stevens & Company, A. C. Williams, Kenton Hardware, and the Wing Manufacturing Company. Most of these cast-iron representations of office safes were painted or decorated with simplified stenciled motifs. They were made in a variety of sizes. Many bore such impressive names as Jewel Safe, Army Safe, National Safe, and Household Security Safe. Some models opened only when the hands of the clock were set at the appropriate hour. Occasionally, one could be classified as a semimechanical bank, such as the Watch-Dog bank with its barking semimechanical dog. *Value guide: safe, Daisy, cast-iron, $60; safe, Security Safe, 4¾" tall, $75.*

Security Safe Deposit Bank

SATSUMA

Boatloads of richly ornate Satsuma reached American shores from Oriental ports in the second half of the 19th century. Reportedly, the ware was named for a war lord who brought Korean potters to Japan in the 1600s. Ceramic critics regard it as the most exquisite faience ever produced. Functional and decorative objects, usually cream or ivorycolored, were enlivened with enamel colors and gold. Earlier pieces were more delicate and restrained. After 1854, when Admiral Perry opened trade with Japan, entire surfaces were covered with brightly enameled depictions of Japanese legends. Figural Satsuma was made specifically for the export market. From buttons to boxes, Satsuma sells on sight. *Value guide: bowl, multifloral design, 7" diameter, $165; chocolate pot, decor of children, $220.*

SAVORY ROASTERS

Over 3 million Savory roasters from the Republic Metalware Company of Buffalo, New York, were in use by the early 1920s. This maker of fine kitchen utensils, was justifiably proud of this handsome dark porcelain roaster. The Savory was touted as being the "Original self-basting, self-browning, time and trouble saver!" The results were easy and quick. Their mouth-watering ads mentioned that the "juices of the meat constantly trickled over the roast, giving it that delicious, rich meaty Savory flavor that one misses with ordinary roasters." *Value guide: Savory, circa 1923, $45.*

SCARLET O'HARA DOLL

Scarlet O'Hara, the belle of Tara, was immortalized in doll form by the Alexander Doll Company of New York City. This beautiful doll

Scarlet O'Hara Doll

was based on Margaret Mitchell's famed heroine from the novel *Gone With The Wind*. The all-composition plaything was marketed in several sizes. It had a jointed neck, shoulders, and hips, green sleeping eyes, closed mouth, and black wig. She was dressed in a gown worthy of her Southern heritage. Cinema buffs compete with doll devotees over Scarlet O'Hara dolls, thus they rate as big ticket items at the flea market box office. *Value guide: doll, original clothes, 18" tall, 1939, $350.*

SCHLEGELMILCH PORCELAINS

The Schlegelmilch porcelains marked R. S. Prussia, R. S. Germany, R. S. Suhl, R. S. Tillowitz, and R. S. Poland were produced between 1861 and 1918. They were made at their respective factories in the Germanic provinces of Prussia, Thuringia, and Silesia. The various R. S. marks often denote the political upheaval of the era. The wares were manufactured under the guidance of Erdmann and Reinhold Schlegelmilch. A nephew, Oscar, started a factory in Langewiesen, Thuringia, about 1892. The majority of this finely modeled and beautiful porcelain was factory decorated. A few blanks were furnished for home decorating. Pieces marked R. S. Poland suggest a date of production between 1916 and 1918. Although the red-marked "R.S. Prussia" pieces are sought, the other "R. S." wares also command collector attention. Recently fakes have been reported in the form of new decal marks and transfers. *Value guide: R. S. Germany bowl, church scene, 9½" diameter, $200; R. S. Poland vase, swans, 7½" tall, $265; R. S. Prussia, plate, castle scene, 8½" diameter, $650.*

R. S. Prussia Tankard

SCHNEIDER, CHARLES

Charles Schneider (1881-1962), famed French art deco glass artist, studied his craft at Nancy and Paris. He did designing work for the Daum Brothers. Schneider established his own works, the Cristallerie Schneider, in Epinay-sur-Seine, near Paris, in 1913. Utilitarian and decorative objects often revealed themes involving color flecks, or streaks between two layers of glass. Some glass vessels were blown into wrought iron mounts for the Daum factory. Unusual colors dominated his output, such as reds shading to orange, orange to yellows, green to blue or smoke, and crystal. Signed Schneider specimens attract the eye of serious glass seekers. *Value guide: compote, amethyst, knobbed stem and pedestal, 9" tall, $300; vase, mottled blue and amber, metal holder, 7½" tall, circa 1925, $285.*

Schneider Vase

SCHOENHUT, ALBERT

Albert Schoenhut, born in Germany in 1849, arrived in America some 17 years later. His family had been involved in woodcarving, a career that was also pursued by Albert. In 1872, he established a factory in Philadelphia. In 1903, the Humpty Dumpty Circus appeared, followed five years later by Max and Moritz. Subsequently, a Farmer and Milkmaid on a Farm set and Mary Had a Little Lamb set appeared. Another Schoenhut toy, Teddy's Adventures in Africa, had 53 pieces, including a portrait doll of Theodore Roosvelt.

It was Schoenhut's first spring-jointed doll. Price lists of 1911 featured "All-Wood Perfection Dolls" painted in enamel colors. Upon Schoenhut's death in 1912, he was succeeded by his six sons. Toy pianos were made in over 40 different sizes. Numerous toys, some based on comic strip characters, were made in the 1920s and 1930s by this still-active concern. *Value guide: toy piano, swivels, $150; Roly Poly Clown, $525.*

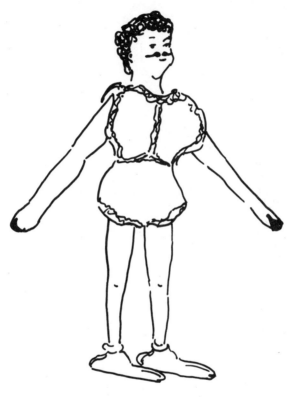

Schoenhut Acrobat

SCHOOLHOUSE CLOCKS

Schoolhouse clocks adorned the walls of American homes, schools, and offices between the 1880s and 1930s. Seth Thomas, Gilbert, Waterbury, E. N. Welch, Ansonia, and the New Haven Clock Company offered them in a variety of sizes. Makers used various woods, favoring oak, pine, cherry, rosewood, mahogany, and walnut. Variations abounded as makers endeavored to lend some individuality to schoolhouse clocks. As a general rule, the drop below the face of the clock was either four or five sided. The clock works varied from eight-day, time only, time with strike, and time with calendar. Caution is advised, for the current Japanese and Korean reproductions defy detection. *Value guide: Ansonia, eight day, oak case, 26", $360; New Haven, satinwood inlaid with oak, 27", $275.*

Schoolhouse Clock

SEA CHESTS

Sea chests of 19th century origin were frequently handcrafted by the sailors who depended upon them for storage. As a general rule, early chests had sloping sides to provide stability on stormy seas. Flat tops were favored, for many doubled as worktables or seats in crowded quarters. While American versions were customarily of unpainted wood, it was not unusual to find the inner lids either carved or painted. German or Dutch chests were normally carved or painted on the interior and exterior. Intricate, handmade ropework handles suggest an authentic specimen. Sailors arriving home from Oriental ports often brought brass-fitted camphor wood chests to American shores. *Value guide: chest, hinged lid, fitted inside, camphor wood, 42"× 17", circa 1880, $650.*

SEBASTIAN FIGURINES

Prescott W. Baston started production on Sebastian figurines in 1938 in Marblehead, Massachusetts. As a source of inspiration, he was influenced by characters from literature, history, children, or scenes from everyday life. From the outset, his figurines were made in limited editions. Most measured between 3 and 4 inches in height. These handpainted, lightly glazed figurines possess enormous charm. In 1981, the first figurines designed by his son, Woody, reached the marketplace. At present, the Sebastian Studios are located in Hudson, Massachusetts. *Value guide: clown, 6205, $150; Sidewalk Days, $95.*

SEROCO CARPET SWEEPER

The distributors of the Seroco carpet sweeper waged a vigorous advertising campaign in the early 1900s. People were advised that it "took more dust and dirt than any broom." It was handsomely finished in a number of durable woods, complete with fine quality metal trim. Work-weary homemakers found that the newly improved roller bearings enabled it to "run far easier than an ordinary sweeper." Sears, Roebuck, & Company even provided a guarantee of satisfaction with this super sweeper. Who could ask for anything more for $2.48? *Value guide: Seroco Sweeper, working condition, circa 1910, $40.*

SEWING BIRDS

Sewing birds often fall into the realm of confusing collectibles. Homemakers were indefatigable sewers, thus sewing birds were essential items for the sewing set. A spring mechanism on these aids kept one end of the fabric taut while being sewn. This saved sewers hours of agitation. Brass, plated silver, iron, wood, and other materials were used in constructing these attachments for clamping onto a table or stand. Sometimes a scrimshaw version crafted by a sailor on a long voyage could be found perched atop a sewing machine or worktable. *Value guide: brass, embossed, $120; steel, clamp-on type, 1880s, $180.*

Brass Sewing Bird

SHARON PATTERN

Sharon, a chip-mold pattern, was kept in production between 1935

269

and 1939 by the Federal Glass Company. Local five-and-ten-cent stores stocked it in green, amber, pink, and crystal. Because cabbage roses dominated the design, some collectors call it Cabbage Rose. Borders boasted garlands of roses divided by six spokes. Covered cheese dishes, candy jars, and large water pitchers rate as the pick of the crop with collectors. *Value guide: candy dish, covered pink, $40; salt and pepper shakers, pair, green, $50.*

Sharon Covered Candy Dish

SHAWNEE POTTERY

The Shawnee Pottery of Zanesville, Ohio, began operations in the late 1930s. Until 1950, Addis Hull of the Hull Pottery was in charge of production. Shawnee took the commercial route, selling everyday pottery pleasers through five-and-ten-cent stores and Sears, Roebuck, & Company. Special order, decorated pottery was available to consumers. Flea marketeers find their Corn King and later Corn Queen lines most appealing. These dishes, ashtrays, and kitchen wares are easily recognizable because they resemble an ear of corn. When the pottery closed in 1961, pieces made the transition from dining room tabletops to flea market tabletops! *Value guide: cookie jar, owl, $60; teapot, Corn King $60.*

SHEET MUSIC

American songs began to be illustrated with lithographed covers in the late 18th and early 19th centuries. Hand-colored examples are coveted. Sheet music cover art, designed primarily to help sell a song, reflects the social fads, attitudes, political events, and cultural mores of the nation during the 19th and 20th centuries. By the late 1800s, hundreds of lithographers were engaged in printing sheet music; among the prolific were Currier, Prang, Bouve, Sharp, Bufford, Pendleton, Endicott & Sweet, John Penniman, and Edward Weber, and Blake & Willis. Photography had supplanted hand designs by the turn of the century. Interest in early 1900s sheet music often centers around innovative cover designs and photographic records of the performers who sang the songs. Desirable artists include Rockwell, Flagg, Gunn, King, Frew, Manning, and Buck. For many collectors, the thrill of old sheet music lies primarily in its sentimental value. *Value guide: Euphonic Sounds, Joplin, $90; Little Annie Rooney, Pickford cover, 1925, $20.*

SCHUCO

Schreyer & Company of Germany, one of the world's foremost toy concerns, was founded in 1912. From its inception, Schuco was adapted as the company's trademark. Interestingly, some early clockwork toys were wound by turning the arms or tail, rather than the conventional key. Realism prevailed, especially during the 1920s, when a Dancing Mouse, Pick-Pick Bird, and Trotting Dog vied for crowded playroom floor space. Another Schuco sensation, cleverly constructed sports cars, based on Mercedes racing cars, came complete with miniature tool kits. Their Steerable Driving School Car, with a starting crank, changeable tires, differential gears, and rack-and-pinion steering also chalked up considerable carpet mileage. *Value guide: Three Little Pigs, felt covered, clockwork, 4½" tall, $300; robot, wind-up, shoots sparks, $60.*

Schuco Bulldog Toy

SIERRA PATTERN

The highly regarded Sierra depression pattern was introduced by the Jeanette Glass Company in 1931. It was an eye-catching pinwheel design that created a three-dimensional effect. Some collectors prefer the more descriptive name Pinwheel. These distinctive art deco tablewares were marketed in pink, green, and crystal. Problems evolved, however, that necessitated the withdrawal of the line from production in 1933—the sharply pointed edges proved prone to chipping, which explains why Sierra falls into the "short supply" category. *Value guide: cup and saucer, pink, $9; plate, 10" diameter, green, $7.*

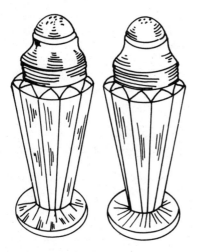

Sierra Pattern Salt & Pepper Shakers

SILVER DEPOSIT GLASS

The silver deposit process was developed in the 1880s. A decade later, glass articles exhibiting naturalistic motifs gained a substantial audience. The technique involved depositing silver, through electroplating, on a silver flux design that had earlier been applied to the glass. Clear and colored backgrounds were chosen to blend with the prevailing themes. The Alvin Manufacturing Company of Providence, Rhode Island, scored major accomplishments in this field. Glass connoisseurs never withdraw from purchasing a piece of silver deposit glass. *Value guide: decanter, tulips, green, 10" tall, $140; vase, florals, cobalt, 6" tall, $65.*

SNOW BABIES

In the early 1900s a collecting fad developed for the 1" to 2 inch tall Snow Babies. They were typically dressed in sugary white snowsuits. These skiers, skaters, dancers, and sled riders frolicked in a hundred happy antics. As their fame spread, they appeared on postcards, Royal Bayreuth china, and other ceramic novelties. Originally, they were known as "Zucker Puppen" (sugar candy dolls) throughout Germany. At Christmas time they were hung on trees or stood in creches. A confectioner prevailed upon a porcelain maker to fabricate them in bisque, to be used as window decorations. China emporiums found themselves knee deep in Snow Babies through the 1930s. *Value guide: figurine, on polar bear, $95; pitcher, quart size, Royal Bayreuth, $285.*

SNOW WHITE

Walt Disney received another Academy Award for the feature that premiered at the Cathay Circle Theater in Hollywood, on December 21, 1937. Profits from the feature were used to build a new home for Disney Productions. The release of "Snow White and the Seven Dwarfs" unleashed a barrage of character merchandise. Within a year, people were purchasing handkerchiefs from the Bernard Wolf Company or silverplated forks or spoons from the International Silver Company. Dolls depicting Snow White and her cavorting crew were made by Richard G. Krueger, the Ideal Novelty & Toy Company, and the Knickerbocker Toy Corporation. The Alexander Doll Company pulled more than a few strings with its set of marionettes. Perhaps one of the most unusual items was the Emerson Snow White radio, which youngsters could turn on to listen to "Whistle While You Work." *Value guide: doll, composition, Knickerbocker, molded hair, 12" tall, $185; radio, Emerson, $550.*

Snow White Doll

SOCIABLE BIKE

Talk about riding in tandem! The Sociable Bike of the 1890s placed riders side by side with sufficient space between for a sibling or umbrella. Thus, it could be easily converted into a bicycle for two, or even three. On this daringly different bicycle, both riders shared the peddling and steering chores. Credit for this ingenious design must be given to the Punett Cycle Company. This form of togetherness, however, failed to attract an audience. It was withdrawn from production after only a short time; therefore, a Sociable Bike is rarely bargain priced nowadays. *Value guide: Sociable Bike, working condition, $1,500.*

SOUVENIR SPOONS

Souvenir spoon collecting started in the 1890s, when vacationers began returning from a holiday with a spoon remembrance in hand. It developed into a nationwide trend, much to the delight of American silversmiths. Sterling silver souvenir spoons were made in teaspoon, coffee spoon, and orange spoon sizes. Others were of silverplate. Historical spoons pertaining to cities, states, places, and people abounded, along with other commemorating events, theatrical personages, or holidays, including Easter or Christmas. Zodiac spoons were available to those having an astrological bent. Good Luck, Wedding, Friendship, and Love spoons were also available. Several companies issued Engagement spoons under such titles as "The Cupid Engagement" and "The Oracle of Love." *Value guide; Boston Tea Party, sterling silver, $28; Liberty Bell, sterling silver, $35.*

SPARKLING ORANGEADE BOTTLES

During the 1920s, Canada Dry marketed a refreshing drink known as Sparkling Orangeade. Based on existing reports, it is believed that these marigold bottles in the carnival glass tradition originated at the Northwood Glass Company. While the bottles appear on a regular basis, few have survived with their paper labels intact. The smaller top label read: "Turn upside down before opening. Contains orange juice, aroma of the peel, a dash of lemon juice, pure cane sugar, and carbonated water." That mouth-watering full-size lower label picturing one full and one cut orange bore the words, "Canada Dry's Sparkling Orangeade, with the natural fruit pulp." *Value guide; bottle, labels intact, marigold, $15.*

SPEAKING DOG BANK

The highly respected Speaking Dog mechanical bank was subjected to a lengthy production run. A patent for this pleasing plaything was received by Peter Adams and Charles G. Shepard in 1885. The original manufacturer was the Shephard Manufacturing Company of Buffalo, New York. When the firm was absorbed by the J. & E. Stevens & Company, this bank was kept in production. A lever in front of the dog is pressed to activate the bank. A girl wearing a red dress and yellow hat drops a penny into a tray, at which time the dog's mouth opens and closes as if he were speaking. In addition, his tail begins wagging. The base of the bank bore the wording "Speaking Dog." *Value guide: Speaking Dog Bank, cast-iron, 7¼" tall, $575.*

SPIRAL PATTERN

The Hocking Glass Company introduced the Spiral depression pattern in 1928. Two years later it had all but vanished from the scene. Those swirled lines forming a pinwheel effect around the borders gave it a thoroughly modern appearance. Caution is advised, for several glasshouses sold very similar designs. During its brief production run, green table settings were marketed. The earlier creamers and sugar were straight sided, but later, footed versions were made. Prices on Spiral pattern mixing bowls, syrup jars, ice buckets, and sandwich servers have been spiraling ever higher. *Value guide: butter, covered, green, $14; salt and pepper shakers, green, $30.*

SPOON HOLDERS

Receptacles for holding spoons appeared in a variety of shapes in

Double Spoon Holder

the second half of the 19th century. Spoon holders of the double-handled type won all popularity contests in the 1850s and 1860s. A decade later, fancier versions dotted silver catalogs, including some involving bells or of the revolving type. They were somewhat taller and slenderer than waste bowls. Spoon holders can be distinguished from sugar bowls because there was no rim where the lid rested. Double spoon holders were the rage of the 1880s. Practically every major maker produced them in countless styles, including Reed & Barton. This company listed 45 different styles in 1885. Many were sold as part of a tea service. Combination sugar bowl/spoon holders, spoon boats, and spoon trays were holding spoons from night to noon by the 1890s. *Value guide: Bell spoon holder, cherub, Reed & Barton, 1885, $150; double spoon holder, squirrel decor, Wilcox, 1880, $145.*

STANGL BIRDS

John James's *Audubon's Birds of America*, with its 435 plates showing 480 species of American birds, was published in England, by Havill, between 1827 and 1838. Practically overnight, ceramic artisans began fashioning birds in Audubon's style. During World War II, the Stangl Pottery of Trenton, New Jersey, offered finely modeled birds based on his prints. They generally bore the artist's initials in underglaze blue. In addition to the pottery birds, a few porcelain representations appeared. Each bird bore a paper string tag noting its name, along with the potter's name and location. All birds were stamped with the potter's mark on the base, such as "Stangl Pottery Birds," "Stangl," or "Stangl Pottery," depending on the size of the subject. *Value guide: Key West Quail Dove, No. 3454, $300; Parakeets, double, No. 3582d, blue, $200.*

STARLIGHT PATTERN

By the late 1930s, customer enthusiasm for colored glassware was declining in America. But this fact did not deter the Hocking Glass Company from issuing the Starlight design. It twinkled only briefly, however, remaining in production from 1938 to 1940; thus starlight accessories are in short supply. Pieces have been uncovered in crystal, pink, cobalt blue, and opaque white. The round plates bore waffle centers, surrounded by a crossed-over stipple border. This stippling created a plaid effect. Depression buffs gleam at discovering a set of Starlight salt and pepper shakers. *Value guide: bowl, crystal, 11½" diameter, $11; plate, white, 9" diameter, $4.50.*

STAR TREK

American television viewers caught their first glimpse of "Star Trek" when it premiered on NBC on September 8, 1966. By the second season the "Enterprise," along with its cast of recognizable characters, were threatened with possible cancellation. Star Trek fans, however, (known as "Trekkies"), mounted a mail campaign that extended the show for another season. Even 100,000 letters each week failed to convince NBC executives to continue the flight of the "Enterprise." Mr. Spock, Captain Kirk, and their entourage were sent into syndication, where they triumphed admirably in the United States and around the world as well. Basically, Star Trek collectibles fall into three categories: those attributed to the original NBC television program; items issued in the wake of syndicated reruns, and those which pertain to the successful film versions. *Value guide: lunch pail with thermos, $75; Tracer Gun, $15.*

STEIFF, MARGARETE

The Steiff Company, active since 1880, originally made stuffed elephants. Later donkeys, horses, pigs, and camels were produced. By the turn of the century a menagerie of animals were originating at this German establishment. Dolls with felt heads, characterized by a seam down the middle of the face, were introduced in the 1890s. By 1903, Steiff operated outlets in Berlin, Hamburg, Leipzig, London, Paris, Amsterdam, and Florence, ultimately winning a Grand Prize for their display at the St. Louis Exposition of 1904. Teddy bears were featured in this exhibit. By 1908, when 2,000 employees were employed by the company, Margarete personally inspected every doll and animal that left the premises. A jointed, mohair Teddy Bear was selling at the annual rate of 974,000 pieces by 1907. When Margarete's nephews assumed control of the business following her death in 1909, the bear's head became the firm's symbols and the "Button in the Ear" trademark was adapted. *Value guide: kangaroo, baby in pocket, 20" tall, $500; cat, early, 12" tall, $150.*

STEREO CARDS

The stereo illusion can be achieved from photographs on metal, transparent tissue paper, glass, and, most commonly, from albumen prints mounted on cardboard. These view-worthy collectibles, capable of creating an illusion of depth, were introduced to America by such early photographers as the Langenheim brothers. The initial efforts, as well as theme cards, fetch the fanciest returns. Any attributed to a celebrated photographer is also prized. A glass stereo plate is more valuable than a paper stereo card, while the tissue transparencies are preferred over paper prints mounted on cardboard. *Value guide: Austria, with map and book, 75 cards, $65; San Francisco earthquake, 75 cards, $200.*

STEREOSCOPES

The stereoscope became widely accepted when Queen Victoria

expressed an interest in it at the Great London Exhibition of 1851. A short time later, the London Stereoscopic Company was formed, using as its slogan "No home without a stereoscope." Based on advertisements, the company had 100,000 photographs in stock. Adults used the more sophisticated brass and mahogany, velvet-lined viewers, while children were given the inexpensive versions of hardwood with folding handles and sliding view-holder or the pocket-sized models. This optical instrument was to become a standard form of Victorian parlor amusement. Millions of stereo-scope views were published. *Value guide; Keystone, Monarch, aluminum hood and lens, $85.*

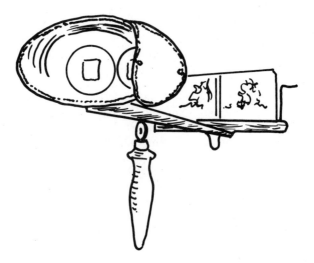

Stereoscope

STERLING CUT GLASS COMPANY

In 1904, Joseph Phillips and Joseph Landenwitch founded the Ster-ling Cut Glass Company of Cincinnati, Ohio. Their timing was on target, for Brilliant Period cut glass kept the cash registers ringing during this period. Through 1950, the company created numerous cut glass patterns, each one more intricately cut than the next. Glass cutters in their employ demonstrated their dexterity with patterns such as Arcadia. Later Mr. Phillips acted as a sales rep-resentative for the Rookwood Pottery Company. Cut glass objects bearing the company's name in script or block print rate as sterling investments. *Value guide: compote, Arcadia, covered, $325.*

Sterling Cut Glass Butter Dish

STICKLEY-BRANDT FURNITURE COMPANY

Around the turn of the century, the Stickley Brothers carved a niche for themselves in the annals of American furniture. Functional oak objects in the Mission style became synonymous with the Stickley name. Charles Stickley broke with tradition, however, favoring late Victorian styles. Many of his Golden Oak forms bore traces of the Eastlake influence. In 1884, he formed a partnership with the Brandt family of Binghamton, New York. They operated under the title Stickley-Brandt Company. Charles suffered a fate similar to Gustav's—by 1919 his factory was forced into bankruptcy (see below). *Value guide: desk, ladies, cylinder roll, Eastlake, oak, $850.*

STICKLEY BROTHERS

The Stickley brothers, Albert and George, established a furniture factory at Grand Rapids, Michigan, in 1901. Operating as the Stickley Brothers they concentrated on Craftsman furniture, along with pieces imitative of the English Cottage style. They sought mass marketing techniques, thus differing in strategy from brother Gustav's concepts (see below). Furniture bearing the title "Quaint Furniture," or "Arts and Crafts" accompanied by the "Stickley Brothers" indicates a find from this factory. In 1907, the year the factory shuttered, George published *The Craftsman Home. Value guide: dining table, oak, oval top, 44" diameter, circa 1905, $150.*

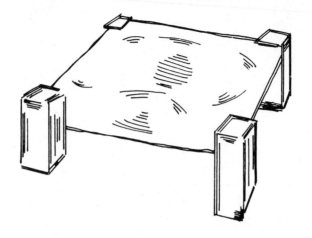

Gustav Stickley Footstool

STICKLEY, GUSTAV

Although Gustav Stickley founded a furniture factory in Eastwood, New York, in 1898, the first public showing of his Craftsman forms occurred in Grand Rapids, Michigan, in 1900. Commenting on the style, he stated, "I had no idea of attempting to create a new style, but merely tried to make furniture which would be simple, comfortable, and fitted for the place it was to occupy and the work it had to do." His Mission pieces were crafted of native American woods, often oak, with coverings of leather, canvas, or simple cloths, and fittings of copper or iron. By 1913, Stickley was advising the public to look for his trademarks: "Craftsman," the shop mark of the motto

Stickley Manufacturing Company Desk

"Als ik kan" (As I Can), or the written Stickley signature. Despite the warnings, competitors forced him into bankruptcy by 1916. *Value guide: bed, five vertical slats on headboard and footboard, circa 1910, $3,750; chest of drawers, oak, three long graduated drawers, paper label, 43" tall, $3,300.*

STICKLEY MANUFACTURING COMPANY

Gustav Stickley's brothers, Leopold and J. George, opened a furniture factory in Fayetteville, New York, in 1900. Their output, suggestive of Gustav's Mission furniture, bore the "L. & J. G. Stickley" name in red. Following in their brother's tradition, they favored veneers and laminated woods. Included in their line was the ever popular Morris chair. They also crafted a quantity of reproductions. Other forms were based on Frank Lloyd Wright designs. In 1916, they acquired the Gustav Stickley factory and operated it as the still-flourishing Stickley Manufacturing Company. *Value guide: armchair, wing, oak, clamp decal mark, circa 1910, $450; magazine rack, oak, rectangular decal mark, 45" tall, $475.*

STILL BANKS

Still banks have been fabricated of pottery, glass, tin, iron, wood, paper, and various metal alloys. Some of the earliest pottery types were fashioned by country potters. Many of the metal models date from the late 1800s and early 1900s, their popularity coinciding with the somewhat more valuable mechanical banks. The J. & E. Stevens & Company, A. C. Williams Company, Kenton Hardware Company,

Pottery Still Bank

Billiken Still Bank

and Arcade Manufacturing Company were among the principal makers. Some of the most imaginative lithographed tin banks have been ascribed to Chein Industries of New Jersey. The cast-iron types were often produced at foundries, some painted, others treated to a "gold bronze" or "aluminum bronze" finish. The subject matter was almost endless, with a special emphasis on animals, buildings, and figures. Historical and comic characters were featured in the latter category. Still banks still manage to fetch fancy returns. *Value guide; pig, blue glass, circa 1910, $40; Santa with tree, cast-iron, circa 1900, $120.*

STRAUSS, FERDINAND

Around the turn of the century, Ferdinand Strauss was responsible

Strauss Leapin' Lena Car

for American toy trunks bulging beyond belief with imaginative playthings. This prolific producer manufactured clockwork, wind-up, and other tin toys in sizable quantities. (Louis Marx was initiated into the toy business while in the employ of Strauss.) Many toys were based on popular personalities of the period. Emerging from this New York-based concern were such toys as the Walking Camel, Leaping Lena Car, Ham & Sam, Jazzbo Jim, and Jenny the Balking Mule. Their Negro toys and band toys were innovative enough to spur similar themes from rival companies. Strauss toys in working condition are capable of activating any toy buff. *Value guide; Ham And Sam, $265; walking camel, $240.*

STRETCH GLASS

Stretch glass, with its iridescent onion skin surface, was manufactured by numerous respected American glasshouses, such as Cambridge, Fenton, Imperial, and Northwood. Even the eminent Steuben Works added it to production schedules in the early 1900s. Stretch glass seekers scour the marketplace for bowls, compotes, perfume bottles, candlesticks, rose bowls, trays, and plates. American-made pieces typically bore mold marks, while the blown glass imports had pontil marks. Shoppers stretch their necks and dollars endeavoring to locate a find in this field. *Value guide: bowl, gold, 11½" diameter, $70; sherbet, red, melon, ribbed, $60.*

STRING HOLDERS

Budget-minded collectors are likely to become unstrung over some of the prices being posted on vintage string holders. A century ago, holders of various materials such as silver, pewter, iron, tin, wood, glass, and brass were household essentials. The familiar beehive shape held its own against fanciful fruit, animal, floral, or figural variations. The costliest holders had their own cutting blades. Those desiring to tie one on at the local general store often did so with an advertising model. Like calendar plates and calendars, some string holders traveled the well-worn premium giveaway route. *Value guide: beehive, clear glass, cobalt rim and collar, circa 1890, $175; apple, iron, circa 1900, $35.*

STROMBERG-CARLSON TELEPHONES

It was Alexander Graham Bell who singlehandedly turned the general store into a communications center in the late 19th century. Stromberg-Carlson telephones with hang-up receivers, adjustable mouth pieces, and crank handles were a newfangled contraption to rural communities. Many early oak and walnut telephones sported silverplated or brass-trimmed receivers. Examples with a shield or plate identifying the maker as Stromberg-Carlson fetch prices that

Stromberg-Carlson Telephone

suggest collectors are dialing for dollars! *Value guide: candlestick-type, nickel plated trim, dial, $150; wall-type, oak case, plain, $225.*

STUDENT LAMPS

Kerosene-burning student lamps, designed to give a soft light, won the approval of scholars in the late 19th century. A typical model had a central stem set on a base, branches that held the oil tank on one side, and a font on the other. Although various metals were used, most makers favored bronze or brass. Single and double styles were characteristically fitted with long, narrow chimneys. The double types were most impressive. Brass reflectors or green glass shades were preferred by students intent on burning the midnight oil. *Value guide: single style, green glass shade, circa 1890, $300.*

STUDIO CABINET CARDS

The studio cabinet card had its major American exposure between the mid-1860s and 1900. Generally, these posed-for portraits, usually measuring 6½ × 4½ inches, were mounted on polished cardboard. As a means of subtle advertising, most bore the photography studio's name along with the photographer's name. A recognizable name generates increased collector interest. Theatrical personages, military leaders, political figures, and other celebrated characters often had their names on the front beneath the portrait. Studio cabinet cards displaying unusual subjects, period furniture, vintage toys or dolls, or fabulous fashions of the era never draw a negative response from photography buffs. *Value guide: Buffalow Bill, $70; child, Sarony Studio, $10.*

SUNBONNET BABIES

The beloved Sunbonnet Babies were created by Bertha L. Corbett. Early black and white drawings of the babies, Mollie and Mae, adorned Valentines and Christmas cards. A colored primer, *The Sunbonnet Babies Primer*, written by Eulalie Osgood Grover and illustrated by Corbett, became a best seller in the first decade of the 20th century. Sequels followed, as the fame of the babies spread. Color reproductions of the Sunbonnet Babies chores—Washing Day, Ironing Day, Mending Day, Scrubbing Day, Sweeping Day, and Baking Day—were published in 1904. The postcard series depicting these views are sought. The babies, whose faces were forever hidden by their bonnets, were issued on Royal Bayreuth children's china, including mugs, plates, pitchers, candlesticks, and dresser trays. *Value guide: book, "Sunbonnet Babies in Holland," Grover, 1915, $120; pitcher, Royal Bayreuth, Doing Washing, 3 3/5" tall, $265.*

Sunbonnet Babies Bell

SUPERMAN

Two 17 year olds, writer Jerry Siegeland and artist Joe Shuster, have been credited with creating the superhero, Superman. The strip soared into *National Comic's Action* in June, 1938, which made Superman the original costumed hero. The strip had three dominant themes. These included a vision from another planet, the superhuman being, and the dual identity. A daily strip was initiated in 1938, and three years later it was billed as "The World's Greatest Adventure Strip Character." The Man of Steel's fame spread into other areas, including a radio program in 1940, animated cartoons,

Superman Toy Figure

several series, a television series, a Broadway play, and immensely successful films. Superman buttons, comic books, gum cards, toys, timepieces, games, and puzzles are acquired by flea marketeers faster than you can say "Clark Kent." *Value guide: bank, ceramic, $75; doll, wood jointed, 1940s, 12" tall, $450.*

SWIRL PATTERN

The Swirl depression design swirled into prominence in 1937. Just one year later, this Jeanette Glass Company design was discontinued. Flea market shoppers have unearthed over 25 different tableware accessories in pink, ultra-marine, and Delphite (blue-opaque). The swirl motif was achieved by incorporating concentric circles with characteristic border swirls. Swirl pattern candlesticks, footed consoles, and vases cause questers to break into a quickstep. Salt and pepper shakers, especially those with their original domed tops, are capable of spicing up any antiquing adventure. *Value guide: butter dish, ultra-marine, $200; salt and pepper shakers, pink, $25.*

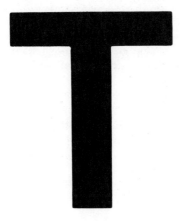

T

TAMMANY BANK

The Tammany mechanical bank from the J. & E. Stevens Company positively drips with political overtones. Needless to say, the introduction of this penny saver dating from the 1870s, coincided with headlines involving Boss Tweed and New York City's Tammany politicians. When news pertaining to the scandals subsided, the bank was renamed "Fat Man." Under one title or the other, it remained in production for about 40 years. The seated figure on this cast-iron creation wore a yellow vest, gray pants, and blue jacket. The coin was deposited into his vest with his right hand as he

Tammany Bank

graciously nodded a "thank you" to penny depositors, one and all. *Value guide: Tammany bank, circa 1880, $200.*

TARZAN

Early Tarzan comic strips by Hal Foster and Burne Hogarth have been subjected to repeated reprints in paperback and hardbound form. The strip was an outgrowth of Edgar Rice Burrough's books, which in themselves rate as choice acquisitions. Tarzan buffs seek the 50 card set, "Tarzan and the Vault of Isis," conceived for the Schutter-Johnson Candy Corporation in the mid-1930s. Another set of strip cards, "Tarzan of the Apes," was issued by Stephen Slesinger, Incorporated., without stories on the reverse side. The Blue Ribbon Books, Incorporated pop up books, as well as the Big Little Books featuring Tarzan, Jane, Boy, and Cheeta, have also been swinging into collections. *Value guide: Big Little Book, "Tarzan and the City of Gold," $14; map, Tarzan Jungle Map and Treasure Hunt, 1933, $275.*

TEA ROOM PATTERN

The decidedly art deco Tea Room depression glass pattern was produced by the Indiana Glass Company between 1927 and 1931. This heavy, machine-made glass was conceived for use in restaurants, soda fountains, and ice cream parlors. Of course, pieces were also sold for home use. Over 25 forms appeared in pink, green, amber, and crystal. That geometric shape, so reminiscent of the era, was achieved by a Block Optic style. Various size tumblers were made for holding Coca-Cola, malted milk, and iced tea. The banana split boat, sundae, ice cream, and sherbet holders are scooped up by nostalic antique buffs. *Value guide: ice bucket, pink, $40; salt and pepper shakers, pair, green, $45.*

TEA STRAINERS

When tea drinking experienced an upsurge in popularity during the 19th century, commercially made tea strainers sprung up in general stores. The handsome silver versions captured the hearts of the wealthier members of the "tea-for-two" set. Internationally renowned potters added them to production schedules, favoring florals as decorative themes. Some of the more ornate porcelain types bore the Nippon backstamp, suggesting Japanese production. Simple tin-sided types, with embossed or printed advertisements, were favored as premium items. Those attributed to C. D. Kenny represent refreshing finds. Tea imbibers were agog in 1902 when Sears, Roebuck, & Company sold "an extra fine wire gauge with enameled handle" model for 5 cents. *Value guide: brass, puffed handle, circa 1900, $35; Nippon china, roses, $65.*

Metal Tea Strainer

TECO GATES

William D. Gates founded the Terra Cotta Tile Works of Terra Cotta, Illinois, in 1881. The company originally manufactured drain tile, architectural terra cotta bricks, and pottery. In 1902, the Teco line, derived from the "te" in terra and the "co" in cotta was introduced. Experiments were undertaken to perfect the art pottery with special emphasis on marbled or mottled surfaces, and green matte on red, buff, or brown finishes. A metallic luster was developed about 1898. Teco Pottery vases and garden ornaments were marketed; the artisans were influenced by surrounding natural lake and wooded settings. By 1911, over 500 designs were available in the Teco line. Through the 1920s, Teco Pottery was

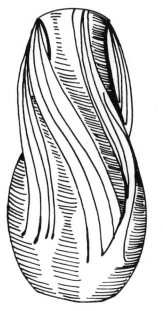

Teco Gates Vase

offered for sale. George A. Berry acquired the works in 1929. *Value guide: vase, apple, green matte, urn, 15½" tall, $1,100; vase, blue-green, square, pierced stem feet, 13" tall, $600.*

TEDDY BEARS

The Teddy Bear legend dates from 1902, when a cartoon drawn by Clifford Berryman for the *Washington Evening Star* depicted President Teddy Roosevelt refusing to shoot a defenseless bear cub. Morris Michton and his wife of Brooklyn, New York, were inspired to create The Teddy Bear based on this cartoon. They obtained permission from the president to use his nickname. Early Teddy Bears generally had humps on the back, jointed limbs, elongated muzzles, and oversized feet and paws. Most had glass eyes with pin-backs or black shoe buttons. Mohair was preferred by American and German makers, many of whom used excelsior stuffing. Firmer models often had wood-wool, while softer ones were stuffed with kapok. The black noses and mouths were usually embroidered into the fabric. Teddy Bears, even the post-World War II versions, are treasured. *Value guide: mohair, jointed limbs, round face, England, 16" tall, 1920a, $225. Steiff, jointed limbs, humped, 14" tall, 1915, $450.*

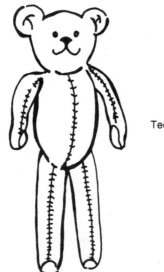

Teddy Bear

TEMPLE, SHIRLEY

When six-year-old Shirley Temple sang "Baby Take a Bow" in Hamilton McFadden's 1934 *Stand-Up and Cheer* American movie-goers lost their hearts. She repeated this accomplishment the next time around in Alexander Hall's *Little Miss Marker*. Then 20th Century Fox starred their all dimples and curly top box office champ in David Butler's *Bright Eyes*. Movie audiences sailed out of theaters singing "The Good Ship Lollipop" after watching this moneymaker. Shirley went on to enchant screen buffs in such films as *Wee Willie Winkle, Heidi,* and *Rebecca of Sunnybrook Farm*. Her screen efforts continued into the '40s. Manufacturers cashed in on her popularity with such items as dolls, paper dolls, school bags, teapots, trunks, and cobalt blue cereal sets featuring her photograph. Shirley Temple items, one and all, attract a vast audience of flea market shoppers. *Value guide: doll, composition, Ideal, 27" tall, $500; sheet music, "Good Ship Lollipop," $18.*

Baby Shirley Temple Doll

THE ROAD IS OPEN AGAIN

The tunesmiths of Tin Pan Alley have honored many American

presidents throughout the years, and Franklin D. Roosevelt received more than his share of recognition from those who dally in ditties. *The Road Is Open Again* was performed by Dick Powell in a propaganda short subject film for the National Reconstruction Administration. He is pictured on the sheet music, along with the president. By featuring these two beloved Americans on the cover, nationwide patriotic sales were guaranteed. *Value guide: "The Road Is Open Again," good condition copy, $15.*

THISTLE PATTERN

Thistle motifs on glassware met with enduring acceptance in the late 19th century. The MacBeth Evans Glass Company tested the Thistle market with depression-plagued consumers in the early 1930s. Their mold-etched variation was available in crystal, yellow, pink, and green. As might be expected, thistles and foliage were the dominant decorative elements. This thistle rendition proved far from fertile, failing to attract an audience. It was discontinued after a short production run. Although a dozen or more shapes were made, accumulating a complete set requires equal amounts of patience and persistence. *Value guide: berry bowl, green, 5½" dimeter, $12; cup and saucer, pink, $14.*

THOMAS, SETH

Seth Thomas must be acknowledged as a major force in the history of the American horological industry. He formed a partnership with Eli Terry and Silas Hoadley, two other celebrated clockmakers, in 1807. Hoadley withdrew from the association in 1813 to form his own works. Terry and Thomas exercised their expertise by working together on an order for 4,000 timepieces. Thomas formed the renowned Seth Thomas Clock Company of Plymouth, Connecticut, in 1853. By 1860, over 125 employees were working around the clock. In the closing decades of the century, Seth Thomas calendar clocks (1863), lever escapement clocks (1866), and round alarm clocks (1875) were second to none in American timepieces. *Value guide: kitchen, Oxford, oak, eight-day, half-hour strike, 27" tall, $225; steeple, Sharon, mahogany finish, eight day, 19½" tall, $200.*

THONET CHAIR No. 14

In 1859, those clever Thonet brothers of Austria (see below) introduced the bentwood No. 14 side chair. It is still in production. These beechwood chairs were made in six parts—namely, a long rod looped to form the chair back and the back legs, a smaller loop inside the back for strength, a hoop providing a framework for the curved seat, a smaller hoop used as a stretcher below the seat, and two gently tapered and bent rods for the front legs. The rods were

Thonet Bentwood High Chair

ingenuously joined by ten screws. The chairs were inexpensive, lightweight, and quite portable. The public adored them, for by 1910 over 50 million No. 14 side shairs were in use throughout the world. *Value guide: bentwood, No. 14, side chair, circa 1900, $225.*

THONET, MICHAEL

Michael Thonet (1796-1871) gave a new twist to furniture forms in the 1840s when his bentwood patents were granted in France, England, and Belgium. Between 1842 and 1849, he entered into a partnership with C. Leistler, making lightweight, elegant, laminated wood chairs. He established his own factory in Vienna, Austria, by 1849. His five sons, Franz, August, Josef, Michael, and Jacob joined him in 1853, operating as the Thonet Brothers. They designed, manfactured, and exported Bentwood furniture to America. Mass production methods ensued, with chairs, tables, sofa beds, and other forms being given numbers indicating chronological order of production. By the 1870s, this presently active firm was recognized as the world's largest furniture factory. The Thonet name, representing varying styles, has been used by the factory. *Value guide: bed, circa 1890, $850; table, 24" diameter, circa 1900, $475.*

THREADED GLASS

Various European and American glasshouses, active in the late 19th century, endeavored to sew up the threaded glass market. Various colors were used, and many pieces had applied portions. On early objects, the threads were painstakingly applied by hand. But in 1876, an English worker discovered a technique for applying the threads mechanically. The result? Mass production methods were undertaken, causing prices to tumble into the affordable category. Countless shapes were conceived by a galaxy of glassmakers. Attribution to a specific factory can furrow the brow of an expert, for few makers bothered to mark their output. *Value guide: basket, opalescent interior, circa 1900, $125; tumbler, cranberry on clear glass, circa 1890, $90.*

THREE LITTLE PIGS

Following the premiere of Walt Disney's Silly Symphony, *The Three Little Pigs,* on May 27, 1933, everyone was afraid of the Big Bad Wolf. It earned Disney a second Academy Award for the best cartoon subject of the 1932-33 season. Additionally, it added four more characters to the list of merchandising possibilities—Fiddler Pig, Fifer Pig, Practical Pig, and the Big Bad Wolf. Sheet music sales of "Who's Afraid of the Big Bad Wolf" soared. *Fortune* magazine even hinted that it should become Technicolor's theme song, for it was "Walt Disney's successful gamble with Silly Symphonies in color that drove the wolf from Technicolor's door." The feature prompted a barnyard full of mementos ranging from bisque figurines to greeting cards. *Value guide: playing cards, complete, $35; wristwatch, Ingersoll, $250.*

TIFFANY, LOUIS COMFORT

Louis Comfort Tiffany (1848-1933) ranks as the outstanding exponent of the American Art Nouveau style. He was the son of the founder of Tiffany & Company. After studying in Paris, he developed an interest in interior design. Working under various titles and partnerships, he excelled in the decorative arts, notably glass, tiles, stained glass, lamps, pottery, furniture, and copper and bronze creations. Tiffany mastered the technique of iridescent glass, marketing it in a rainbow of colors under the term Favrile. Peacock feathers, trailing vines, and lily pads were among the distinguishing decorative elements. In addition, he designed jewelry, including "art jewelry," which was either privately commissioned or made for exhibitions. His lamps, typically having cast bronze stems in naturalistic forms, along with opaque multi-colored Favrile glass shades in overall tree or flower motifs, were other notable Tiffany triumphs. *Value guide: compote, Favrile, turquoise, signed, 5" tall, $450; lamp, table, turtle back, leaded green shade, 16" diameter, signed, $6,000.*

TIFFIN GLASS COMPANY

Alexander J. Beatty purchased an existing glass factory at Steubenville, Ohio, in 1851. The venture evolved into a family affair when he was joined by his two sons, Robert and George, in the mid-1870s. By 1888, the glasshouse had undertaken a successful move to Tiffin, Ohio. Some four years later it became amalgamated with the United States Glass Company, operating as factory R. When black satin glass was boosting profits in the 1920s, Americans were dancing to the black bottom. Between the 1930s and 1970s, a legion of lovely stemware patterns brought them fame, but seldom fortune. In fact, bankruptcy proceedings were instituted in 1963, followed by several unsuccessful reorganizations that extended the life of the firm until 1980. *Value guide: pitcher, Shawl Dancer, $90; vase, black stain, poppies, 9" tall, $50.*

TINTYPES

From the 1850s through the 1920s, tintypomania seized the American populace. They were also known as melanotypes, ferrotypes, gems, and bon tons. Originally, they were housed in late daguerrean cases of leather, thermoplastic, or paper. These early tintypes are regarded as choice examples of photographic art. At present, few are found enclosed in cases, although some still have their original paper protectors intact. The sizes varied considerably, the most popular being 4¼ × 2½ inches. They fit ideally into family albums. Later versions were lighter in weight, similar to the thickness of a playing card. As for the subject matter, it ran the gamut from bathing beauties to babies. *Value guide: Civil War soldier, Union Case, $70; poker players, paper protector, $35.*

TOILET SETS

From the 1870s, practically every major and minor American silversmith fabricated toilet sets. Their present scarcity, however, would belie this fact. These dresser-top delights consisted of silverplated stands conceived to hold a varying number of bottles for toiler water, puffs, and powder. The Meriden Britannia Company, Reed & Barton, and Middletown Plate Company were among the list of makers who marked their wares. As for the bottles, they were conceived in eye-catching enameled, engraved, and etched motifs suitable for a lady's dresser top. Some had Mary Gregory-type figures. Those who toil after toilet sets seek complete ensembles from renowned silver concerns. *Value guide: Reed & Barton, four jars, enameled florals, arched stand, circa 1885, $185.*

Silverplated Toilet Set

TOOTSIETOY

The first Tootsietoy, a small 47 millimeter limousine, was marketed in 1911. Just three years later, the Dowdst Brothers Manufacturing Company of Chicago, Illinois, introduced a Ford Touring Car. The Tootsietoy name, honoring Tootsie Dowdst, the daughter of the company's president, was registered in 1924. It first appeared on cars in 1926. Some early models remained unmarked until about 1931. Initially, many cars had open-spoked turning wheels. By 1933, white rubber tires on metal rims were in general use, while post-World War II vehicles boasted black rubber wheels. Between 1926 and 1961, the title Dowdst Manufacturing Company was utilized. It operates at present as the Strombecker Corporation. Bartering shifts into high gear over such Tootsietoy rarities as the Funnies Series, based on comic characters: La Salles; the 1925 panel truck; the J. C. Penney truck; and Graham automobiles. *Value guide: airport hanger, two planes, original box, $450; Oldsmobile Brougham, 1920s, $30.*

Andy Gump Tootsietoy

TRANSVAAL MONEY BOX

John Harper and Company, Ltd., English bank makers, produced a score of mechanical banks in the late 1800s. Their Transvaal Money Box has a tinge of historical significance. The bank depicted Paul Kruger, or "Oom Paul," as he was known, who fought the British in the Transvaal in the closing decades of the century and was Transvaal's president between 1883 and 1900. Because of its limited action, some call it a semimechanical bank. Kruger was bedecked in a brown jacket, yellow vest, and black top hat. The hat bore the phrase "Transvaal Money Box." Since the pipe in Kruger's mouth moved with or without inserting a coin in the slot on the hat, it performed even for the penniless. *Value guide: Transvaal Money Box, 6" tall, circa 1895, $450.*

TRICK DOG BANK

The Trick Dog mechanical bank from the Hubley Manufacturing Company of Lancaster, Pennsylvania, was kept in production for almost half a century. It was patented on July 31, 1888. The casting on the side of the base reads "Trick Dog." The lever for releasing the dog is located on the right side of the base. When a penny is placed in the dog's mouth, he jumps through a hoop held by a clown and deposits the penny into a barrel at the far side of the base. Would he do it a second time? Of course! For another penny. By the 1940s, this trick bank was being sold by leading retailers for $1.19. On this later version the bank's title, "Trick Dog," appeared on the top of the base, rather than on its side. *Value guide: Trick Dog Bank, circa 1900, cast-iron, 7¼" tall, $150.*

Trick Dog Bank

TRICK PONY BANK

Children got a kick out of the Trick Pony bank patented by Peter Adams and Charles G. Shephard in 1885. This mechanical marvel was manufactured by the Shephard Hardware Company. The handsome and presumably well-trained animal was painted brown, with a red and yellow saddle. The red base bore the wording "Trick Pony" in gold lettering. When a penny is placed in his mouth and a lever pulled on the right side of the base, the pony lowers his head, and the penny falls into the trough in front of him. Locating the Trick Pony bank in pristine condition is a trick in itself. *Value guide: Trick Pony Bank, cast-iron, 7¾" tall, circa 1890, $550.*

TRUNKS

Flat or slightly rounded trunks covered with leather were preferred by overland travelers from the late 1700s into the mid-1800s. Many were ornamented or reinforced with nailheads or studs. Their interiors were typically lined with cloth, wallpaper, or newspapers, which can serve as dating guides. Others bore painted motifs. The Jenny Lind trunk had a flat top, rounded corners, and studded metal bands around the edges and in the center. Its popularity coincided with the Swedish singer's triumphant American tour in the early

1850s. Later in the century, canvas-covered and decorated sheet metal trunks appeared with flat tops or high, rounded barrel stave tops. Most had square or rounded corners with iron bottoms. Some were iron bound for added security. In the early 1900s, embossed metal coverings came into general use with American travelers. *Value guide: domed lid, hide covered, 41" × 21", $125; leather, studded with brass tacks, $800.*

Leather-Covered Trunk

TWO FROGS BANK

The patent for the Two Frogs Bank was granted to James H. Bowen in 1882. On this mechanical bank from the J. & E. Stevens & Company, two frogs are poised to perform a penny escapade. Mother Nature would have been pleased with the design, for the two shiny green frogs are depicted amidst lush green foliage. When a coin is placed on the smaller frog's tray, and a lever is pressed behind the larger frog, his mouth opens. His small companion kicks the penny into his mouth. The result? Children absolutely leaped with joy. *Value guide: Two Frogs Bank, cast-iron, 4⅛" tall, circa 1890, $325.*

Two Frogs Bank

UKELINS

The ukelin, patented in 1926, was an offshoot of the ukelele and violin. The exclusive maker of this musical instrument was the International Musical Corporation of Hoboken, New Jersey. Even an amateur could amuse listeners with this unique music maker. It was played by placing it on the lap, plucking zither-type strings with one hand, while simultaneously bowing a different set of strings with the other hand. Apparently, with this instrument, it paid to let your left hand know what your right hand was doing! The ukelin heard its swan song in 1963, when production was abandoned. *Value guide: ukelin, good condition, circa 1935, $125.*

UNCLE SAM BANK

Peter Adams designed this patriotic mechanical bank for the Shephard Hardware Company of Buffalo, New York, in 1886. An Uncle Sam, attired in red, white and blue, stands on the base of the bank next to his carpetbag. There is a depiction of an eagle on the base. The lever that must be pushed to activate the bank is located behind Uncle Sam's umbrella. A penny placed in Uncle Sam's hand disappeared into the carpetbag, while his lower jaw and beard move accordingly. In fact, the motion continued long after the coin had been deposited. Reproductions abound, therefore caution is advised when investing in an Uncle Sam Bank. *Value guide: Uncle Sam Bank, cast-iron, 11½" tall, $525.*

UNEEDA BISCUIT DOLL

Uneeda Biscuits were developed by National Biscuit Company's A. W. Green in 1898. He sought to establish a brand name that would successfully compete against the anonymity of the standard cracker barrel. Undoubtedly, the country needed a flaky soda cracker, for Uneeda Biscuits took a bite out of competitors' profit margins. Just prior to World War I, the Ideal Novelty & Toy Corporation introduced the Uneeda Biscuit boy doll. It had composition head, arms, and legs. This 16-inch tall doll boasted molded brown hair, painted blue eyes, and a closed mouth. Further detail was provided in the form of molded black boots, bloomer suit, yellow slicker, and a rainhat. Of course the doll carried a box of Uneeda Biscuits. *Value guide: doll, good condition, 16" tall, $135.*

Uneeda Biscuit Boy Doll

UNGER BROTHERS

In the early 1870s, the Unger Brothers of Newark, New Jersey, established a works for the sale and production of hardware specialties. A decade later, thanks to Eugene's wife, Emma, they became immersed in the sterling silver jewelry trade. Their sinuously curving naturalistic configurations displaying art nouveau effects bedazzled the eye. As their output grew, American dresser tops and tabletops sparkled under the brilliance of Unger silverware. Jewelry boxes held brooches, buckles, pins, and other baubles from this silversmith. Collectors hunger for silver items bearing Unger's interlaced "U. B." trademark. *Value guide: brush, He Loves Me, $85; mirror, Love's Dream, woman with cherubs, $275.*

Unger Brothers Brooch

UNITED STATES WATCH COMPANY

The Nutting brothers began manufacturing watch tools and machinery at Waltham, Massachusetts, about 1879. Charles Vander Woerd, an ingenious mechanic, joined them in the venture shortly thereafter. When a decision was reached to enter into the watch business, Woerd gained the financial support of E. C. Hammer. Woerd's initial watch design failed to stimulate the public's response, however, causing him to exit from the firm. Despite efforts to promote a more conventional product, their watches failed to find mass appeal, and all production ceased in 1901. After reorganization attempts, it was sold to the Keystone Watch Case Company of Philadelphia, in 1905. *Value guide: pocket watch, dome-type 16 size, 7 jewels, gilt case, $275.*

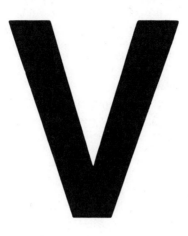

VAN BRIGGLE, ARTUS

Born in Felicity, Ohio, in 1869, Artus Van Briggle founded a pottery in beautiful Colorado Springs, Colorado, in the shadow of Pikes Peak, in 1899. After working at the Avon and Rookwood potteries, he traveled to Paris in 1892. While in France, he met Annie Lawrence Gregory, an art student from Plattsburg, New York. He relocated to Colorado because of ill health and married Annie in 1902. The artwares he fashioned from native clays had a marble glaze.

Van Briggle Lady of the Lily Vase

The colors, indigenous to the region, were based on sunset hues, turquoise skies, and vari-colored mountains. Upon his death, his widow continued to operate this still-flourishing pottery. A cypher mark of two "A's" representing Artus and Annie has long identified the Van Briggle pottery. *Value guide: mug, leaf and berry decor, handled, green on yellow, 1905, $335; vase, beige ground, stylized tulips, 10¾" tall, 1903, $565.*

VASA MURRHINA GLASS

Vasa Murrhina glass was patented by the Vasa Murrhina Glass Company of Sandwich, Massachusetts, in 1884; however, it was also made by a dozen other glasshouses in America and Europe in the closing decade of the 19th century. The transparent body of the glass was enhanced with imbedded particles of colored glass and mica flakes. A completed object bore a resemblance to ancient Roman vessels carved from *murra*, a semiprecious stone. Skilled glassmakers dazzled the public with delightful color combinations on items ranging from cheese dishes to rose bowls. *Value guide: bowl, white lining, silver specks, 7" diameter, $185; vase, amber, gold flecks, 10" tall, $165.*

VERRE DE SOIE

The Vernon pattern had a short production at the Indiana Glass Company during 1931, making it difficult for depression glass disciples to find. Originally, it was known as the firm's Number 616 pattern. Approximately ten different shapes have been discovered, most frequently in green, crystal, and yellow. The latter was initially referred to as Topaz. On luncheon plates, this mold-etched design has a snowflake center motif surrounded by four lattice panels alternating with florals. Collectors relish locating a bargain-priced, three-section Vernon relish dish. *Value guide: cup and saucer, green, $14; tumbler, footed, crystal, 5" tall, $10.*

VERRE de SOIE

Chalk up this glass achievement to Frederick Carder, of Aurene fame. He introduced this iridescent milestone while in the employ of the Steuben Glass Works of Corning, New York, in 1905. Iridescent glass novelties were experiencing a vogue during this time. On Verre de Soie, crystal glass was characteristically treated to a rainbow with a trace of iridescence. The applied portions were colored. Quite frequently fruit and floral clusters served as handles. Adventuresome glass artisans strove for variations; thus some engraved and etched effects were used. A similar glass was being produced by European factories; so definite attribution of an unsigned specimen is a task best reserved for an expert. *Value guide:*

Verre de Soie Frog Bowl

bowl, etched flowers, amber edge, 10" diameter, $190; compote, blue edge, 6" tall, $75.

VOGUE DOLL COMPANY

Mrs. Jennie Graves established the Vogue Doll Company after

Vogue Ginny Doll "Toddles"

World War I. Through the 1930s, she concentrated her efforts on making doll clothes. Later she started importing dolls from Germany. The Vogue name became a household word with the introduction of the Ginny doll. Ginny became the most successful of the 8-inch plastic dolls. She could walk and had 52 separate outfits. Ginny also had a trunk with her name on it, along with such accessories as a shoebag filled with shoes, and four pairs of eyeglasses. Other dolls, wardrobes, furniture, and related items were marketed as the company expanded. When the Tonka Corporation purchased Vogue in 1973, Ginny was kept in production. *Value guide: Dearest One, 1967, $45; Ginny Baby, bent limbs, original clothes, 8" tall, $55.*

WAFFLE IRONS

To facilitate cooking chores, many of the cast-iron waffle irons used on coal stoves had ball-and-socket joints that enabled them to be turned over with relative ease. Some makers were still manufacturing Waffle irons for coal stoves through the 1920s. The Fanner Manufacturing Company, Wagner Manufacturing Company, Stover Manufacturing and Engine Company, and the Griswold Manufacturing Company made and marked these tasty acquisitions. Most came in 7-, 8-, and 9-inch sizes to fit snugly into various-sized stove lid openings. To bedazzle batter makers, they were offered with round or square pans in pie, heart, and star motifs. *Value guide: cast-iron, Fanner, circa 1900, $40; Keen Kutter, $60.*

Waffle Iron

WAGNER MANUFACTURING COMPANY

The Wagner Manufacturing Company of Sidney, Ohio, cast a spell over consumers with its cast-aluminum cooking accessories in the early 1900s. Every piece "was cast solid in a mold, not sheet metal or stamped." Some of Wagner's originally designed tea kettles such as The Colonial, Grand Prize, Sidney, and Priscilla models had been in use for "fifteen or twenty years." Kettles were described as being "the heart of kitchen equipment." Company advertisements stated that Wagner-cast aluminum items were sold by the "best dealers everywhere." *Value guide: Grand Prize tea kettle, 1920s, $35.*

Wagner Colonial Tea Kettle

WARWICK CHINA COMPANY

The Warwick China Company of Wheeling, West Virginia, was founded in the late 1880s and flourished until 1951 because the firm's tablewares and toilet articles were affordably priced, thereby making them available to the masses. From the outset, the company specialized in vitreous glazed wares. Aware shoppers seek the handpainted pieces, which are somewhat more scarce than the decal-ornamented wares. Portrait objects rate as favorites, with monks and Indians prompting instant collector patronage. Other items bore bird, animals, and fraternal emblems. The first backstamp incorporated a helmet and crossed swords, followed between 1893 and 1898 by the Warwick Semi-Porcelain mark. Later the wording "Warwick China" identified the company's creations. *Value guide: mug, fisherman, "IOGA," $75; vase, monk decor, 13" tall, $350.*

WATCH FOBS

The watch fob was conceived to facilitate the removal of a watch from the narrow pocket of a vest or waistband. These small, dangling tags, or *fobs*, appeared in an infinite variety. Some collectors preferred specialization, concentrating on the commemorative, campaign, souvenir, fraternal, or political types. Advertising fobs proliferated as promotional items from various business establishments. One-of-a-kind versions exist, for affluent gentlemen shunned the mass-marketed varieties. Time has been kind to the watch fob, especially the beaded and crocheted varieties attributed to members of the craft contingent. The industrial examples are also viewed with admiration by fob fanciers. *Value guide: Columbian Exposition, 1893, metal, $75; Indian decor, sterling silver, circa 1900, $70.*

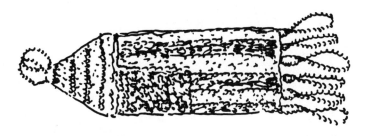

Beadwork Watch Fob

WATERBURY WATCH COMPANY

The Waterbury Watch Company was formed with a capital investment of $400,000 on March 1, 1880. By May of the following year, over 600 watches were being produced each day. Within a few years that number had escalated to 1,000. Daniel Buck's long-wind watch was discontinued when a short-wind model appeared. In 1898, the company was reorganized as the New England Watch Company. Under this title, they produced mainly duplex escapement watches without jewels. A ladies watch, the Elfin, was the smallest watch ever made in America at that time. The Waterbury Watch Company operated independently from the Waterbury Clock Company, although they were both an outgrowth of the Benedict and Burnham Manufacturing Company. The Waterbury Watch Company never made watches for R. H. Ingersoll; they were made by the Waterbury Clock Company. *Value guide: Series T, Oxford duplex, $100; Waterbury, long-wind, skeletonized, $325.*

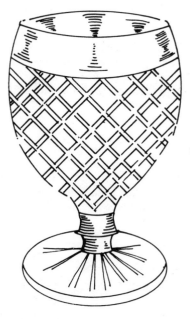

Waterford Pattern Goblet

WATERFORD PATTERN

The fad for colored glass tableware articles was waning by 1938 when the Hocking division of the Anchor-Hocking Corporation introduced the Waterford pattern. It remained on production schedules through 1944. Those having a weakness for Waterford have located pieces in crystal, pink, white, and yellow. A few articles have also been unearthed in forest green. The plates boast radial sunburst lines separated halfway by a triple concentric circle of small blocks. The unusual rims have a waffle motif, which explains why some collectors prefer the more descriptive term Waffle. *Value guide: butter dish, covered, pink, $35; goblet, crystal, $10.*

W. C. FIELDS SPOONS

Spoon seekers swoon at the sight of the W. C. Fields spoon. In fact, many collectors have displayed a preference for spoons featuring theatrical or screen luminaries. This 8-inch long Fields silverplated stirring spoon receives stellar billing from cinema buffs. The star is depicted in the outfit worn by him in the MGM classic film, *David Copperfield*. His Mr. Micawber attire consisted of top hat and tails. It makes the spoon an easily recognizable acquisition, particularly to viewers of late-night television. The Fields spoon stirred up considerable attention at the Chicago World's Fair of 1933-34, where it was distributed as a souvenir item. *Value guide: W. C. Fields spoon, $15.*

WELLER WARE

Samuel A. Weller operated a small factory at Fultonham, Ohio, from 1873. He specialized in making flower pots and similar objects. As the business prospered, several moves were undertaken, including the purchase of the former American Encaustic Tiling Company building in Zanesville. Art wares appeared in 1893, beginning with William Long's Lonhuda. When Long left the company, Weller made a similar art ware naming it Louwelsa. Charles Babcock Upjohn introduced Dickensware in 1900. Two years later, Jacques Sicard developed a pottery with a metallic luster known as Sicardo. Prior to 1906 Aurelian, Aurora, Turado, Escocean, Etna, Floretta, Jap-Birdimal, Dresden, Etched Matt, Hunter, and Art Nouveau were included in Weller's art pottery accomplishments. The Weller factory was regarded as the largest in the world by 1915, employing 40 salesmen and hundreds of workers. Following World War I, Weller introduced a new line every year. The factory shuttered in 1948. *Value guide: bowl, Ardsley, 6½″ diameter, $135 vase; Bonita, 8″ tall, $100.*

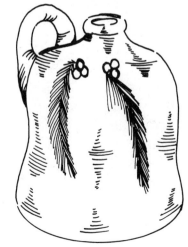

Weller Jug Vase

WHO'S NEXT FAN

The shield-shaped, "Who's Next," fan dating from the Taft-Bryan campaign, receives an affirmative vote from political memento collectors. In addition to the two candidates, it pictures every president from George Washington to Theodore Roosevelt; thus it qualifies as a mini history lesson. An advertisement appeared on the reverse side, this being the hey-day of freely distributed campaign items. Despite its collector appeal, the fan was actually a poor predictor of presidential possibilities. This became evident when Woodrow Wilson accumulated sufficient votes to become the next president of the United States. *Value guide: "Who's Next" fan, good condition, $85.*

WICKER

Ornately structured pieces of rattan and bamboo began arriving on American shores from the earliest days of the China trade. When makers discovered that the pitch, or reed, of rattan (which had previously been discarded) was able to be bent into various shapes, designs became more imaginative. Eventually, wicker replaced rattan as the choice material for crafting this light and airy furniture. In the post-Civil War era, Rococo, Gothic, Classical, and other styles appeared. Natural, stained, or painted pieces often reflected Oriental themes. The hourglass chair was the chair of the hour following the Centennial Exposition of 1876. Subdued designs were favored by the turn of the century, when complete sets found favor. Removeable seats and upholstering, along with a small diamond

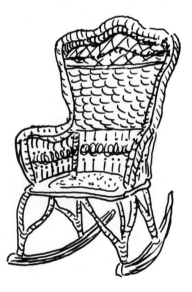

Wicker Rocker

motif in a contrasting color, denote an art deco specimen. *Value guide: armchair, rolled arms, round seat, circa 1890, $325; rocker, platform, circa 1900, $325.*

WILLIAM TELL BANK

Russel Fris received a patent for his story-telling William Tell mechanical bank in 1896. This marksman's delightful bank was manufactured by the J. & E. Stevens & Company of Connecticut. Bank buffs regard it as one of the finest quality shooting banks. It is set in motion by placing a penny on the barrel of Tell's rifle. The marksman's right foot is set to trigger the action. As the penny whizzes through the air, the apple drops from atop his son's head and is deposited through the slot in the castle behind the boy. Just to complete the action, a bell rings, providing this mechanical marvel with a penny's worth of amusement. *Value guide: William Tell Bank, cast-iron, 6¾" tall, $450.*

WINDSOR PATTERN

Early advertisements for the Windsor depression glass design featured a depiction of Windsor Castle. Between 1936 and 1946, this Jeanette Glass Company creation surfaced in pink, green, and crystal. About 1940, the pink line was discontinued. Diamond-shaped facets with a center circle of radial ribs provided plates with a majestic appearance. Some collectors prefer the name Windsor Diamond. Formidable finds in this pressed pattern include the square relish dish, pyramid candlesticks, boat-shaped bowl, and covered powder jar. *Value guide: pitcher, 16-ounce, crystal, $14; sugar and creamer, pink, $18.*

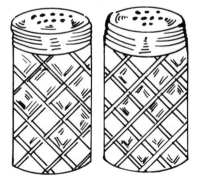

Windsor Pattern Salt & Pepper
Shakers

WIRE FURNITURE

Wickedly wonderful wire furniture twisted its way into American interiors in the late 19th century. Its popularity coincided with the craze for cast-iron creations. Because wire could be twisted into untold fanciful forms, American gardens blossomed under its spell. Chairs, tables, carts, flower stands, baskets, and trellises were held in high esteem by horticulturists. Numerous manufacturers competed for sales with a full array of accessories. Among the first under the wire in this race was M. Walker of Philadelphia, who featured over 53 wire accessories in a single catalog. *Value guide: armchair, fancy, circa 1890, $275; table, round top, 24" diameter, circa 1900, $250.*

Wirework Chair

WITCH BALLS

Why could glass spheres be found hanging in windows throughout England by the 18th century? Supposedly they warded off the "evil spirits." Others were hung near the fireplace to catch demon spirits descending from the chimney. Colored and multi-colored types were produced by leading glasshouses. Since superstition knows no boundaries, the fame of the witch ball spread to America. Especially elusive are those attributed to the glass craftsmen of South Jersey. These whimsies appeared in many sizes, with most measuring between 3 and 8 inches in diameter. Some early types had silvered interiors, which reportedly really kept those witches flying in the opposite direction. *Value guide: cranberry, 5" diameter, circa 1880, $75; Nailsea glass, aquamarine with white loopings, 6" diameter, circa 1900, $250.*

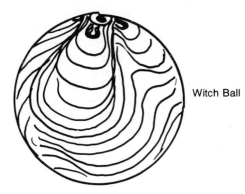
Witch Ball

WOOTEN DESKS

Indianapolis, Indiana, became the home of the William S. Wooton furniture factory in the 1870s. The awesome desk, known as "Wooten's Patent Cabinet Office Secretary" was patented on October 6, 1874. These heavy desks, made with bracket feet for portability, furnished endless space with innumerable cubby holes and drawers that could be locked by night for maximum security. Four grades were advertised: Ordinary, Standard, Extra, or Superior. Each grade was crafted in three sizes, ranging from 4 feet 7½ inches to 5 feet 1½ inches. These Eastlake style desks, possessing ornate carving, sold from $90 to $750. When Wooten's factory closed in 1884, similar desks were marketed by Canadian and English manufacturers. *Value guide: Wooten desk, No. 101, $7,500.*

WRIGHT, RUSSELL

Russell Wright, noted American industrial designer, is acknowledged as a chief exponent of the art deco style. During the 1930s, Wright could do no wrong with his blonde furniture, spun-aluminum cooking accessories, chrome, glass, and pottery articles executed in Deco themes. His bold and beautiful modern dinnerware items were presented in muted shades such as seaform blue, spruce green, and chutney. Innovation was the order of the day—dishes were rimless and cups turned in at the rim. Practically overnight, the Wright name developed into a household word, appearing on the backstamp of various potters including Steubenville Pottery Co., Harker China Co., Iroquoise Chine Company, and Justin Therod. *Value guide: coffeepot, pink, $30; teapot, gray, $50.*

WROUGHT IRON FURNITURE

Wrought iron furnishings boasting art deco styles enjoyed a decade of desirability between 1925 and 1935. This attention was generated in part by exposure in *La Ferronerie Moderne,* by Henri Clouzot, published in 1925. Of course, Paris-based designers, notably E. Brandt, captivated consumers with chairs, tables, fire screens, consoles, and decorative panels. Glass or marble surfaces were frequently supported by wrought-iron legs. When decorative elements were required, as on decorative panels, stylized birds, animals, clouds, crosses, and diamonds were utilized. By the late 1930s, fickle buyers were already showing a preference for chromium-plated tubular steel and strip steel furniture. *Value guide: armchair, wrought iron, ornate, French, circa 1930, $450.*

YELLOW KID

The hero of America's first true comic strip, which was created by Richard Felton Outcault, appeared in the *Sunday New York World*

The Yellow Kid

on May 5, 1895. About a year later, the Kid became more noticeable when he began wearing a yellow shirt. The nameless child who captured the public's attention was dubbed "The Yellow Kid." The strip continued running under the title "Hogan's Alley." When Outcault joined Hearst's *New York Journal*, the Yellow Kid label was applied to the panel. Following legal battles and other difficulties, Outcault returned to free-lancing in 1898. But the memory of the Yellow Kid persisted into the 20th century, with Outcault using him, along with a pet goat, on advertisements. An army of Yellow Kid artifacts beguiled kids around the turn of the century. *Value guide: button, Outcault, 1896, $12; toy, Yellow Kid in goat cart, cast-iron $275.*

ZANESVILLE ART POTTERY

Around the turn of the century, Zanesville, Ohio, was affectionately dubbed the "Clay City." About 1900, the Zanesville Art Pottery began operating in a town teaming with potteries. Initially, utilitarian objects were potted. Following in the tradition of neighboring potteries, however—including Weller, Roseville, and Owens—art pottery lines were initiated. One notable achievement in this direction was La Moro, a handpainted art ware ornamented under the glaze. High-glaze and matte-glaze pieces, often possessing the La Moro block print mark, typically bore floral designs. Samuel A. Weller purchased the works in 1920, naming it Weller Plant No. 3. *Value guide: jug, whiskey, pansies, La Moro, 5½" tall, $160; vase, clover blossoms, La Moro, 7" tall, $225.*

ZANE WARE

Adam Reed and Harry McCelland, two progressive potters, acquired the assets of the Peters and Reed Pottery of Zanesville, Ohio, in 1921. Following in the tradition of the original owners, They initiated art pottery lines. Descriptive titles such as Sheen, Powder Blue, Drip, and Crystalline were chosen to designate the lines. Horticulturists purchased their wares with vigor, because garden accessories dominated their output. The partners remained active through 1941, when Lawton Garner became the owner of the pottery. Looking for tomorrow's antiques? Then begin accumulating pieces marked Zane Ware today. *Value guide: jardinere, Mon-*

tene, two handles, variegated green glaze, 14½" tall, $175; vase, Aztec, 8" tall, $65.

ZDEKAUER, MORITZ

Moritz Zdekauer, a Czechoslavakian ceramic wizard, acquired an existing porcelain factory at Altrohau, Bohemia, in 1844. Through 1909, beautiful wares in a bewildering array of shapes emerged from this works. Zdekauer turned a profit in porcelains simply by concentrating on the healthy American market. Brides of the era were usually presented with one or more treasures bearing the "M.Z. Austria" backstamp. Most specimens bore the symbols of an eagle and coronet, sometimes accompanied by the location, Altrohau. From 1909, the factory has flourished under the direction of the Hutschenreuther dynasty. *Value guide: cookie jar, roses, satin finish, 9" tall, $100; portrait plate, Constance, scalloped edge, 9⅜" diameter, $135.*

CROSS REFERENCES

Art Glass
Aurene, 15
Berry Bowls, 28
Cambridge Glass Company, 52
Carnival Glass, 60
Custard Glass, 88
Daum Nancy, 92
Degenhart Glass, 94
Durand Glass, 103
Fenton Glass, 111
Fostoria Glass, 119
Fry, H. C., 123
Goofus Glass, 130
Heisey Glass, 140
Holly Amber, 144
Imperial Jewels, 157
Jack-in-the-Pulpit Vases, 160
Kemple Glass, 164
Lalique, Rene, 169
Loetz Glass, 176
McKee Glass Company, 192
Monroe, C. F., 201
Moser, Ludwig, 206
New Martinsville Glass, 210
Normandie, 213
Parrot, 227
Patrician, 227
Quezal Glass, 245
Red Block, 250
Ruby Stained, 259
Schneider, Charles, 266
Silver Deposit Glass, 272
Stretch Glass, 283
Threaded Glass, 293
Tiffany, Louis Comfort, 294
Tiffin Glass Company, 295
Vasa Murrhina, 304
Verre De Soie, 304

Witch Balls, 314

Banks
Bad Accident, 19
Bismarck, 30
Bowling Alley, 37
Boy on Trapeze, 38
Boy Robbing Bird's Nest, 38
Bulldog, 46
Calumet Baking Powder, 51
Chein Industries, 68
Clown, Harlequin, and
Columbine, 74
Creedmoor, 85
Darktown Batter, 91
Eagle and Eaglets, 105
Elephant, 107
General Butler, 126
Girl Skipping Rope, 128
Globe Savings, 138
Hall's Excelsior Bank, 137
Humpty Dumpty, 150
Li'l Abner, 172
Lion and Two Monkeys, 173
Magic, 183
Magician, 185
Mickey Mouse, 194
Monkey and Coconut, 201
Novelty, 215
Paddy and the Pig, 223
Punch and Judy, 243
Reclining Chinaman, 249
Registereing, 250
Safe Bank, 263
Speaking Dog, 274
Still Banks, 281
Superman, 285
Tammany, 287

328